Nationalism in the Vernacular

Nationalism in the Vernacular illuminates the relationship between orality and nationalist politics. In doing so, it provides a new angle to the understanding of nationalism by looking at the popular support and participation of ordinary people in the construction of Mizo nationalism—in short, the vernacularization of nationalism. The book examines this process of vernacularization at two levels: first, the process of creating a vernacular language to express nationalist ideas and, second, the irrepressibility of the oral against the Indian state's violent response to the nationalist movement. Drawing from multiple sources, the book—through the rich oral narratives and archival material, including government and media reports— shows how Mizos have remained active agents in asserting and claiming their rights to define ideas of nationalism in their own terms by making them distinctively Mizo.

Roluahpuia is Assistant Professor of Sociology in the Department of Humanities and Social Sciences, Indian Institute of Technology, Roorkee (IITR). He was a recipient of the Arvind Raghunathan and Sribala Subramanian Visiting Fellowship (2018– 2019) at the Lakshmi Mittal and Family South Asia Institute, Harvard University. His research interests broadly concern identity, nationalism, development, and borderland studies. His latest article, 'Unsettled Autonomy: Ethnicity, Tribes and Sub-National Politics in Mizoram, Northeast India' (2021), was published by the journal *Nations and Nationalism* and was awarded the 2020 Association for the Study of Ethnicity and Nationalism (ASEN)–*Nations and Nationalism* essay prize in memory of Dominique Jacquin-Berdal.

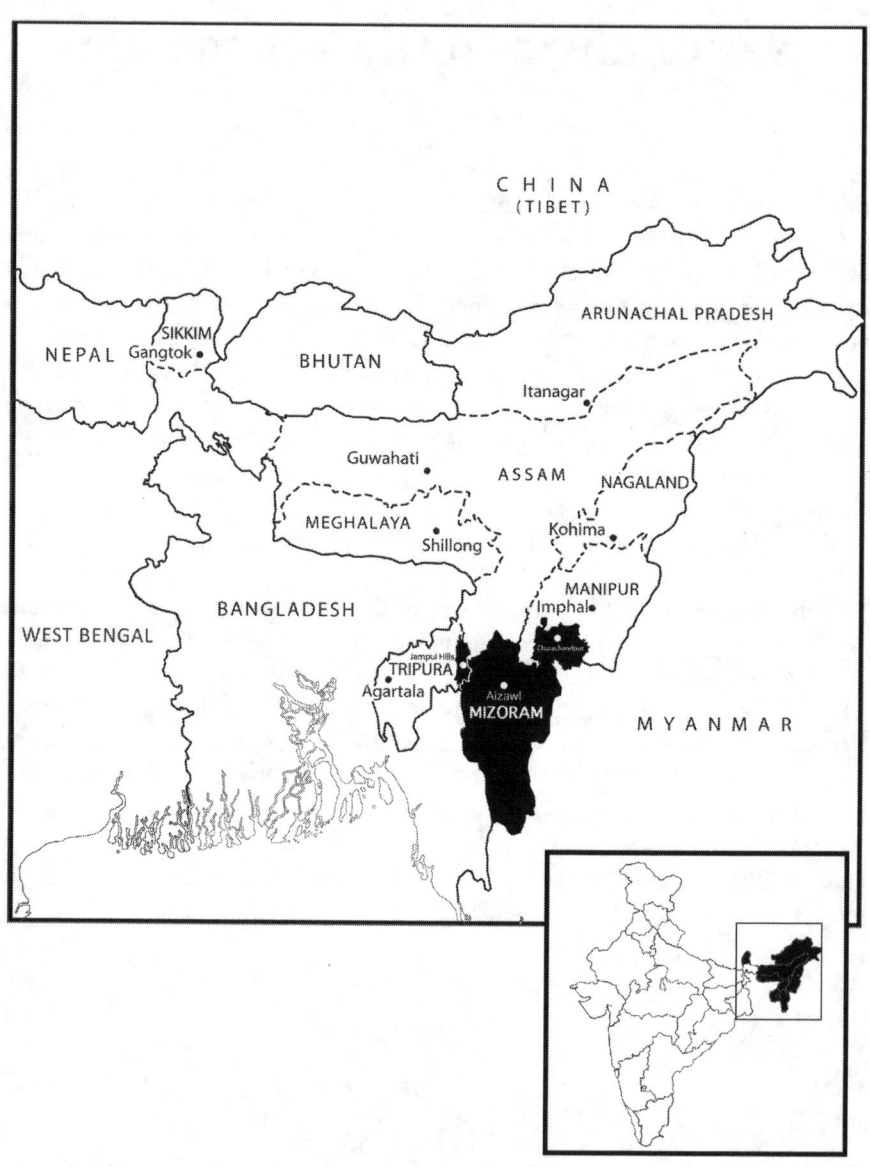

Map of northeast India

Source: Map prepared by Benjamin V. Jamkhanpau.

Note: Map not to scale and does not represent authentic international boundaries.

Nationalism in the Vernacular

State, Tribes, and the Politics of Peace
in Northeast India

Roluahpuia

CAMBRIDGE
UNIVERSITY PRESS

CAMBRIDGE
UNIVERSITY PRESS

Shaftesbury Road, Cambridge CB2 8EA, United Kingdom

One Liberty Plaza, 20th Floor, New York, NY 10006, USA

477 Williamstown Road, Port Melbourne, vic 3207, Australia

314 to 321, 3rd Floor, Plot No.3, Splendor Forum, Jasola District Centre, New Delhi 110025, India

103 Penang Road, #05–06/07, Visioncrest Commercial, Singapore 238467

Cambridge University Press is part of Cambridge University Press & Assessment, a department of the University of Cambridge.

We share the University's mission to contribute to society through the pursuit of education, learning and research at the highest international levels of excellence.

www.cambridge.org
Information on this title: www.cambridge.org/9781009346078

First published 2023
Reprint 2023, 2025

Printed in India by Thomson Press India Ltd.

A catalogue record for this publication is available from the British Library

ISBN 978-1-009-34607-8 Hardback

To my mother, for her love and sacrifice

Contents

List of Figures		ix
Preface		xi
Acknowledgements		xiii
List of Abbreviations		xvii
Notes on Transliteration and Translation		xix
1	Introduction	1
2	The 'Tribal Question' in India: Problem of Inclusion	30
3	The Emergence of Mizo Nationalism: The Formative Phase	48
4	The Mizo National Front and the Vernacularization of Nationalism	81
5	Violence, Counter-Insurgency, and the Transcript of Resistance	112
6	Discord, Accord, and the Politics for Peace	141
7	Conclusion	165
Glossary		170
References		172
Index		190

Figures

1.1   Leaders of various Mizo organizations on the stage of the protest during the Mizo *hnam hnatlang* (voluntary action to save the Mizo nation), 2018   2

1.2   Mizo *hnam hnatlang* (voluntary action to save the Mizo nation) in Aizawl, Mizoram, 6 November 2018   3

2.1   Map showing tribal boundaries in northeast India (provisional), 1946   39

3.1   The first Mizo Union (MU) assembly, 24 September 1946   53

3.2   Members of the District Advisory Council with L. L. Peters, 1948   58

3.3   Jawaharlal Nehru with Mizo District Council leaders   61

3.4   Block officers and councillors of the Mizo Union (MU)   65

3.5   Banner by the Manipur Mizos extending support to the demand for territorial unification of Mizo-inhabited areas   68

3.6   Office bearers of the Mizo Union (MU), Manipur: (*left to right*) Pu Chhunngenga, Pu Sabuta, Pu H. Darkhuma, Pu Lalchhawnzova, Pu B. Lalhnuna, and Pu T. L. Sangliana   69

3.7   The first Mizo District Council members, 1952–1957   71

3.8   Members of the Pawi-Lakher Regional Council (PLRC), along with other political leaders and officers of the Mizo Hills   72

4.1   Hill and plain areas of Assam showing the areas demanded by the All Party Hill Leaders Conference (APLHC) for the creation of a separate hill state, 1960   85

4.2   Mizo National Front (MNF) rebels in their camp in East Pakistan
        (now Bangladesh), 1970–1980   103

4.3   Mizo National Front (MNF) leaders and armies with Laldenga
        (*second from the left*) and his wife, Biakdiki, 1970–1980   106

5.1   A family in a grouping centre, Saitual, Mizoram, 1970–1980   121

5.2   Central Reserve Police Force (CRPF) men arresting a Mizo civilian
        for violating the curfew rule, 1979   124

5.3   Public rally against the violence in Aizawl, 1980   126

5.4   Coffins of the Mizo National Front (MNF) rebels who died during
        the period of the movement, 1986   132

6.1   Rally in demand for the resumption of peace talks   149

6.2   Mizoram Congress leaders meeting Rajiv Gandhi,
        the then prime minister of India, regarding renewed peace talks,
        in New Delhi, mid-1980s   150

6.3   Mizoram church leaders meeting Rajiv Gandhi, the then
        prime minister of India, regarding peace talks, in
        New Delhi, 1982   154

6.4   The signing of the Mizo Accord, with (*left to right sitting*)
        Lalthanhawla, R. D. Pradhan, and Laldenga, 30 June 1986   155

6.5   Mizo National Front (MNF) rebels on their way to peace camps, 1986 155

6.6   Rajiv Gandhi (*centre*), the then prime minister of India, inaugurating
        Mizoram as the 23rd state of the Indian Union, 1987   156

6.7   The public welcoming the Mizo National Front (MNF) rebels and
        the martyrs in Aizawl, 1986   157

6.8   Mizo women giving tributes to the coffins of Mizo National Front (MNF)
        rebels after the signing of the peace accord   158

6.9   Celebration of Remna Ni in Aizawl, 2019   158

6.10 Memorial stone of Mizo National Front (MNF) martyrs in Nghathal village,
        Manipur, 2020   161

6.11 Martyr Thlanmual (Martyr Cemetery) in Luangmual, Aizawl, 2021   161

Preface

This book focuses on Mizo nationalism in northeast India. In 1966, the Mizos, through the Mizo National Front (MNF), declared independence from the Indian Union through an armed struggle that lasted for two decades. As a study of a national movement, the book addresses key questions and theories concerning identity, nationhood, violence, peace, and post-conflict transformation. To explore this, it examines the significance of oral culture and how it is imbricated in nationalist politics. The book traces this at two levels: first, the creation of vernacular language and idioms, which reframes and reconstructs Mizo nationalist ideas and the politics of peace; second, the irrepressibility of oral vernacular idioms and practices against the state's violent response to the Mizo nationalist movement. It brings into analytical focus the multiple oral forms of expression such as *party hla* (party songs), *hnam hla* (national songs), and *rambuai hla* (songs of troubled times). It argues that this was vernacularization at work, where political ideas and imaginations, idioms and practices, and loss and suffering were articulated in the local idiom that reflected the agency of the Mizos.

The period of the MNF movement (1966–1986) is pivotal in Mizo political history, and most often it is with the MNF that Mizo nationalism is associated. The rise and emergence of the MNF are linked to the famine that hit the Mizo Hills in 1959, causing mass anger and disenchantment directed at the Assam government. Hence, one explanation looks at the greed or grievance factor to explain the rise of Mizo nationalism. The other common explanation is the colonial isolation policy of the hill areas, particularly regions inhabited by tribal communities. The prevailing understanding is that colonial policy prevented the penetration of the Indian national consciousness by keeping the tribes in isolation. This was further aided by the Christian missionary interventions that fuelled the secessionist mindset among the tribals. The book goes beyond such arguments by taking a more *longue-durée* perspective in analysing the emergence of Mizo nationalism. It argues that the Mizo nationalist impulse was foregrounded by the vernacular consciousness, idioms, and language of *ram leh hnam* (territory and nation), the groundwork for which was laid much prior to the emergence of the MNF.

In 1946, the first political party in the form of the Mizo Union (MU) was established. The party championed the cause of the majority commoners against the despotic rule of the chiefs, who were backed by the British. The chiefs, who earlier were the primary source of authority and the protector of the people's interests, were reduced to mere administrators by the colonial state. This changing role resulted in antagonism between the chiefs and the majority of commoners who demanded the immediate end of the chiefs' rule. Led by the MU, the movement to overthrow the chiefs, or the anti-chieftainship movement, saw the support of the vast majority of the commoners, who questioned and challenged the colonial state. Unlike conventional understanding, the case of the Lushai Hills demonstrates how tribes kept in administrative isolation were politically active in articulating their aspirations. With the support of the commoners, the MU took charge of articulating the political aspirations of the Mizos in independent India. Political consciousness, in as much as it was aided by colonial intervention, was home-grown, where the Mizos, both elites and commoners, articulated and asserted themselves politically. It is the evolution of this consciousness, and how it shaped the political culture up to the launching of the independence movement, that I trace in the book.

The political mobilization under the leadership of the MU has had a lasting influence on Mizo society and politics. It altered political configuration by displacing the old political authority and instituting a decentralized form of politics, whose success was only enabled due to the participation of the masses. More significant for our purpose here is how the grammar of Mizo politics was laid down, grounded within the oral world of Mizo society. The MU volunteers used songs to protest and challenge their rival political parties. Even as the leadership of the MU was largely drawn from the elites, the tone and tenor of Mizo politics were set by the songs whose composers and singers were from diverse backgrounds. This continued up to the rise and emergence of the MNF, which began to employ what is now known as *hnam hla* to spread the ideas and ideologies of Mizo nationalism. During the period of counter-insurgency, another genre known as *rambuai hla* emerged as a genre of songs that captured the Mizos' lived experiences under terror and violence. Drawing upon the multiple genres, we acknowledge the role of non-MNF members and non-elites in the articulation and imagination of Mizo nationalism. From song composers to rebels, one finds that orality facilitated the extensive dissemination of ideas of nationalism beyond borders and across regions.

Acknowledgements

This book began as a doctoral project at the Tata Institute of Social Sciences (TISS) in Guwahati in the year 2013. Evidently, it has been a long journey, and I have incurred many debts over the years. However much has changed in terms of contents and materials, the core idea remains the same. I am grateful for the support I received from faculty and friends at the TISS, who shaped my intellectual thinking. I owe a great debt to my doctoral supervisor, Professor Virginius Xaxa, particularly for his patience and understanding towards my project. My post-PhD stopover in multiple places gave me the opportunity to rework and refine the work—first at the Centre for the Study of Developing Societies (CSDS), New Delhi, followed by fellowships at Harvard University, at the Indian Institute of Technology (IIT), Guwahati, and at IIT Roorkee (IITR), my current institutional affiliation, which provided me the space to complete the work. At the CSDS, I got the opportunity to work and focus exclusively on my work. I greatly benefitted from the resources within Delhi, such as the National Archives of India (NAI), the Institute of Defence Studies and Analysis (IDAS), the Nehru Memorial Museum and Library (NMML), and the library at Jawaharlal Nehru University (JNU).

Outside academic spaces, I am fortunate to have received support and company from friends while conducting fieldwork. My thanks go to those who gave me so much of their time, accompanying me in my interviews and helping me locate and find documents: to Lalnunpuia, for guiding and driving me around in Aizawl and to Pu J. D. Mawia and his family for hosting me in the Jampui Hills, Tripura. Yet all of this is possible only because of my research participants, and I thank each one of them for sharing their experiences and stories with me. The names of my research participants have been changed to maintain confidentiality. At the time of writing this, the project has just entered its eighth year, including my time as a doctoral student. For all these years, the more I learned, read, and researched Mizo politics, the less I felt I knew, with my confidence dipping every time I sat to think and write. Hence, the work was always in progress, and by the time I finished the book it had expanded quite significantly. This was only possible because of the continued support from friends who helped me collect and ship materials that I needed, ranging from books to photographs, and to my research participants who made themselves available online and on phone calls on occasions when I was unable to travel and visit the field. I feel extremely privileged to have gotten all the support that I have needed, always on time.

In 2018–2019, a one-year post-doctoral position at the Lakshmi Mittal and Family South Asia Institute, Harvard University, was critical to the fruition of this work. At Harvard, the academic support and resources were instrumental in my revision and reworking of various chapters of the book. Upon arriving at the university, my excitement knew no bounds, what with the libraries at Harvard housing a range of vernacular Mizo books, some of which I painstakingly borrowed and carried along with me for my research! I thank the staff and faculty at the university for their support during my fellowship: Andrea Wright for inviting me to Brown University for a talk at the Center for Contemporary South Asia and Susan Laurence, Paula Lee, and Bertrand for hosting me with love, care, and support. From day one at Harvard, Susan ensured that I receive full support and utilize the university resources to the fullest. I remain thankful to her!

I returned to Guwahati in 2019, which was re-enlivening and, at the same time, challenging. Within a month of my joining IIT Guwahati, my mother was diagnosed with cancer, which had greatly affected all of our family. We are fortunate to have received love and support from friends, although my work had to take a back seat. However, I am glad that the book is finally seeing the light of day. Dixita Deka, Pavei, Sangay Tamang, Savio, Jitu Kumar, and faculty at IIT Guwahati, Dr Ngamjahao Kipgen and Professor Sambit Mallick—their friendships and presence were invaluable; they helped me through one of the most challenging times of my life.

A rewarding part of academic life and work is the people we meet, the new friendships and the network it offers. This book is an outcome of such meetings and camaraderie developed across regions and continents, and this I consider to be one of the greatest perks about being in this profession. In this spirit I am grateful to friends, old and new, for the academic and friendly conversations in different places: Ashutosh Kumar, Aashish Xaxa, Benjamin V. Jamkhanpau, Jasnea Sarma, Dolly Kikon, C. Zonunmawia, Gangsim Eon, Japheath, Johannes Maakar, Joy Pachuau, Lalhriatchiani, Suanmuanlian Tonsing, Paul Lalchhanhima, V. Pumkhansiam, Sanjay (Xonzoi) Barbora, Ramengmawia, and Raile Rocky. Special thanks to my friends Ngarin Singlai and Pragya Gautam for helping me collect archival materials and guiding me in Delhi. Professor Kham Khan Suan Hausing, Hyderabad Central University, provided unstinted support since my time as a doctoral student. If there is anyone who played a key role and oversaw my academic work, it is Professor Kham Khan Suan Hausing (commonly addressed as Professor Suan or U Suan) for me and many others. I am also glad to have met and known Professor Duncan McDuie-Ra, University of Newcastle, Australia, whose words of advice and support have been extremely helpful and motivating. My sincere thanks to Sawmtei Chongthu and Thara Tlau for helping me with the translation work and to Lalthlanchhuaha for the cover design. I am especially grateful to Lalruatkima, Academy of Integrated Christian Studies (AICS), Aizawl, whose close readings of the book have helped in strengthening its structure. My sincere appreciation to Peace Accord MNF Returnees (PAMRA) leaders and Pu L. R. Sailo for willingly sharing with me their photograph collections and to Lalpekhlui, Tarun Bhartiya, and Lalnupuia for their timely help in finding photographs.

Various sections of the chapters were presented at multiple platforms—at the CSDS, JNU, Brown University, Yale University, Mizoram University—and on various occasions in the form of seminar papers. The comments and critique received at these forums enabled me to rework and refine the arguments in the book. I express my sincere gratitude to Qudsiya Ahmed, the head of academic publishing, and Anwesha Rana, my commissioning editor, at Cambridge University Press India, for believing in the project and their kind exigence. To Priyanka Das and her team at the Press, I am grateful for their editorial prowess that has greatly refined the book in its present form. However, any mistakes in the book are entirely my own.

Finally, my greatest debt is to my family for their patience and for teaching me perseverance; I owe deep gratitude to them. Even in the most difficult of circumstances, I was never asked to quit, and this book in its entirety is the fruit of that. Last but not least, I thank my wife, Ruati, for being with me and seeing the project through its completition.

Abbreviations

AFCO	Anti-Famine Campaign Organization
AFSPA	Armed Forces (Special Powers) Act
AIR	All India Radio
AMPO	Assam Maintenance of Public Order
APCC	Assam Pradesh Congress Committee
APHLC	All Party Hill Leaders Conference
AR	Assam Rifles
ASC	Advisory Subcommittee
ATC	Aizawl Theological College
BJP	Bharatiya Janata Party
CA	Constituent Assembly
CADC	Chakma Autonomous District Council
CEO	chief election officer
CHTs	Chittagong Hill Tracts
CI	circle interpreter
CIJW	Counter-Insurgency Jungle Warfare
CNF	Chin National Front
CYMA	Central Young Mizo Association
DoI	Defence of India
ELAs	Extended Loop Areas
HNU	Hmar National Union

HPC	Hmar People's Convention
HPC-D	Hmar People's Convention (Democratic)
HRC	Human Rights Committee
INC	Indian National Congress
JP	Janata Party
KNA	Kuki National Assembly
MCS	Mizo Cultural Society
MKHC	Mizoram Kohhran Hruaitute Committee
MLA	member of legislative assembly
MNF	Mizo National Front
MNFF	Mizo National Famine Front
MNVs	Mizo National Volunteers
MNA	Mizo National Army
MSA	Mizoram State Archives
MSU	Mizo Students Union
MU	Mizo Union
MZP	Mizo Zirlai Pawl
NAI	National Archives of India
NC	National Council
NGCs	New Grouping Centres
NNC	Naga National Council
NNL	Naga National League
PAMRA	Peace Accord MNF Returnees Association
PC	People's Conference
PLRC	Pawi-Lakher Regional Council
PLTU	Pawi-Lakher Tribal Union
PPVs	Protected and Progressive Villages
RC	Regional Council
RSS	Rashtriya Swayamsevak Sangh
SF	Special Force
STs	Scheduled Tribes
UMFO	United Mizo Freedom Organization
UT	union territory
VCP	village council president
VGCs	Voluntary Grouping Centres
YMA	Young Mizo Association

Notes on Transliteration and Translation

I have not followed any standard guidelines or conventions of translating Mizo into English in the book. The songs, in particular, have been taken from a mix of published and unpublished sources, both online and print. As such, diacritical marks and other writing conventions in the Mizo language are not strictly followed and, in most cases, omitted. In many instances, I have observed differences in the lyrics of the songs, and in such cases I have tried to retain the essence of the original by cross-checking them against two or more sources. The translation work has been undertaken collectively, and I appreciate the support of friends and colleagues who have assisted me.

1 Introduction

In November 2018, a protest engulfed the state of Mizoram, demanding the removal of the state's chief election officer (CEO), S. B. Shashank (Figure 1.1). With just a month away from the state's assembly election, the protest came in the wake of the CEO's attempt to allow Bru refugees to vote in the election. The Mizos perceived the move as being politically motivated by the Bharatiya Janata Party (BJP) trying to gain support of the Brus and alienate the Mizos against the non-Christians of the state. Ethnic relations between the Mizos and the Brus have been strained since the 1990s, resulting in conflict and displacement, with many Brus fleeing to the neighbouring state of Tripura (Roluahpuia 2018a). The case of the Mizo–Bru tension is embroiled with the state electoral issue, particularly after the coming of the BJP in power at the centre in 2014. Given the party's ideology, the BJP did not find much appeal among the dominant Mizos, who are predominantly Christian. With this, the party shifted its focus onto the ethnic minorities of the state, the Brus, including the Chakmas—who mostly practise animism and Buddhism—as its support base. The final blow came when the centre agreed to the transfer of the state's principal secretary, Pu Lalnunmawia Chuaungo, a Mizo bureaucrat. This had further intensified the discontentment among the Mizos with major organizations, such as the Central Young Mizo Association (CYMA), the Mizo Zirlai Pawl (Mizo Student Federation) (MZP), and state celebrities, including sportspersons, coming out in the open to extend solidarity. An online campaign on various social media platforms demanding Shashank's removal galvanized like-minded netizens. Mizos from Manipur, Tripura, and different parts of India released a press handout to mark their solidarity.

Figure 1.1   Leaders of various Mizo organizations on the stage of the protest during the Mizo *hnam hnatlang* (voluntary action to save the Mizo nation), 2018
Source: Explore   Mizoram,   https://www.exploremizoram.com/2018/11/hnam-chhan-hnatlang.html (accessed in November 2022).

In Mizoram's recent past, the protest to oust Shashank is one of the few political mobilizations that the state has witnessed on such a massive or extensive scale. It demonstrates that local politics, both electoral and ethnic, are entangled with the interplay of regional and national political interests. This is particularly true in the case of the Mizo–Bru ethnic tension. The case of the ethnic tension between the Mizos and the Brus has a longer history. Since the eruption of the conflict in 1997, various organizations such as the Rashtriya Swayamsevak Sangh (RSS) and the Vanvasi Kalyan have operated in the refugee camps of the Brus, mobilizing the community. The Bru community conveniently fits into the right-wing narrative that projects tribal communities as 'backward Hindus'. The success of the RSS and its sister organizations was soon felt as the Brus began to project themselves as 'Hindus' suffering at the hands of the majority Christian community.

Two crucial features mark the protest (Figure 1.2). First, the protest was held under the name Mizo *hnam hnatlang*, a call upon the public to come out together in protest against the CEO of the state to save their *hnam* (clan, tribe, or nation),[1] Mizo. The Mizos' sense of being a community is informed by their idea of *hnam*. The *hnam* consciousness can refer to or relate to a clan, tribe, ethnicity, or nation. The Mizos' sense of nationalism is closely intertwined with their *ram*[2] (territory or land),

Figure 1.2 Mizo *hnam hnatlang* (voluntary action to save the Mizo nation) in Aizawl, Mizoram, 6 November 2018
Source: Reuben Lalmalsawma, Aizawl, Mizoram.

commonly referred to as Zoram (Zoland) or Mizoram (land of the Mizos). Hence, their idea of nationalism has to do more with Mizo nationalism and not necessarily state nationalism, or, in this case, Indian nationalism. The protest brought to the fore, once again, the question of the Mizos' integration into the Indian Union, an issue that remains an undercurrent in Mizo politics.

Second, a lesser recognized and unacknowledged aspect of the protest is the circulation of *hnam hla* (national songs) during the protest. Social media was flooded with verses of patriotic songs, and artists were invited to sing popular *hnam hla* on the day of the protest. In Mizo political history, *hnam hla* were a vital source of mobilization and continues to be sung in important sociocultural and political events. Specific to the protest, it was the songs composed by Rokunga that became one of the most sung and circulated. Rokunga is a known composer whose songs became widely popular at the dawn of India's independence. As India's independence drew near, various *hnam hla* were composed through which the Mizos expressed their political aspirations. Rokunga's songs swept the hills of Mizoram, Manipur, and Tripura. His song 'Ro Min Rel Sak Ang Che' (Be Thou Our Counsellor) remains widely popular today. Largely, the case of *hnam hla* demonstrates the persistence of a strong *hnam* consciousness among the Mizos.

Hnam hla have an important lesson for us in the way we understand nationalism. *Hnam hla* in Mizo history were particularly significant and widely popular during the Mizo struggle for independence. For this reason, *hnam hla* were closely associated with the Mizo National Front (MNF). For the MNF, *hnam hla* were an important node for transmitting nationalist ideas. *Hnam hla* proliferated particularly after the outbreak of the conflict with composers mostly being MNF members themselves. Both the MNF and non-MNF members composed songs that shaped the idea of Mizo nationalism. The influence of composers aids our understanding of nationalism and their contribution. In fact, in post-colonial Mizo society, modern electoral politics have engendered an offshoot genre of *party hla*[3] (party songs), where political parties use songs to mobilize support and counter their rivals. *Hnam hla* are political narratives that contain a rich source of information about the ideas and ideology of nationalism.

Another aspect of this is the cultural context that underpins why *hla* (songs) have such a strong resonance. The use of *hla* in general and *hnam hla* in particular needs to be understood within the sociocultural milieu of Mizo society. At its heart, Mizo society is an oral society. The practice of orality has a strong cultural context where knowledge and histories are transmitted orally. For a society that primarily relied on oral communication, the practice is deeply interwoven into the social fabric and easily adaptable to the larger community. *Hla* in Mizo society occupy a central place in understanding the history, literature, and culture of the community. Historically, various genres of *hla* emerged in Mizo society, and such genres reflect the specific time, period, and context to understand Mizo society. For instance, historians used *hla* as a means to periodize Mizo history according to the form and style of the *hla*. The Mizo historian Lalthangliana (1993) categorized *hla* in Mizo society according to the time period in which they were composed; accordingly, he noted more than 30 types of *hla*. Likewise, Chhuanvawra (2011) noted more than 50 types of *hla* whose history dates back to way before colonial rule. While not all types of *hla* are sung any longer and nor are their tunes followed, different forms of *hla* continue to survive and remain significant to this day.

Historical studies analyse how *hla* reflect the sociocultural change and transformation in Mizo society. This is particularly evident from the time the Mizos converted to Christianity, beginning in the late nineteenth century. While there was no fundamental break between the pre-Christian and post-Christian eras in terms of the songs, the tune and tenor of the *hla* were influenced by Christian hymns composed by the missionaries as well as local Mizo composers. On the centrality of Christianity, Thirumal, Laldinpuii, and Lalrozami (2019: 15) note that 'the connection between script and scripture was established through the singing of Christian hymns and the introduction of performative culture instead of a textual culture'. During this period, new styles of singing, such as *puma zai* and *kaihlek hla*,[4] began to be popular. Both genres of songs emerged at a time when religious revivals, locally referred to as *harhna sang*,[5] spread across the hills. The Christian Mizos quickly adapted to the new religion and made Christianity their 'own' religion, and soon, they repudiated other forms of traditional rituals and singing, with *lengzem hla* (love or romantic songs) being one. The songs that were sung were strictly monitored, and the church leaders decreed against any form of singing or songs that were not Christian hymns.

What made this history significant to understand is that it directly influences the tune and tenor of *party hla* and *hnam hla*. The tone of much of the *party hla* composed by the Mizo Union (MU) supporters were sung using the tune of the gospel hymns. This was the case with *hnam hla* as well. In fact, in the case of *hnam hla*, what has become quite pronounced is the Christian symbolism, showing the profound influence Christianity has had on the Mizos' sociocultural and political world. In all this history, it was in *hla*—in other words, the 'oral'—that Mizos expressed their experience of change. The place of the 'oral' has increasingly gained significance in scholarly studies on the Mizos. More recent studies have examined not the 'oral' per se but the forms and narratives of Mizo oral culture. Often, they are categorized as *thawnthu* and *chanchin*. The former encompasses a wide array of oral practices such as folktales, lore, and myths, while the latter is mostly used to refer to stories, literal and historical (Thirumal, Laldinpuii, and Lalrozami 2019: 21). Others take orality as a way of tracing the history and myths of origin (Zama 2005). *Hla*, in particular, remain imperative in these narratives of history as a specific genre of songs was composed to define an event or emerged as a specific response to historical events (Lalthangliana 1998). Of this, *hla* provide a vital resource to trace and locate the historical agency of the Mizos. In other words, *hla*, in the form of *zai* (singing), were the predominant means of expression (Thirumal, Laldinpuii, and Lalrozami 2019: 18).

In the broader context, songs and nationalism are widely studied fields. If nationalism shapes the sound of music, songs themselves also shape the way nationalism is defined. Such literatures have focused more on the relationship between music and nationalism and their significant role in shaping ideas about national identity and culture (Bohlman 2004, 2010; Gooptu 2018; Subramanian 2020). From national anthems to anti-colonial resistance, songs have been effectively used to mobilize the masses. In important national events and commemorations, songs are sung with much valour and pride. Such is the centrality of songs in the national life of the country that even in sporting events, national anthems are played, and today, there is no nation-state without anthems. Anti-colonial movements were infused with songs, and in many cases, it was songs that inspired such movements. In India, too, it was song composers that stirred the movement for independence. Writing on Tagore, Chakrabarty (1999: 31) notes that his poetry offered a mode of expressing and experiencing intense feelings for the nation, a feeling that transports the body beyond the remits of historical time. The imagination of free India was expressed in songs that were later on used by nationalist leaders to mobilize the public.

Within nationalism studies, the study of national songs occupies a central place. The historiography examines the connection between national songs and state nationalism (Bohlman 2004; Riley and Smith 2016). This is true of both European and formerly colonized countries. As formerly colonized societies gained independence, anti-colonial songs were elevated to national songs. They became essential ways by which states infused nationalism through their institutions, extending from schools to government-run institutions. The production and performative aspects of such songs demonstrate how elites used them as a mechanism to govern their citizens. Such songs often carry the imaginaries about the state, usually defined by grandeur, with the intention to stir sentiments. Citizens emotionally connect with them, and this is what makes such songs powerful and relevant in nationalist politics.

National and popular leaders have effectively used songs to mobilize and garner political support. Subramanian (2020) has demonstrated how M. K. Gandhi retorted to public prayers and music as a way to communicate and mobilize the public. In such cases, Gandhi was able to weave his idea about the India he imagined, a multi-faith country. The songs and music he chose were drawn from different regions and religions, displaying the diverse communities that inhabit the country. In this, song composers played a critical role in arousing anti-colonial sentiments and used them to counter colonial policies. Patriotic songs are influenced by the cultural context in which they are composed. The tune and lyrics are rooted in the sociocultural and religious contexts. However, the case has been mostly that such studies tend to focus on the musical work and familiar composers (Curtis 2008; Riley and Smith 2016). It is also the case in India, where composers and poets considered 'national' are mostly familiar composers. This is often at the behest of marginalizing regional composers.

This book situates *hnam hla* and the rise of *hnam* consciousness among the Mizos of northeast India. It argues that the idea of *ram leh hnam* (territory and nation) and *hnam* consciousness is pivotal to understanding Mizo nationalism. The idea of *hnam* encompasses the Mizo sense of 'self'—being 'Mizo' and the distinct way in which 'Mizoness' is articulated in everyday language. It is common to encounter terms and sayings such as 'Ava Zo[6] em' (It is very Zo), Zopa (Zo man), and Zonu (Zo woman) that all point towards a distinct sense of Mizo identity. They are expressions that define Mizoness. It can be ways of talking, appearance, and dressing. This distinctiveness permeates national thinking, which is best encapsulated when one explores how the vernacular language shaped the Mizos' political life-worlds.

The book locates the rise and emergence of Mizo national consciousness by examining various literary sources, with *hla* being one of the most prominent. The lyrical content of *hnam hla* and their tones fit into what are mostly known as patriotic songs. In the book, *hnam hla* are examined within the context of the Mizo oral culture. It further extends into how the Mizos conceive their idea of nation and nationalism, and *hnam hla* represent the 'long term process of vernacularization' (Michelutti 2008: 18). National movements are often associated with tall leaders and the organizations involved in leading such movements. A reading of *hnam hla* shows how the composers of such songs included both MNF and non-MNF members, elite and non-elite. Not all Mizos are members of the MNF, and non-MNF members equally have a strong *hnam* consciousness and consider themselves nationalists. The vernacularization of nationalist ideas and ideals expands our understanding of nationalism in general and Mizo nationalism in particular.

The MNF has used vernacular expressions such as *ram leh hnam* and *zalenna* (freedom) through which it localizes the nationalist expressions in a language understandable to all. This vernacularization of nationalist ideas further shows how the Mizos reshape modern notions of nation and nationalism in the local. The language of the movement and the ideology that underpins it are framed as *zalenna* and the struggle as *ram leh hnam tan* (for our land and nation). *Zalenna* becomes the core ideological base and the political motive of the movement. The use of *zalenna* contrasts the existing and predominant analytical frames by which the MNF movement is studied, such as insurgency, regionalism, and ethnic movements. Adopting and examining the vernacularization process enables us to appreciate and acknowledge the agency of the so-called rebels. The projection of their struggle as *zalenna* is pivotal in the writings of MNF leaders such as Laldenga and Zoramthanga. *Zalenna* also found its usage in songs, and that formed the core ideology of the movement.

More than the study of the songs per se, the book interrogates the relationship between orality and nationalist politics and shows how the oral and print cultures were mutually constitutive. It examines this through the vernacularization of politics and nationalist ideas by exploring the divergent ways in which Mizos localize expressions by using terms such as *zalenna*, *ram leh hnam tan*, and different genres of *hla* to express and articulate their aspirations, dissent, and disenchantment. Specific to politics, *hla* were one of the first mediums through which political ideas were transmitted. The political visions of individuals and political parties expressed their political desire and articulated their aspirations through *hla*. In this way, the book locates the rise of *hnam* consciousness preceding the emergence of the MNF.

While the MNF did lead the movement for independence, the case of *hnam hla* has a deeper legacy rooted in the political culture of the Mizos. The MU used songs as a weapon of protest against the British political superintendent and the continuing rule of the chiefs. Under democratic India, the party advocated the abolishment of chieftainship and used *party hla* for electoral mobilization against their rival, the United Mizo Freedom Organization (UMFO). Furthermore, the significance of orality becomes evident in how the Mizos resort to *hla* to express their grief and suffering during the period of counter-insurgency. Now known as *rambuai hla* (songs of troubled times), local communities fell back to oral culture, and there was a proliferation of songs about suffering and sacrifice, pain and loss. With media censorship and high surveillance, *rambuai hla* emerged as a form of oral expression through which experience and encounters of violence are moved to the oral domain. This makes the oral vital to understanding Mizo politics. Hence, the emergence of various genres of *hla*—namely, *party hla*, *hnam hla*, and *rambuai hla*—are means through which the Mizos record and express political ideas, imagination, and discontent. *Hnam hla* and *rambuai hla*, in particular, soon caught the attention of the state and were then subsequently banned from being sung in public. Most of *hnam hla* as such were disallowed on the radio. Today only a few recordings of both the *hnam hla* and *rambuai hla* are done. Likewise, any print materials related to the MNF or politics were also burned, if not banned, during the period of the MNF movement.

The case of the Mizos also raises important questions about how nationalism emerged in backward regions with limited literacy. There was no 'high culture', to use Ernest Gellner's expression, when Mizo nationalism emerged. Moreover, the northeastern part of India, except for Assam, did not experience any form of industrialization, even during the colonial period. The areas inhabited by the Mizos, the 'savagery tribes' in the colonial lexicon, were left out of the colonial economy and excluded from any meaningful political participation. This, however, is not to undermine the presence of print culture and the influence of modern education. Moreover, Mizo society was largely agrarian with a subsistence economy, and during the 1950s and the 1960s, there were no communication links and industrialization. A modernist explanation is inadequate to explain the rise of Mizo nationalism.

Furthermore, various common theoretical approaches have been used to explain Mizo nationalism. However, such works, more than writing about Mizo nationalism, have to do with analysing the MNF movement, its rise, and its fall. In this context, secessionism is one of the common ways through which the MNF movement is studied. In fact, secessionism is a prominent issue in northeast India. Its geographical location and isolation have made it a periphery, both in the ideas and imagination of the national leadership and the powers at the centre. This follows the explanation of the emergence of nationalism in peripheral regions and among minority groups. Prominent examples of this are the Basque Country in Spain, Quebec in Canada, Papua in Indonesia, Karen, Kachin, and other ethnic minorities in Myanmar, and similarly among ethnic and religious minorities in various regions of India such as Punjab, Jammu and Kashmir, and Tamil Nadu, among others. Such cases are often referred to as 'peripheral nationalism', where secessionist tendencies have emerged due to the exploitative tendencies of the core region, leading to an uneven and unequal pattern of development (Hechter 1975; Nairn 1977). Peripheral regions and minority groups feel alienated, and this becomes more pronounced when they have a strong sense of cultural identity. Hence, the desire for independence from the core emerges and often translates into nationalist movements aspiring for independence.

Another trend of studies examines nationalist conflict within the broad framework of the conflict between official nationalism of the state and regional nationalism. In India, this has been widely approached as a tension between pan-Indian nationalism and regionalism (A. Guha 1982; U. Phadnis 1989; Baruah 1999). From this perspective, it is common to see cultural explanations of nationalism. Hutchinson (1987) examines the significance of how the Gaelic revival stimulates a thinking that promotes an identity consciousness with the potential to recur even after the establishment of nation-states. The argument is that nationalism is not only a political movement alone, as it has a strong cultural aspect. This explanation has a strong influence within the field of nationalism studies (Hroch 1985; Smith 1986, 2008; Hutchinson 1987; 1994; P. Chatterjee 1993). They stress the role of myths, symbols, art, tradition, the *ethnie*, according to Smith (1986), and how they are appropriated by cultural nationalists that get regenerated from time to time. With nationalism thought to wane and fade away with modernity and become irrelevant under the forces of globalization, its persistence is explained by the strong presence of cultural nationalism.

Hardly has there been any real effort to approach the Mizo case within the studies of nationalism. In the context of South Asia, and India in particular, such movements are commonly approached as insurgency or ethnic movements. While most nation-states claim the national question as resolved or the issue of national integration as settled, communities such as the Mizos continue to have a strong sense of being a distinct nation. This distinct sense is emblematic of how they govern, organize, and perceive themselves apart from their Indian counterparts. In other words, the *hnam* consciousness fosters an idea of belonging that is not only imbued with a strong sense of difference vis-à-vis 'Indians' but also involves the assertion of a pan-Mizo identity. A pan-Mizo social network in the form of institutions such as the Young Mizo Association (YMA) fosters an ethnic belonging that transcends national borders, both inter and intra. However, the prevailing view is that *hnam* consciousness is considered a mere identity consciousness, and ethnic mobilizations in the form of protests are relegated as sporadic outbursts and reactionary.

Even today, Mizo nationalism is associated with the MNF movement, and the end of the armed struggle is considered the end of Mizo nationalism. In pursuing my study on Mizo nationalism, I commonly encounter the question 'What is there left to study given that the movement is already over?' In seminars and academic gatherings, this question continues to linger. The point here is not so much about the naivety of the question but how it reflects the way we look at contemporary Mizo society, politics, and nationalism, generally. Following this, a question that began to bother me was 'Does the MNF only signify the emergence or end of Mizo nationalism?' The MNF today, as a political party, has proclaimed itself as the guardian of Mizo nationalism. One may also ask: What did Mizo nationalism mean to the non-MNF members before, and what does it mean today? How do ordinary people perceive and construct their sense of Mizo nationalism?

In writing about nationalism, Billig (1995) argues that what we understand as nationalism is inherently limited and biased. In his critique of the existing theories of nationalism, he writes: 'Nationalism is equated with the outlook of nationalist movement and when there are no such movements; nationalism is not seen as an issue' (Billig 1995: 16). In *Banal Nationalism* (1995), Billig demonstrates that even in established liberal democracies where nationalism is so routinized and familiar, it goes unrecognized as expressions of nationalism, such as the 'un-waved flags'. He argues that the banality of various acts and events are ways by which the state reminds its citizens of their national place. Succeeding studies on nationalism have attended to the more mundane and quotidian aspect of nationalism, dealing with 'everyday nationhood'. Two significant contributions of these studies are that they have introduced what is now commonly referred to as 'bottom-up' studies of nationalism and put the masses at the heart of nationalism studies.

This book is not necessarily concerned with the everyday practices of nationhood in the Mizo context. However, what is relevant is that the way we think and perceive of nationalism, including that of the Mizos, is underpinned by the fact that it is seen only in the form of an extremist movement—in this case, armed struggle. From this viewpoint, Mizo nationalism is irrelevant and non-existent in contemporary times. There are certain caveats inherent in this explanation. To begin with, it is restrictive because it equates Mizo nationalism with the MNF, thereby denying the contribution and participation of the non-MNF members and ordinary Mizos in shaping the idea of Mizo nationalism. Furthermore, this view is unhelpful in explaining the contemporary tensions about national identity and nationhood in India. As already noted, the Mizos continue to have a strong sense of being a distinct *hnam* in the Indian Union. Most importantly, the nationalist impulse was foregrounded through the consciousness that was expressed in the vernacular notion of *ram leh hnam*, the groundwork for which was laid prior to the emergence of the MNF. Needless to say, the Mizos' sense of being a distinct *hnam* is strongly attached to the notion of *ram*, which, in turn, is deeply connected to the emergent political consciousness that began to take shape during the colonial period.

Today, the Mizos are collectively recognized as Scheduled Tribes (STs) under the Constitution of India. In northeast India, they inhabit a compact geographical area, although they are divided by state and national boundaries. Within northeast India, the predominant population is concentrated in Mizoram, with a much smaller number in Manipur, Tripura, Meghalaya, and Assam. Contemporary Mizo consciousness and the conception of Mizo identity are rooted in the long history of their encounters and negotiations with the colonial and post-colonial states. They are a 'product of the specific long-term historical and cultural process', as J. Pachuau (2014: 7) puts it. For instance, there is an intricate connection between the consolidation of Mizo identity and the aspirations for the territorial unity of all the Mizo-inhabited areas under one administrative unit. Furthermore, the choice to rename the place from Lushai[7] Hills to Mizo Hills and subsequently adopt 'Mizo' against 'Lushai' for self-identification was intentional—an act and assertion to define a sense of collective belonging. Hence, in this book, I locate Mizo agency through the study of Mizo politics with a focus on the MNF movement in northeast India.

Mizo Politics: Background and Context

Politically, the MU first used the term 'Mizo' when it changed the name of the then party, Lushai Commoners Union, to MU. Established in 1946, the MU leaders, belonging to diverse clans and tribal groups, favoured the use of 'Mizo' over 'Lusei', the name of the tribe who were also the ruling and dominant chiefs in the Lushai Hills. This usage gives further credence to the aspirations for territorial unity, what they called 'Mizo inhabited areas', under one administrative unit. Heavily backed by the Mizo public, the MU's anti-chief stance popularized the party among the majority of the commoners. At the dawn of India's independence, it was able to project itself as representing the voice of the people to the British and Indian national leaders. A counter-mobilization by the chiefs and their supporters was made by another party, the UMFO, led by Lalbiakthanga. The political competition became evident in the demands made by the two parties, with the MU opting for integration with the Indian Union while the UMFO sought to join Burma (present-day Myanmar).

Amid this divide, there were also individuals and groups within the MU who aspired for the independence of Mizoram. Both the MU and the UMFO continued to be the main rivals until natural interruptions, in the form of the famine of 1959, led to the gradual downfall of the MU, the more popular of the political parties in the Mizo Hills.[8] Despite their political rivalries, one of the demands of the parties was for territorial integration of the Mizo-inhabited areas into a single administrative unit. Yet, between 1947 and 1960, various Mizo leaders felt a sense of cultural loss due to economic and cultural dominance by the *vai* (plains people). It was during this time that the Mizo Cultural Society (MCS) was established to protect and safeguard the traditions and customs of the Mizos. Notable leaders among them were Laldenga, R. B. Chawnga, R. Zuala, and R. Vanlawma.

The activities of the organization were directed towards protecting and safeguarding the existing Mizo culture. In 1959, the MCS organized a rally in Aizawl to condemn the neglect and ineptitude of the Assam government towards the incoming famine in the Mizo Hills. The rally, however, cost the leaders of the movement—from being suspended if not arrested—as they were government employees, such as its president Chawnga and Laldenga, employed under the Mizo District Council (Chawngsailova 2007: 2–3). In 1959, the MCS was converted into the Mizo National Famine Front (MNFF), focusing entirely on relief and rehabilitation. By this time, Laldenga had emerged as the organization's face. With the famine receding after two years, the MNFF rechristened itself as a political party and openly proclaimed independence. The loss of lives during the famine reinforced the Mizo view of the need for self-reliance and self-determination and convinced the leaders of the MNF that independence was the only way out (Aplin and Lalsiamliana 2010: 22). In 1961, as the MNFF was transformed into the MNF, it openly expressed the goal of achieving *zalenna sang ber* (the highest form of self-determination). The demand for independence took a violent turn in 1966 when the MNF declared independence at midnight on 28 February 1966.

Broadly speaking, there are two dominant perspectives regarding the emergence of political consciousness among the Mizos. The first view reflects the total reduction of the common people to passive actors, thereby silencing their voices. For instance, in commenting on the Mizos' options of integration and independence at the dawn of India's independence, B. B. Goswami (1979: 135) notes, 'The common people, many of them though literate, did not have the competence to grade the intricacies and the consequences of these problems.' The second perspective is the oft-repeated argument that the colonial exclusion policy of tribes, such as the Mizos, brought about a rift between them and the mainland Indians. Hence, this created fertile ground for secessionist movements. Therefore, the conclusion is that colonial policy and religious proselytization were the reasons for the unrest in the region. On this line, S. Chatterjee (1994: 7) observed, 'The secluded line confined the intellect of the Mizos to narrow limits. They did not take very seriously the changes that were brought about by World War I. They had practically no idea about the political dynamics of their own country.' This seclusion of the Mizos not only isolated them from the larger Indian society but also 'sowed the seeds of hatred between the rest of the Indians and the Mizos' (Goswami 1979: 136).

Contrary to such a view, this book demonstrates how the Mizos were conscious political actors and actively involved in the politics of their time. In this process, the role of the traditional and educated elites remains significant. For the Mizos, this was activated through their demand to recognize Mizo identity (*hnam*) and for the autonomy of their territory (*ram*), either within the Indian Union or outside of it. Likewise, the trend was similar in other tribal areas of northeast India, where issues of identity and autonomy were two central concerns. The task of this book then is to explain how this was envisioned and articulated and how and why this idea has become internalized and embedded, even in contemporary Mizo society. Additionally, Mizo identity and nationalism found resonance beyond the territorial borders of Mizoram. This book therefore probes what made this political transgression of boundaries possible. Furthermore, it seeks to explore what enabled the emergence of a strong political consciousness, leading to the struggle for independence, given the backward economic condition of the Mizos in the 1950s and the 1960s.

Edensor (2002) states that the major theories of nationalism have focused mainly on the dominant elite culture, often equating them with the national culture.

One of the most salient aspects of Edensor's argument is what he calls the 'cultic milieu', which he uses to show how the various cultural elements are dismissed as 'wild', 'vernacular', 'traditional', and 'irrelevant'. However, to Edensor, they can, in fact, be the main determining factors of contemporary national identity. In a similar vein, Fahmy (2011), in the case of Egypt, notes that the emergence of national identity did not occur merely around the high culture or the literate masses. Rather, he argues that it was through the Egyptian colloquial language that the masses were exposed to a national culture that further helped create a modern Egyptian national identity. In concurring with Edensor, Fahmy shows how news, rumours, jokes, and gossip, which he calls 'oral sources and direct social interactions', effectively reach a broad audience—literate and illiterate.

Cueing in on Edensor and Fahmy's observation, this book focuses on two key issues. First, it looks at the critical role of the oral to understand Mizo politics. This is examined in two forms. The first is songs as a form of oral expression, examining the emergence of various genres of *hla* that are now known as *party hla, hnam hla,* and *rambuai hla.* All of them are tied to nationalist politics. In fact, one of the most visible manifestations of this is how songs play a pivotal role throughout the Mizo national movement. Prior to the outbreak of the conflict in 1966, numerous songs were composed with a strong nationalistic fervour. The MNF made skillful use of the songs composed by individuals such as Rokunga and Laltanpuia and later on by the MNF rebels themselves. The second is the oral narration as a way of uncovering the diverse voices in relation to the movement. Studies on violence and nation-making show that oral narratives have a unique capacity to unearth both the voice and testimonies of hitherto silenced persons and histories that official records suppressed (Butalia 1998; Saikia 2011). Oral narratives of the MNF rebels provide insight into the contestations and complexities surrounding the question of peace, violence, and the movement at large.

Second, the MNF used local idioms to construct and circulate nationalist ideas. For instance, for every member of the MNF, the struggle was for *zalenna* and the sacrifice for *ram leh hnam.* This book then explores the vernacular notion of *zalenna* and *ram leh hnam* to engage Mizo nationalism. Using local terms such as *zalenna* and *ram leh hnam* is what I call 'vernacular nationalism', which reframes and reconstructs the nation in local terms, making it distinctively Mizo. I adopted the idea of vernacularization within the body of scholarship that examines how democratic and nationalist ideas are embedded in the people's everyday consciousness and how the elites and non-elites are involved in the creation of this vernacular work (Michelutti 2008; Wouters 2014). The vernacularized expressions, *zalenna* and *ram leh hnam,* formed the core of the ideology of the movement and, by extension, Mizo nationalism. In other words, *zalenna* is the ideology that underpinned the MNF movement. The MNF leaders articulated their idea of *zalenna* in their speech and text, which in turn padded the idea more coherently. As early as the 1960s, the idea of *zalenna* figured prominently in the political discourse, with leaders such as Laldenga referring to it both in his speeches and writings. A particular mention can be made of his 'Zalenna Thuchah' (Message of Freedom). Likewise, leaders of the movement, such as Zoramthanga and Lalhmingthanga, put *zalenna* at the core of their analyses in their writings, using *Zalenna Lungphum* (Foundation of Freedom) (1980) and *Exodus Politics* (2009 [1965]), respectively. In reading such texts, this book uncovers how the MNF leaders constructed the idea of *zalenna*, the context of their articulation, and the meanings attributed to it.

The use of songs and the vernacularization of nationalist expressions are closely interrelated as they overlap quite significantly. This is so because both vernacularization and the use of songs work in tandem with each other. On the one hand, vernacularization means that songs are easily received by the people, irrespective of their status or literacy level. On the other hand, it grants agency to the Mizos by showing how they assert and self-define ideas of nationalism on their own terms. Furthermore, oral narratives are vital in revealing people's experiences, particularly in cases and situations involving violence and human rights abuse. In the Mizo case, too, the effectiveness of songs and oral narratives was demonstrated by their survival even in times of heightened counter-insurgency. Numerous songs were composed against the backdrop of the violent counter-insurgency response, and these are now testaments of violent encounters and experiences.

Over the years, the Mizo experience has attracted attention due to the stability that Mizoram has experienced since the signing of the Mizo Accord (1986) between the MNF and the government of India (Roluahpuia 2018b). While the 'peace' in the post-MNF period has been remarkable, this book critically examines the making of said 'peace' and what the signing of the accord means for the former rebels in contemporary Mizo society. The oral testimonies from the former rebels challenge the singular frame in which peace and peace-making are understood as an act of ending the conflict. It uncovers how the making of peace was interlocked within power equations in the MNF and how the peace-making process was accompanied by a contest of power and position, often exploited by political and rebel actors, local and national. The complexity of the accord-signing process is underscored by the fact that the making of peace in regions of conflict is not only about achieving stability but also guided by multiple interests for which the benefits are often unevenly distributed.

The Mizos: History and Identity Formation

The Mizos are a trans-border community. Inhabiting territories that border three different countries—India, Bangladesh, and Myanmar—the Mizos live in marginal regions in all the states they inhabit. Within northeast India, the Mizos inhabit the states of Manipur, Tripura, and Mizoram, with a smaller population in states such as Meghalaya and Assam. Their cross-border presence within the states of northeast India has determined their sense of identity and how they define and position themselves.

The actual origin and meaning of the term 'Mizo' is a vexed one. However, the general understanding is that 'Mizo' is a transliteration of two words—*mi* meaning people and *zo* meaning highland. Mizo then means hill men or highlanders (Nunthara 1996: 33; U. Phadnis 1989: 149). While one may question the appropriateness of the term (Thanga 1978: xii), it has become entrenched in the consciousness of the people who now collectively identify themselves as Mizo. The sense of a Mizo self is produced and reproduced in different forms, at different sites, and through various interactions and exchanges. In all this, multiple agencies and institutions, such as the YMA, churches, and student bodies, collectively help create and recreate the Mizo sense of self.

Scholars have used the term 'Mizo' as a broad appellation. For example, Nunthara (1996: 33) uses the term to include all those who identify themselves as Mizos, and all the related branches or sub-groups of the Mizo tribes now scattered over the neighbouring territories are relatively fluent in the use of the Lusei language. Along similar lines, U. Phadnis (1989: 149) notes that the term 'Mizo' cuts across tribal boundaries and have wider territorial connotations. This has been more or less the general understanding in Mizoram. However, Nunthara (1996) further adds that this excludes tribal groups, such as the Chakmas and the Brus of the state, while also acknowledging the contestation surrounding the acceptance by the Lai and Mara tribes of being identified as Mizo. Others, like Lalthangliana (2005), use the term as a collective name to refer to the various clans and tribes of the state of Mizoram. These include the Hmar, Paite, Lusei, Ralte, Lai, and Mara, among others.

Colonial rule was premised on gathering information on colonized subjects and recording and documenting them (Dirks 2001). The power of the colonial state was built around the production of knowledge and its dissemination, which become pivotal to colonial strategies of rule and domination. In this way, Mizo history is closely bound with colonial ethnography, and even today colonial texts remain indisputably the main source of Mizo history. Considered in this way, colonialism marks the beginning of written history for the Mizos—a break from the oral tradition. Like anywhere else, colonial writings disaggregated populations based on clans and tribes, which began to fix both administrative boundaries and the identity of the communities.

In a sense, the term 'Mizo' was not a colonial invention, even though its formal usage appeared during the colonial period. Colonial writers primarily used 'Lushai', an Anglicized version of 'Lusei', to designate populations living in present-day Mizoram. This use of 'Lushai' to identify and classify the people subsequently became a part of the official administrative language of the colonial state. Examples of how this term was used by many colonial writers can be seen in John Shakespear's

The Lushei Kuki Clans (1912) and A. G. McCall's *Lushai Chrysalis* (1949). Both writers show how 'Lushai' became the official term used by the colonial state. Every clan and tribe under the present district, excluding the Chakmas, Lais, and Maras, who inhabit the southern district of present-day Mizoram, are collectively identified under the term 'Lushai'.

The use of 'Lushai' by the colonial state was no surprise. At the time of the expansion of the colonial state, the Lusei chiefs ruled the majority of areas in the Lushai Hills, and so it was through them that the British consolidated their rule in the Lushai Hills. Even though clan and tribal identifications predated British colonization, it was either the chiefs or the village through which people identified themselves. The encounter with colonialism created a rupture where identity began to take on a homogenous character. Consequently, in the colonial accounts, the land and the people came to be recorded as 'Lushai'—hence, Lushai tribes and the Lushai Hills. The Duhlian language, which was also the language of the Lusei tribes, began to be used in colonial bureaucracy and was later extended to missions and educational institutions.

The propagation of the Duhlian language by the British significantly contributed to its popularization, making it eventually the common language for the disparate tribes and groups. The customs and language of the Lusei were codified to govern and rule the hills. Putting aside the customary practices, language has become one of the most significant markers of Mizo identity. This is particularly the case with the Mizos of Manipur and Tripura, where language is an important ethnic marker. In fact, one of the most visible imprints of colonial rule is the standardization of language. In administration, education, and missionary activities, the language of the Lusei became popularized and intrinsic to Mizos' ethnic consciousness. The close association between missionary activities and education efforts also played a pivotal role in entrenching the Mizo identity (Kipgen 1997; L. Pachuau 2002). Given the situation, religion and language became essential markers of Mizo identity formation.

The act of naming communities was a part of the larger colonial enterprise. This was evident among the tribes of India, as naming was also a means of 'anthropologizing them'. Influenced by the orientalist discourse of their time, colonial authors produced a wealth of writings on the Mizos, emphasizing their culture, customs, and histories. This was carried forward in the post-colonial period when the study of tribes was largely undertaken by non-tribals or the state. Such accounts gave nearly similar findings to those left by the colonial agents and so, in many ways, ended up reinforcing colonial biases and stereotypes (L. Jenkins 2003).

Given the dominance of the Luseis and the adoption of their language and culture, there is a strong association between Lusei and Mizo identity. As noted earlier, this has also been the view in scholarly research. While there is an element of truth in it, it ignores the longer history of absorption and assimilation and the incoming and outgoing of the clans and tribes. Colonial accounts of the Mizos are essentially tilted towards Lusei history and are not necessarily about the disparate clans and tribes. Of course, exceptions exist, as in the case of Shakespear's *The Lushei Kuki Clans*, where he discusses non-Lusei clans. What is interesting to note from Shakespear's account is how such clans have adopted the Lusei manners and customs. These include clans such as Chawhte, Chawngthu, Khiangte, Ngente, Pautu, Vangchhia, and Zawngte (Shakespear 1912: 130–135). Shakespear (1912: 136–147) also notes various other clans, such as the Fanai, Ralte, and Paite, among others, who came under the influence of the Luseis and had gradually adopted the Lusei manners and customs. In short, during their role as chiefs, the Luseis could absorb smaller clans and tribes into their fold (Nunthara 1996: 235). This influence of the Lusei upon the non-Lusei clans remains a significant part of Mizo history and ethnic identity formation.

In addition to this, the suzerainty of the Lusei chiefs spread beyond the present territorial borders of Mizoram to regions such as Tripura. As a result, even as 'Mizo' was largely adopted in place of 'Lusei', it has become generally accepted in areas and among groups influenced by the Lusei tribe. The situatedness of Mizo identity in terms of its acceptance and rejection underscores this fact. In areas where Lusei chiefs held dominance, particularly in the northern areas of Mizoram and the Jampui Hills of Tripura, Mizo identity was gladly accepted. In the now southern regions of Mizoram inhabited by the Mara and the Lai tribes, Mizo identity was considered Lusei-centric, thereby limiting its acceptance. This contest over identity continues to mark the sociopolitical processes in the state of Mizoram.

By the 1940s, the Lusei language was already well developed, even in the field of literature. Books and writings in the vernacular made their appearance outside the interests of the church (missionary activities) and the colonial state. The issue of Mizo history and identity was the focus of such vernacular writings. The title of books published began to carry 'Mizo' in place of 'Lusei' or the colonial term 'Lushai'. The first Mizo history book was written by Liangkhaia, entitled *Mizo Chanchin* (Accounts on Mizo) (1938), and was followed by numerous others such as *Mizo History* by V. L. Siama (1953) and *Mizo Pi Pute Leh An Thlahte Chanchin* (The History of Mizo Ancestors and Their Descendants) by K. Zawla (1964). It is no surprise that the bulk of literature focused on Mizoram, given the high concentration of Mizos in the state, while there are very few works on the Mizos of Manipur and Tripura (Zairemthanga 1992; Darkhuma 2009).

Early Mizo historians and writers have stressed the significance of the myth of origin and cultures as the defining characteristics of the Mizo identity. Of these, the Chhinlung narrative is one of the most profound ones. Therefore, it is common to see terms such as 'Chhinlung *chhuak*' (people of Chhinlung origin), with Chhinlung, as the myth goes, believed to be the root of the origin of the Mizos. One of the common claims is the ethnic similarities of those identified as 'Kuki', 'Chin', and 'Mizos', or collectively as 'Zo', by some scholars (Vumson 1988; Khai 1995). The claim of ethnic similarities is based on their similar histories of migration and the myth of origin.

The Mizos' sense of self is therefore evolving and being constructed over time. Scholarly research on ethnicity and identity has increasingly focused on the construction of ethnic identities. This is a tradition in the studies of ethnicity initiated by Barth (1969), where he argues that ethnic groups get constituted through the maintenance of boundaries. The notion of the 'self' and the 'other' is fundamental to how the Mizos construct and conceive the notion of themselves. This ethnic 'othering' is constructed against the perceived outsider such as the *vai* or the people from Burma and among those who identify themselves as Mizo. J. Pachuau (2014) has cogently delineated and successfully showed how the sense of 'being Mizo' was an outcome of a long historical process intertwined with the production of historical writings and how the Mizos' sense of self is connected to their micro (*veng*, or locality) and macro reality. In this context, on the one hand, the Chhinlung narrative is utilized to articulate a sense of pan-Mizo identity and belonging beyond borders; on the other hand, the social practices of burying the dead define the attachment and belonging of a person as members of the *veng*—hence, inclusion and exclusion at the local or micro level.

Up until the publication of J. Pachuau's *Being Mizo* (2014), there had been no significant research done on Mizo ethnicity. Mizo identity has often been projected as 'given' and 'homogeneous'. Such studies have largely left the political history untouched, leaving aside how identity assertion and political aspiration were interlinked. Even though this book is not on Mizo ethnicity per se, it attempts to show how the consciousness of being a *hnam* is concomitant to the construction of the Mizos' ethnic self. It brings into focus the political construction of Mizo identity and the role of political parties in the entrenchment of Mizo identity. This is explored through the exploration of the historical specificities of the construction of Mizo identity, its adoption, and the demand for recognition and how it came—not merely as an identity in itself but also how the Mizo engaged and negotiated with the state.

Mizo Nationalism, the MNF Movement, and Nationalism Studies

Three broad paradigms can be identified in the studies of Mizo nationalism—namely, the ethno-nationalist, the constructivist that focuses on the role of the elites, and the studies that examine the relationship between religion and Mizo nationalism. Of them, the most common theme is the ethno-nationalist paradigm (B. B. Goswami 1979; U. Phadnis 1989; Nunthara 1996). A basic characteristic of ethno-nationalism is its focus on the ethnic, and therefore, ethno-nationalism is a manifestation of the politicization of ethnicity premised on the 'politics of difference' (Wilmsen and McAllister 1996). It is therefore not surprising that explanations of Mizo nationalism through this frame focus on the ethnic dimension—that is, the politicization of Mizo identity. To an extent, such studies located the rise of the MNF movement within the change that the Mizo communities were undergoing with colonial intervention, particularly in the fields of culture and education.

It is noteworthy that ethnic interpretations of the movement remain the dominant theme in scholarly studies. There is a burgeoning literature on ethno-nationalism, particularly after the 1990s when nationalism rebounded to haunt most established nation-states, particularly in Eastern Europe (Ignatieff 1993; Brubaker 1996). This goes against the common wisdom that ethnicity and nationalism would wane due to technological and economic development making them irrelevant. Connor (1972), writing as early as the 1970s, is one of the scholars who argued about the potency of ethno-nationalism.

Until the 1990s, scholars overlooked the issue of ethnicity and nationalism. As Connor (1972) observes, scholars associated with the theories of 'nation-building' have tended to either ignore the question of ethnic diversity or treat the matter of ethnic identity superficially as merely one of a number of minor impediments to state integration. Connor's understanding of ethno-nationalism is also different from the dominant view, as he treats ethno-nationalism as being synonymous with nationalism. As he defines it, the nation 'connotes a group of people who believe they are culturally related', and nationalism means identification with and loyalty to one's nation. He further notes that the terminological confusion between state, nation, patriotism, and nationalism contributes to the haziness within the study of nationalism (Connor 1994: 73). This view goes against the oft-repeated typologies commonly applied in the study of nationalism—that is, civic versus ethnic nationalism (Kohn 1944). Ethnic nationalism is therefore often treated with a suspicion that impedes the understating of the issues and challenges. In India, too, ethnicity was considered a danger and a threat to the unity and integrity of the nation-state (Krishna 1999: 25).

The role of the elite and ethnicity is another primary focus of nationalism studies. The constructivist and modernist theories of nationalism attribute the emergence of nations and nationalism under modern conditions of industrialization (Gellner 1983). This is achieved by promoting a monoculture and education—hence, a homogenous culture and national community. One of the primary contentions of the constructivist view is the role of the elites in the construction of national identities, given their existing privilege to construct and shape national ideologies, often to further their interests. They are usually responsible for the 'invention of tradition' (Hobsbawm and Ranger 1983) and the circulation of nationalist ideas (Anderson 1983) and remain actively involved in the bourgeois public sphere (Habermas 1991).

The constructivist approach also remains dominant in the study of nationalism in India. For instance, Brass (1991) argues that national identity arises from the specific interactions between the modern states and the elites of dominant regional groups. In studies on nationalism in the northeast, too, the role of the elites has figured prominently (Hussain 1993; Datta-Ray 1983); in the context of the Mizos, it was the emergence of the elites that sowed the seeds of unrest, first against the chiefs and the British, led by the MU, and then against the Indian state under the

MNF. The rise of the educated middle class was one of the pivotal foci of such studies (Datta-Ray 1983; Lalrimawia 1995), and this class of individuals were described as 'articulate' (McCall 1949: 217) and 'enlightened' (C. Nag 1999: 18). Consequently, nationalist movements in the region were driven by the elites' interest in power and controlling the resources (A. Guha 1979). Varghese and Thanzawna (1997: 21–23) have noted that Laldenga used the nationalist card to influence the Mizo youth to join the MNF and later the movement.

The elites in Mizo society were not a homogeneous group, and the literate class comprised both secular and religious backgrounds. Both had a strong influence on the social, economic, and political life of Mizo society. In fact, given the missionary roots of education, the early literate Mizos were primarily educated in missionary-run schools, irrespective of their orientation and outlook. Even among those who received higher education, many preferred to serve or be affiliated with the church and so became important and influential members of society. In this way, religion was integral to the Mizo ethnic and national consciousness. In fact, religion was indispensable to the MNF's idea of nationalism and therefore intrinsic to the consciousness of Mizo identity. L. Pachuau (2002) argues that a Christian identity gave the Mizos a sense of collective identity and belonging. This further paved the way for the creation of a unified political identity that overrode former inter-tribal differences.

The religious nature of nationalism is exemplified in the way the MNF propagated Christian identity as a part of its nationalist ideology (U. Phadnis 1989). In some sense, it is not surprising to see that many considered Christianity as one of the catalysts of change among the Mizos. Fernandes (2009: 131) further argues that evangelical activities paved the way for the emergence of civic spaces through which the tribals articulated and advanced their political goals in the Indian federalist system. However, there is a danger in reducing the MNF movement to a mere expression of religious nationalism. As L. Pachuau (1997) notes, the impetus for ethno-nationalism among the Mizos was driven by the motive to protect and safeguard the historical, racial, and cultural differences (see Chapter 4). However, when it comes to the church as an institution in Mizoram, it neither advocated any form of secessionism nor lent support to the MNF movement (Lalchungnunga 1994: 52).

Given that the MNF emerged in the late 1960s—first as a cultural society under the banner of the MCS in 1955—the organization's success in terms of its popularity was credited to its intervention during the famine that hit the Lushai Hills and adjoining areas in 1959. In the same year, the MCS was renamed as the MNFF under the leadership of Laldenga, among others, who were involved in recruiting volunteers to help the famine-stricken people. S. Nag (2002) ascribes the rise of Mizo nationalism to the neglect faced by the Mizos during the famine, which resulted in widespread discontent. The popular appeal of the MNF, S. Nag (2002) contends, was the outcome of the Assam government's inept response that drove the Mizo youth to rebellion. Others like Lalchungnunga (1994) view the MNF movement as politics of regionalism. Mizo regionalism, Lalchungnunga (1994) argues, was persistent since the colonial period, and the MNF movement was a manifestation of this regionalism. Both Nag and Lalchungnunga have commented that the correct response to insurgency and regionalism lies in integrating the region into the national mainstream.

Ethnicity, culture, and religion all play a major role in the articulation of Mizo nationalism. In other words, one observes what Appadurai (1996: 15) calls the 'conscious mobilization of cultural difference'. However, as R. Jenkins (2008 [1997]: 164–167) contends, nationalisms, in as much as they are about political projects, are also social productions produced and reproduced by ordinary people in their everyday lives. Over the years, one finds how research on nationalism began to address the intimate, innate, and quotidian aspects of national identity and nationhood. Such studies acknowledge the diverse manifestations of nationhood and national identity while simultaneously recognizing the universal manifestation of nationalism (Billig 1995; Edensor 2002).

These scholarly studies are helpful in understanding the rise of the MNF into mainstream Mizo politics. For instance, the MNF's use of songs for nationalist mobilization, even though this was not unique to the Mizo situation, introduced a new idiom into the political life and culture. The composers of the songs were ordinary and educated Mizos engaged in different professions, with the most notable being Rokunga. Rokunga himself was employed by the Presbyterian Synod and never joined or participated in the activities of the MNF. The point here is not about his affiliation with the MNF but how individuals like him were pivotal in shaping the ideas of Mizo nationalism. During the period of the movement, numerous songs continued to be composed by the rebels, advocating the Mizo national cause that further (re)produced the imaginings of the nation. This demonstrated the need to diversify the voices by incorporating the non-elites into the historical narratives of the national movement (Fahmy 2011: xi). The idea and meaning of nationalism did not emanate from the Mizo elites alone. The nationalist expressions of *zalenna* and *ram leh hnam* percolated in the minds of the Mizo public and found expression in the songs and speeches of the leaders of the movement. Such terms became embedded in the lives of the people, arousing the passion for struggle and sacrifice for the nation (Smith 2009).

In addition, the caveat for research on Mizo nationalism and the MNF movement is that existing studies are confined to only examining the causes of the movement, particularly the famine and the peace accord. There is now an excessive focus on Mizoram's stability with the signing of the accord. Since the signing of the accord in 1986, the discourse in Mizoram has shifted towards focusing on the 'success' of the Mizo Accord. Political parties such as the MNF and the Indian National Congress (INC) often compete to stake claims to the 'success' (see Chapter 6).

Often, former rebel leaders of the MNF such as Zoramthanga are deputed as a peace ambassador in the region to bring rebel groups to the negotiating table and open doors for other states to follow the Mizo path. In fact, the issue of Mizoram's transition from a conflict-ridden state to a peaceful state has garnered much recognition both in academia and public discourse, and it gives a singular view of the counter-insurgency experience and the peace accord. This again brings back the significance of oral culture in Mizo society, where songs became a way of retrieving the voices of the people who lived through terror and violence. In the heyday of the MNF movement, the Indian state resorted to a counter-insurgency strategy that disrupted the lives of a majority of Mizos through village groupings, physical torture, and everyday violence. Drawing upon the songs and narratives of the people, the oral culture has the potential to unveil the divergent and complex narratives of violence and peace. Most importantly, they are narrations of the lived experiences of the people or 'what these happenings meant to people' (Carye Jr 2017: 196). In short, this book also interrogates what the peace accord means for the survivors and participants of the movement.

On Fieldwork: Arguments and Reflections

The primary data for this work were collected by using in-depth interviews that started in 2015, stretching up to 2017. The Mizos as a community are used to what they call *titi*, an unstructured conversation, and hence, the in-depth interviews made for a suitable choice to conduct fieldwork. There are two critical aspects to this: First, the questions had to be formulated in words familiar to the people. Second, there was no fixed sequence applied to the research participants while conducting an interview (Bryman 2012 [2005]; Denzin 2017: 125). This allowed a more free-flowing interview and tailoring of the questions to fit the specific context of each interview. Interviews were conducted at homes, workplaces, or sometimes in government and non-government offices, and this influenced how the interview process was conducted and the nature of the interaction. In this way, an in-depth interview gives a great deal of freedom to probe various areas (Denzin 2017: 126).

The process was time-consuming, with each interview easily taking up to two hours. In other words, they were 'long interviews' (McCracken 1988). The interviews were also long because they mostly began with *titi* on personal issues such as family background, occupation, and the purpose of the interview. This experience was true across different districts of Manipur, Mizoram, and Tripura, where fieldwork was undertaken. The in-depth interviews were particularly helpful in understanding narratives of the movement, the ideas of nationalism, and the contestation surrounding the movement. In my meeting with former MNF rebels, I realized how many of them identified themselves as song composers. As the interviews and fieldwork progressed, I was informed that many of the MNF leaders composed songs not only of the movement but also gospel hymns, love songs, and Christmas songs. Within the MNF, the genre of songs was popularly referred to as *hnam hla*, and many former rebels trace their inspiration to the songs of composers such as Rokunga. The *hnam hla* reflected the life-words of the MNF rebels and became a critical part of the movement as it was through *hnam hla* that the MNF rebels expressed their aspirations, hopes, and visions. It was from this that I began to draw a close connection between orality and nationalist politics.

Subsequently, I began to locate and identify how different genres of *hla* emerged before and after the movement. Political parties in Mizoram have used *hla* as a medium to connect with the people. The interview process expanded to trying to situate and understand *hla* within the context of their emergence. Political leaders who I interviewed narrated how *hla* were convenient and easily understood by the people. *Hla* democratized the political culture as the composers were drawn from both the literate and non-literate classes, and the vernacular form in which they were composed further aided their rapid spread and popularity. Historically, as noted earlier, *hla* were always the preferred mode of expression, and as such, I analyse *hla* within the oral culture of the Mizos and examine the close relationship between *hla* and modern Mizo politics.

Yet reliance on a single mode of interviews is not enough to capture the dynamics and complexities of the MNF movement. The work also involves heavy realiance on pamphlets, secondary materials, and archival records, and I specifically analyse the written works of three leaders of the movement. Such texts further enable us to understand the ideological underpinnings of the movement. The early educated sections of the Mizo population were active in writing and publishing, despite their limited audience and readership. The texts under analysis provide cues to ideas and imaginations of the movement, particularly the idea of *zalenna*. In my interview with former rebels, the movement was described and referred to as *zalenna sual* (freedom struggle), and this figures prominently in the songs that were composed as well. In the writings produced by the MNF leaders, the idea of *zalenna* is at the heart of it, and for this, I examine three key texts—namely Laldenga's *Mizoram Marches towards Freedom* (2001), Zoramthanga's *Zoram Zalenna Lungphum* (Foundation of Zoram Freedom) (1980), and Lalhmingthanga's *Exodus Politics* (2009 [1965]). Overall, the work draws upon a combination of in-depth qualitative interviews with more than 70 individuals—inclusive of both former MNF and non-MNF members—field notes, and observations, along with the analysis of archival materials from national and international institutions, newspaper archives, and files of personal collections in the form of photographs, diaries, and monographs.

The data sources are diverse, and this reflects my belief in using multiple methods of data collection. This approach is advantageous as the data collected through in-depth interviews or official sources such as government records supplement one another. For instance, the accounts from the interviews provide a rich insight into the movement, enabling one to understand it from the perspective of former MNF leaders and rebels. The archival data are very significant in understanding the anti-chieftainship movement and the struggle for autonomy by the MU leading up to the independence of India. For this, records from the Mizoram State Archives (MSA), Aizawl Theological College (ATC), and the National Archives of India (NAI), as well as library resources of Harvard University, were consulted.

The fieldwork was done in four phases: from January to September 2015; November to December 2015; January to March 2016; and January to February 2017. In fact, as the writing of the book progressed, I continued to remain connected with my field and my research participants and engaged myself with them, only to realize that fieldwork has no real 'end'. It has become a personal endeavour at times as it affects my way of interacting with people in my home state of Manipur and my friends. Given the nature of my work, the fieldwork was carried out in multiple locales, which started off at Aizawl, the capital city of Mizoram, and then extended to different parts of the state, in addition to trips to Tripura and Manipur. Although Mizoram was the epicentre of the MNF movement, the narratives came from across the borders and boundaries of these places. By conducting fieldwork in multiple locations, the intention was to integrate the experiences of the struggle in Manipur, Mizoram, and Tripura. The objective was not to compare and contrast the events and experiences of the different states but to map out how the MNF movement penetrated and influenced the Mizo inhabited areas. It must also be reiterated that the MNF rebels were constantly crossing borders and regions, making it possible that an informer from Manipur might have spent his entire time in the movement in Mizoram or elsewhere. Hence, there is a constant overlap in the nature of the experiences and narratives across state borders.

In the studies of the MNF, the larger trend has been to limit them to the territorial boundaries of present-day Mizoram, particularly the northern part of the state (Lalchungnunga 1994; Nunthara 1996; L. Pachuau 2002), and to urban centres (J. Pachuau 2014). This not only gives a lopsided view of the movement but also silences the support and participation of the Mizos outside of Mizoram. The MNF movement in itself was spread out across multiple regions, and my research participants' experiences were more or less 'partial' for two reasons. First, many of them left the movement before the conclusion of the movement, so they only knew about the movement during the specific period they were part of. Even for those who were part of the movement for the entire two decades, their encounters and experience were limited, depending on the area they lived in. Second, in as much as the movement enjoyed mass support, it also had its fair share of opposition. This came from the MU members and volunteers, from the Lai, Mara, and Chakma tribes, and, to some extent, from the Paite and Hmar tribes in Manipur. For all these reasons, there is a need for a contextual understanding of the problems with the movement, and this book attempts to provide this, although it remains 'partial—committed and incomplete' (Clifford and Marcus 1986: 7).

Even as I was unable to cover the whole area that was under the influence of the MNF movement, the regions I studied, in terms of geography, covered a major part of it. The field was constructed during the time of my fieldwork as I began to identify my research participants and trace their narratives. Given the high concentration of the Mizo population in Aizawl, fieldwork was much easier in the capital city. In addition, collecting documents was also convenient due to the access to major libraries such as the state and district libraries, the ATC library, and the MSA. The archival materials at the MSA and the ATC were particularly useful in understanding the political processes and events. However, personal documents, such as those in Manipur and Tripura, were also helpful, depending on who my research participants were. In short, the depth of data collected and the focus varied from site to site due to the differing levels of accessibility and the nature of the field (Nadai and Maeder 2005).

The nature of my fieldwork also exposed me to multiple encounters that shaped and opened up different avenues of research. In fact, my research participants significantly shaped the way this research was undertaken. In academic discourse, while the MNF movement is more or less known as an insurgency, and as *rambuai lai* (troubled years) in the popular discourse, my research participants repeatedly referred to it as *zalenna sual*. Based on this description, I began to pick up the term *zalenna*, which became a central idea for my research work and writing. Identifying and contacting my research participants was fairly easy as this was done through the networks maintained by the former MNF's armies and leaders. These groups included the Ex-Mizo National Army (Ex-MNA) Associations and the Peace Accord MNF Returnees Association (PAMRA). The MNF party office in Aizawl and other districts of the state were equally helpful in the identification of research participants.

These networks enabled me to connect with research participants from diverse backgrounds, which was evident from how many of them expressed themselves with reference to the MNF as a party and as a movement. While many continued to speak highly of the movement and the sacrifice they had made, some expressed disenchantment arising from the appalling conditions under which they are presently living. This narrative became a central part of the understanding of the peace accord that is discussed in Chapter 5. However, a limitation that I encountered during the study was the difficulty of maintaining sustained interaction with my research participants. This was because I had to move from one place to another, which did not permit me to build close relationships with the participants. Consequently, there were fewer opportunities for face-to-face interactions with them.

In the field, my identity as a Mizo greatly facilitated access to the fieldwork sites and also helped during the interview process. I found out that I was constantly 'renegotiating identities in different sites', to quote Marcus (1995: 113). As a Mizo, I was able to conduct my fieldwork, speaking fluently in the local language. This made it easier to build relationships, and it encouraged conversation. In any research, the insider is presumed to gain deeper insights and greater access to more information.

However, while I acknowledged my privileged position as a Mizo in this regard, in a region where politics is defined along ethnic lines, my ethnic identity often became intertwined with the everyday politics of identity and belonging at my field sites. Furthermore, my knowledge of Mizoram and Tripura was limited, and it was an entirely new place for me, except for the knowledge gained through the reading of secondary sources.

My identity as a Mizo comes in two different ways—first as a Mizo *of* Manipur and second as a Mizo *in* Manipur. This interplay of my identity informed my field site visits. Two events are worthy of mention here. First, in March 2015, the Hmar armed group named the Hmar People's Convention (Democratic) (HPC-D) ambushed a member of legislative assembly (MLA) convoy in the northern part of Mizoram. In the ambush, three Mizo policemen lost their lives while the HPC-D militants fled. This caused widespread anger across Mizoram, with the public demanding a fierce response from the state government. It was not the ambush per se that was significant, but my identity as a Mizo *of* Manipur that was increasingly coming to the fore while conducting interviews. The HPC-D is considered a Manipur-based militant group in Mizoram, and its penetration into Mizoram could turn the state into a conflict-ridden and ethnically divided one like Manipur. From my personal encounters with my research participants and the public in general, it would seem that Manipur is enmeshed in violence with sharp ethnic divisions. The image of Manipur is construed negatively within the state of Mizoram. I often came across people who advised me to settle in Mizoram. Interestingly, my research participants often interviewed me about the issue after the incident rather than me interviewing them (Geleta 2014: 139).

In Manipur, my experience was different, given my belonging to Churachandpur, the district where I was conducting the fieldwork. My knowledge of the district, the people, and the places were generally better compared to that of Mizoram. However, despite my belonging, my research participants related to me not necessarily as an 'insider' but according to my identity. For instance, I was considered as an 'ethnic other', a Mizo *in* Manipur and my identity as an insider oscillated, depending on who my respondent was. To those who identified themselves as Mizo, I was one of them, but not to a Paite or a Hmar. In a state that is highly polarized along ethnic lines, ethnic belonging cannnot be downplayed as irrelevant. In Manipur, ethnic belonging determines not only one's attachment but also one's political allegiance, which further decides the prevailing network of trust and distrust.

I tried to remain sensitive to the local realities and refrained from discussing local politics. This was, at times, challenging, as the first question that my research participants usually asked was about my identity. My name itself is enough to denote my identity as it is a typical Mizo name that is easily identified due to the gender suffix attached to each name: *a* for male and *i* for female. In my case, it is Puia, with Pui being a common name in Mizo, irrespective of gender. On the contrary, in Manipur, my identity as a Mizo gave me an easy entry into the Mizo community. A noted community leader introduced me to his friends as 'one of us, a YMA member'. Being a Mizo and native of Churachandpur itself made me an insider, and by all criteria, I fit within the insider category. For a non-Mizo, I was an insider, but not one of them.

My experience in the Jampui Hills of Tripura was again different from that in Manipur and Mizoram. The Jampui Hills are more or less homogeneous, and the inhabitants are closely connected and predominantly Mizos. Despite being from Manipur, I was considered one of them due to my ethnic belonging. In a multi-ethnic and ethnically polarized region, my identity as an insider or outsider was uncertain. In other words, the boundaries of my identity as an insider and outsider were rather changeable and could be overlapping, depending on the location where I was doing my fieldwork. Apart from this, my encounters and experiences raised the more significant question about identity and belonging among the Mizos in northeast India. This also shows that the static notion of Mizo identity being homogeneous is certainly dismissive of the contextual realities of Mizo ethnic belonging.

Chapter Outlines

The book is organized into seven chapters, with this being the first. Chapter 2 gives a broad outline of national integration in the context of northeast India. In India, tensions over nationality and movements for independence are considered a problem of integration. The chapter points out that more than a problem of integration, the national question in India is an issue of inclusion. Integration underlies assimilation and homogeneity, erasing differences and diversity. This chapter places the issue of inclusion within the framework of the 'tribal question' in post-colonial India. For marginalized communities in India, the issue remains that of being identified as equal members, which the state often tried to address through integration. In this context, the chapter draws upon the current agenda of integration within the Mizo context and the contestation surrounding national integration.

Chapters 3 and 4 focus on Mizo politics, tracing it from the colonial period. Going against the grain, Chapter 3 presents political development and the rise of political consciousness among the Mizos as a transformative act that not only sought the end of the chief's rule but also challenged colonial authority. Even as the leaders of the MU largely comprised of the educated class who later led the anti-chieftainship movement, what was distinctive about Mizo politics was how political consciousness became ingrained in the consciousness of the Mizo commoners. The acts and assertions of the Mizo public against colonial paternalism and the aspirations of autonomy and the struggle against the traditional power structures were expressed through the medium of songs. It was here that *hla* began to take root in Mizo politics. Both parties prominent at that time, the MU and the UMFO, used *party hla* to contest and mobilize the public. In other words, songs, in as much as they were an important political tool for mobilization, were also a medium through which rival political parties contested each other within the political landscape of the hills. Songs became the voice of expression that enabled the transmission of political ideas that transgressed village boundaries and national borders. Rooted in the traditions and ethnic life-world of the people, songs were easily receptible and accessible to the commoners. They were effective for political mobilization and were employed to garner political support.

Songs played a pivotal role in the rise and popularity of the MNF. This resulted in a new genre of songs among the Mizos, which came to be known as *hnam hla*. While the use of songs to articulate, envision, and inspire is not new, in the Mizo context, what was introduced through such songs were the terms that became associated with the MNF movement. For the MNF, the movement was for *zalenna* and *ram leh hnam tan*, and as such, *hnam hla* significantly pointed towards popularizing such ideas. In other words, through *hnam hla*, *zalenna* and *ram leh hnam* became widely circulated and were infused with strong patriotic fervour. Chapter 4 is an examination of nationalist mobilization and expression through a reading of the songs and texts, which demonstrated how the MNF put conscious effort into legitimizing its struggle and political cause by referring to it as *zalenna sual*.

Chapters 5 and 6 address the issue of peace. The background to this lies in the continuing sustenance of peace in the state after the signing of the Mizo Peace Accord, 1986, between the MNF and the government of India. In short, 'peace' or 'peaceful state' is what Mizoram is now associated with. Given this, the Mizo Peace Accord is widely celebrated as a case of a successful peace accord. This is attributed to the counter-insurgency strategy, particularly the village groupings, that staved off the MNF armies by isolating them from the civilian population. In the larger discourse of counter-insurgency, particularly in the official one, there is a silencing of the people's experiences of counter-insurgency. While acknowledging the stability of Mizoram, the chapter shows how the state was unable to repress orality or censor its contents despite mass surveillance and control. Common Mizos and the civilian public resorted to songs to express their anguish and loss as well as their encounters with and experiences of violence.

In Chapter 6, the question of peace is examined, factoring in the various political and power struggles occurring intermittently in the making of peace in Mizoram. The signing of the peace accord was not only about a peaceful settlement between the MNF and the goverment, who were ensnared in local rivalries and the contest for power. Brigadier Thenphunga Sailo's emergence as a prominent political actor, the rise of the People's Conference (PC), and the subsequent fallout between Sailo and Laldenga, the president of the MNF, resulted in fratricidal killings. All of these demonstrate how peace was entrapped in local politics and interests. The party that gained the most from this was the INC, which, through the promise of peace, unseated the PC, the then ruling government, in the state election of 1984. Beyond this, the chapter also seeks to understand what the accord meant to the former leaders and the armies. The divergent narratives that emerged are testimony to some of the unsettled issues in contemporary Mizoram. Chapter 7, the conclusion, is an overall reflection on the arguments of the book.

Notes

1   A *hnam* is often loosely used to refer to a clan, tribe, or even nation. For the purposes of this book, I use *hnam* to refer to nation.

2   *Ram* can be used to refer to land privately or publicly owned, while it is also used to refer to territory, in the more political sense. In this book, my use of *ram* connotes a more political understanding of the term.

3   *Party hla* refer to songs that are composed by members of political parties or individuals in support of specific parties to advance their own party. It is common to find campaign songs and songs of political parties even today in Mizoram.

4   Both *puma zai* and *kaihlek hla* were largely viewed as anti-Christian songs and, as such, hostile to Christian activities, such as the proselytizing activities of the missionaries. However, recent interpretations, particularly on *puma zai*, has shown how it paved the way for future revivals and enabled the consolidation of Christianity with its celebration of singing in the open and in public.

5   *Harhna sang* marked a form of 'revival' or 'awakening', which was accompanied by intense emotional outburst through songs, movements, and actions. The revivals took place in multiple waves, in 1906, 1913, 1919, and 1930, and was an important event in Mizo history that marked the consolidation and spread of Christianity.

6   'Zo' is an ethnic category inasmuch as it is used to refer to distinct attributes and cultural expressions of the Mizo way of being and life. In this case, 'Zo' is used to mean the attributes and cultural expressions that define Mizo-ness.

7   'Lushai' is an Anglicized version of 'Lusei', and I will be using the two terms interchangeably. 'Lushai' will be used when colonial sources are cited and references made to the colonial period. Otherwise, 'Lusei' will be used throughout.

8   'Lushai Hills', 'Mizo Hills', and 'Mizoram' will be used interchangeably in accordance with the time period being referred to. For instance, 'Lushai Hills' was used by the colonial administrator, or during the colonial period, until it was changed to 'Mizo Hills' in 1954.

2 The 'Tribal Question' in India
Problem of Inclusion

The years between 1947 and 1949 were crucial periods in the history of nation-building in India. It was during this period that the integration of the princely states and the tribal regions was undertaken. Across the country, numerous concessions were made to integrate the princely states into the Indian Union through the signing of the Instrument of Accession. There was a mixed response to the integration plan, with some princely states opposing it while others complied without much difficulty. Regardless, the process of integrating the vast geographic regions was regarded as a 'success'. At the same time, large parts of the regions inhabited by communities identified as tribals were loosely administered with certain provisions for self-rule during the colonial period. In the northeast region itself, the tribal regions, which constituted the major geographic area, were put under 'partially excluded areas' and 'excluded areas'.[1]

The STs in India constitute about 8.6 per cent of the total population, which comprises about 32 million of the country's total population. The population of tribes was much smaller during the early decades of independence, making up only a mere 6.23 per cent in the first census of 1951 in post-independent India. Whereas it is generally understood that the terms 'STs' and 'tribes' are a legacy of colonial rule, the communities identified have embraced them as a means of self-identification. Today, the term 'tribe' connotes both an official category of the state as well as community self-identification. The making of the tribal citizen in post-independent India saw how tribes have creatively used the colonial and anthropological discourse to advance their identity and political rights (Upadhya 2011).

At the dawn of India's independence, the 'tribal question' was framed between two opposing positions—the integrationist and the isolationist, or the widely known Ghurye–Elwin debate (K. S. Singh 1982; R. Guha 1996). G. S. Ghurye advocated for the gradual assimilation of tribes within the Hindu fold, while Verrier Elwin saw such efforts as a direct threat to the survival of the tribes and hence pleaded for isolating the tribes. The debate has occupied centre stage within both academia and policy concerning tribes, particularly during the years between 1920 and 1950—that is, up to the Constituent Assembly (CA) debates that saw divergent positions around the 'tribal question'. The debate emerged out of the national anxiety over the question of integration expressed by nationalist leaders. Sociologists and administrator-cum-anthropologists of the time who were active in the study of tribes took the mantle of framing the debate (Bhukya 2021: 14). Quite startlingly, the debate often misses the position of the 'tribes' themselves and how they envision their future in independent India. Whereas it is understood that Elwin did influence India's policy towards tribes, the policy of isolating the tribes was, however, short-lived, given the realities of the tribes. Tribal regions, particularly in mainland India, felt the effect of state and market penetration that sought control of their territories and resources.

The position of the tribes in independent India is best understood in their demand for autonomy. During colonial and post-colonial rule, the tribes gradually began to lose self-rule and autonomy, which hastened the process of their marginalization. This process of marginalization shaped tribal political contours in post-independent India, which the integrationist and isolationists failed to take into account (Bhukya 2017). In other words, the tribal question in India is intricately tied to the issue of autonomy. The demand for autonomy represented an act of self-assertion by the tribes. This takes place at two levels: first, movements that aspire for autonomy within the Constitution, such as the demand for a separate state of Jharkhand and Gondwana; and, second, movements that aspire for independence, as in the case of the Nagas and the Mizos in northeast India. Political mobilization during the colonial period among tribal communities pointed towards protecting their identity, culture, and resource rights over land, among others. The trend continued in post-independent India, where there have been successive movements by the tribals that aspire for independence and, if not, then internal autonomy within states.

There is a tendency to generalize the rise of tribal political movements in the northeast. Most studies have reduced it to a colonial policy of isolation and exclusion of the tribals into enclosed spaces that fuelled the feeling of separatism (Inoue 2005). There is an aversion among nationalists to keeping the tribe in 'isolation', which Gandhi, for instance, expressed as if 'it was their shame that the Adivasis should be isolated from the rest of the nation of which they were an inalienable part' (K. S. Singh 1982: 1320). Others allude to the Christian missionary activities that bred the fear of religious persecution among the newly proselytized Christian tribals of the region. The general and the more widely held view is that they represent the case of the 'problem of integration'. Within this framework, all communities, be it tribes or non-tribes, fit into the explanation where the secessionist movements represent a case of the 'periphery strikes back' (Misra 2002); the tribal question will be solved once they are fully integrated into the national mainstream of the country.

National integration tends to be a centralized initiative—hence, a top–down affair. States continue to relentlessly pursue the integration of minorities or peripheral regions into the mainstream of the nation-state. The question of integration is particularly central for countries where numerous disparate ethnic groups consider themselves as a nation. Sheth (1989) observed that 'nation-building' was closely associated with Third World countries modelled around a European nation-state. This was seen as 'nation-building' as the countries sought to create a sovereign state out of a society that are highly heterogeneous socially, linguistically, religiously, and ethnically. Nonetheless, nation-building through integration was prima facie the locus of the national project for newly independent countries.

The experience of integration has been, however, relatively different across communities and regions. Different communities have articulated and sought political concessions that would safeguard their rights as groups. Despite being granted various provisions and protections, communities such as tribes and Dalits have continued to experience myriad forms of 'national' exclusion or remained excluded from the national life of the country. Such exclusions, in as much as they were political, also had strong social and cultural bases. Guru (2016b) has shown how social distinction based on caste perpetuates an exclusion of the untouchables. The modern nation of India, as Guru (2016a) shows, has failed to dissolve the boundaries that divided caste groups in village, towns, and cities. Drawing from B. R. Ambedkar, Guru notes that India continued to be divided into two: 'Puruskrut Bharat' (ideal, pure India) and 'Bahiskurt Bharat' (actual, polluting India) (Guru 2016b: 34).

Integration is not neutral, and it is articulated through dominant cultures relegating racial, ethnic, and religious minorities as 'outsiders'. The commonly sought way to solve this issue of exclusion is through the integration of such communities with the 'national mainstream' or simply the 'mainstream' in the context of tribes (Chaudhury and Patnaik 2008). Therefore, the 'tribal problem' in India is considered as one of integrating geographically isolated communities into the national mainstream. The sociocultural and political isolation of the tribes during the colonial period blocked the development of national consciousness, which must be redeemed by integrating them with the national mainstream. Even as what comprises the national mainstream is never properly defined, it has shifted the focus away from the central issue as it ignores the exploitative nature of the integration process itself (Saha 1986: 287).

If the colonial state saw the tribes as 'recalcitrant subjects', the post-colonial state viewed them as a 'problem' of national integration. In fact, the framing of tribal communities as a 'problem' draws on a discursive history of 'othering' that they are subjected to. For instance, the socio-anthropological discourse of tribes in India largely views and studies tribes as the 'other'. This 'othering' reinforces prejudicial notions and stereotypical images of 'tribes'. In other words, tribes are socially and politically considered as an internal 'other'. As such, the problem of the integration of tribes is often framed in the language of bringing them into the national mainstream. This presupposes an ideology of expansionism and exclusivism that presumes the existence of those who define themselves as 'insiders' and label the rest as 'outsiders' to the mainstream (Oommen 1986: 56). Mainstreaming the tribes thereby becomes the modus operandi of national integration.

However, political integration, in particular, does not necessarily imply inclusion. In terms of political integration, there are no parts of tribal regions that are not integrated. Even with strong resistance movements, the state has been penetrating and establishing its regime of control and rule. It is the mode and basis of inclusion that is contested as integration is premised on tribes adopting the culture of the national mainstream. The past and present tensions over national identity and nationalism in India demonstrate how the problem is primarily that of the national inclusion of minorities and marginalized communities. It is an issue that is evidently pronounced in the case of tribal communities whose participation and incorporation into the national movement are minimal. The issue here is not merely about colonial isolationist policy, but also about the efforts of national leaders and political parties to seek tribal support and participation. Noted sociologist Xaxa (2016) argues that the tribe and non-tribe relation was one of the reasons that restrained tribes from participating fully in the national movement. This, as he notes, was because of the exploitation of tribes at the hands of non-tribals, who, in fact, were their national brethren. In another instance, Xaxa (2018) shows how the tribals' participation in the formal democratic process remained limited in that they were deprived of positions of importance within political parties. The issue, as one can understand, is beyond merely including tribals in the nationalist narrative.

Very few scholars have examined the question of 'inclusion' in the context of the Indian national experience. The use of inclusion is instructive in the sense that it allows one to engage with the ideas, imaginations, and actors involved in the nation-building process. Aloysius (1998) shows how exclusive caste interests guided nationalist ideas and the leaders of the Indian national movement. In his critique of Indian nationalism, he concludes that Indian nationalism delivered a state but not a nation, as social distinction and social differentiation remained more or less undisturbed. In short, equality and the promise of freedom were far from achieved for the 'submerged masses'. In line with this, Oommen (1986) notes how Indian nationhood is defined in terms of an insider–outsider dichotomy wherein the dominant cultural mainstream, the twice-born Hindu community, occupies the 'insider' status and inhabits the cultural core, while the peripheral communities are relegated to an 'outsider' status. Through this, the voice of the dominant collectivity is legitimized as 'nationalism', and identification with the nation is only possible through identification with the 'cultural mainstream'.

This observation reveals the tension and contradictions that are inherent in the nationalist imagination. To invoke inclusion therefore is to go beyond mere integration, which is often about entrenching the territorial borders of the nation-state or reordering the cultural life of the communities into the 'national mainstream'. Furthermore, what is sought is not merely an inclusion in the historical writings or as subjects of history, but the questioning of normative ideas of nationhood and national imagination that sustain and reinforce exclusionary practices (Guru 2016b). The reason and consequent outcome of exclusion vary across communities and regions. For the majority of tribal communities, the question of inclusion goes beyond simply associating them with Indian nationalism; it instead extends to recognizing their claim to autonomy and their rights over resources.

In this context, the experience of the northeast region and its tribal communities is worthy of attention. Since independence, the case of the tribals of the region and their future status has been under scholarly focus and widely debated. This book presents a more complex history of integration within this context by taking the case of tribal communities, such as the Mizos. This is evident in the continued obsession with 'integration' for a state that, ironically, is being projected as a model for accommodating secessionist aspirations (see Chapter 6). The state continues to direct its efforts towards integrating regions and communities within the national mainstream. This means that the root problem of integration lies not with the state or the dominant culture per se, but with the people at the periphery who are unable to integrate themselves into the wider society.

Considering the case of the tribes and the Mizos, the rest of the chapter shows how integration was entrenched in the national agenda and is still pursued today. In a region like the northeast, the case for integration is justified on the premise that the region's isolation, both geographically and culturally, feeds the feeling of alienation among the people of the region. On the contrary, the experience of the last two decades has shown the opposite, where migrants from the region living in various metropolitan cities are perceived as national 'outsiders'. The issue is now recognized, albeit reluctantly, as a case of racism; nevertheless, it demonstrates how national imaginings have excluded the 'northeastern face' (Wouters and Subba 2013: 131). This has evoked debates about citizenship and national identity and raised the question of national integration in India (McDuie-Ra 2012). As Baruah (2020) notes, the problem of national belonging and unbelonging is a complex question in the context of India. In this context, it is useful to examine the case of secessionists and other political movements as a problem of inclusion.

India's Northeast and National Integration

As India gained independence, the immediate task was to integrate the diverse communities and vast geography into a united nation. What the state sought was unity and the integrity of the nation-state and its entrenchment. One of the staunch challenges of integration came from the northeastern region. Since independence, the

Indian state has resorted to various strategies to incorporate the region by granting special provisions and protections to the communities. However, the response towards the attempt to integrate the region has been mixed and guided by not only an interest in nation-building but also strategic compulsions and considerations.

Nationalist politics in northeast India is premised on a narrative of the struggle for autonomy. There was a common feeling that the process of India's independence and decolonization failed to liberate them (Walker 2019). The experience of decolonization was uneven, and many communities felt that the end of colonialism did not end alien, if not foreign, rule. As such, under post-colonial states, movements for independence sprang up, invoking the language of political sovereignty, similar to the ones popularized by anti-colonial movements across the globe. Many of the region's communities-led secessionist movements share a historical grievance about the manner in which they were integrated into the Indian Union. Besides this, the narratives of the struggles are posited against the region's distinctiveness from mainland India, both socially and culturally. However, the region is ethnically diverse, and unlike other parts of the country, it has a large tribal concentration, which makes it an exception from other regions of India. Tribes in the region are composed of various ethno-linguistic and religious communities that are scattered all across the region. The present regional set-up in terms of state boundaries and autonomous and regional councils cannot be read without understanding the region's tribal politics.

At the time of independence, there were two princely states—Manipur and Tripura—with large parts of the tribal areas put under partially excluded and excluded areas. Such tribal areas were made part of the districts of Assam in post-independent India. The tribals of the region responded differently to the national integration project. In Tripura, while the tribal king agreed to accede to the Indian Union, it was far more contentious in Manipur as the then king, Bodhchandra, was coerced to sign the Instrument of Accession in the year 1949. For the tribal communities of Manipur, a different aspiration was articulated, which was to integrate their territories as a sovereign state or one federal state within the Indian Union, as was the case of the Naga and the Mizo tribes, respectively. The issue for states like Manipur was that the contest for political integration was not merely against the Indian state. Whereas armed groups in the valley areas challenged the integration of the princely states into the Indian Union, the tribal communities inhabiting the hills sought secession from the Manipur state, claiming historical independence from the erstwhile princely state.

Among the Khasis and the Nagas, too, there were voices of resistance against integration, which culminated in an armed movement for independence in the case of the Nagas. In the present state of Meghalaya, the Federation of Khasi States and the Garo and Jaintia tribes were made to sign the Instrument of Accession by coercion. Pressured by the government to complete its annexation, 19 out of the

25 Khasi states under the federation signed, while the Khasi chiefs, such as Wickliffe Syiem, refused to accede and fled to East Pakistan when denied the right to self-determination (Nongbri 2003: 101–102). Likewise, in the Naga Hills, the aspiration to remain independent grew considerably strong under the leadership of Angami Zapu Phizo, popularly known as AZ Phizo. He demonstrated the ability to convince the different Naga groups under the aegis of the Naga National Council (NNC) to support the Naga national cause. In short, the political integration of the region within the Indian Union has remained a bone of contention between the Indian state and the ethnic nationalities of the region (Chandhoke 2006; S. K. Das 2010).

The story of integration did not end with mere political integration. This is because while the state may succeed in political integration, communities within a single state may not necessarily forge a common sense of identity or even national consciousness and be divided around primordial attachments. Geertz (1973) shows that newly independent states are vulnerable to political mobilizations of primordial attachments such as assumed blood ties, race, language, region, religion, and custom. Primordial loyalty supersedes other loyalties as those of class as it 'strikes more deeply and is satisfied less easily' (Geertz 1973: 261). This posed a serious challenge to the territorial unity and integrity of the new states. At the same time, the states themselves often used dominant ethnic symbols and culture to define nationalism. In South-East Asia, as Brown (1988) observes, despite the multi-ethnic composition, nation-states promote the identification of the states with the majority ethnic community of the state. According to Brown (1988), this is the major impediment to nation-building and the factor for separatist movements in South-East Asia. It has often put ethnic minorities in conflict with the central state and its rule. Against this backdrop, Wimmer observes:

> The struggle over the state becomes a struggle *against* the state when the costs of the state activities become very high.... [I]n the eyes of the majority population, peoples of the hinterland stick like a thorn of primitiveness in the body of the nation. To strengthen national self-consciousness, it thus seems legitimate and virtually necessary to subdue 'the barbarians', to fill the 'cultural vacuum, to declare their lands as state property, and to populate them with one's own peoples'. (Wimmer 1997: 645)

For Brown (1988), ethnic separatism in South-East Asia needs to be located within the problem of national belonging and identity. As he notes, 'it is this identification of the state, and thence the nation, with the majority ethnic groups which provide the starting point for explaining the development of ethnic nationalisms amongst the minorities' (Brown 1988: 55). As each nation-state ventures towards nation-building vis-à-vis integration, the concomitant outcome of such agenda is assimilation, pushing smaller ethnic groups to melt towards the dominant culture. Perhaps how smaller ethnic minorities articulate their aspirations or aspire for different states depends invariably on the behaviour and attitudes of the dominant ethnic groups.

Read along this line, the objective of national integration is underpinned by a singular idea of national identity built upon cultural homogeneity. As such, even as territorial unity was the predetermined objective of the national integration process, homogeneity and uniformity were its undeclared objective. Cultural pluralism was seen not merely as an obstacle to integration but also as a threat to national unity. Hence, the unity of the nation-state was to be achieved through the expansion of the dominant culture (Oommen 1986). This was the objective behind the establishment of the Committee on Emotional Integration in the 1960s, which demonstrated how the Indian state tried to homogenize feelings and attitudes. M. S. S. Pandian (2009) outlined this in one of the committee's recommendations on how to sing the national anthem, where the committee proposed that '... [t]o ensure complete uniformity of rendering ... recorded music by the All India Radio should be invariably used as a guide both to the instrumental and vocal rendering of the Anthem' (cited in M. S. S. Pandian 2009: 65). He further observed:

> Given such emphasis on homogeneity and sameness as the source and essence of the nation, the Committee had to repeatedly address the question of difference as the problem to be combatted in nation-making. Hence, it speaks repeatedly of identities based on region (regionalism), caste (casteism) and religion (communal-ism), among others, as threats to the young Indian nation. (M. S. S. Pandian 2009: 65)

The issue of national integration therefore is not confined to political integration. The agenda was elevated to create unity and a feeling of belonging among the people. This was instituted as a part of the official nationalism embracing 'unity in diversity' within a modern nation that came to define 'Indian-ness' (Roy 1999). In outlining post-colonial Indian nationalism, Roy (1999) argued that events such as Republic Day were representative of how India's diversity was not merely a case of displaying its diversity but how the Indian 'state embraces notions of social diversity in its discourse on Indian identity' (Roy 1999: 82). While such views ignored the contestation of the Indian nation-state, a far more problematic assumption was that it considered 'unity' as naturally occurring and equally accepted by all. On the contrary, what was sought in a 'troublesome frontier' was to make them feel 'Indian' through state developmentalism and securing of the territory (Guyot-Réchard 2013). The first prime minister, Jawaharlal Nehru, stated the goal was to 'inspire with confidence and to make them feel at one with India, and to realise that they are part of India and have an honoured place in it' (cited in Guyot-Réchard 2013: 23).

The issue of integration was not unique to the northeastern region. It was equally contentious in the princely states of Kashmir and Hyderabad. Furthermore, there was also strong nationalist mobilization in the southern states. The demand for separate Dravidistan in the southern states, for instance, was made against the linguistic imposition of Hindi that paved the way for a strong regional identity in the mainstream politics of Tamil Nadu. What made the case of the northeastern region unique was the inherent 'postcolonial insecurities' (Krishna 1999) of the central state that defined the attitude of the ruling elites. One of the notable references to this was the letter written by Sardar Vallabhai Patel to Jawaharlal Nehru in 1950, where he said:

> Let us also consider the political conditions on this potentially troublesome frontier. Our northern and north-eastern approaches consist of Nepal, Bhutan, Sikkim, Darjeeling and the tribal areas in Assam. From the point of view of communication, there are weak spots. Continuous defensive lines do not exist. There is almost an unlimited scope for infiltration. Police protection is limited to a very small number of passes. There, too, our outposts do not seem to be fully manned. The contact of these areas with us is by no means close and intimate. The people inhabiting these portions have no established loyalty or devotion to India. Even Darjeeling and Kalimpong areas are not free from pro-Mongoloid prejudices. During the last three years, we have not been able to make any appreciable approaches to the Nagas and other hill tribes in Assam. (Subba 1991: 97)

From the central states' point of view, the region was marked out as an 'insecure region' populated by communities whose loyalty to the 'nation' was questionable. There was a perpetual 'cartographic anxiety', to borrow Krishna's (1994) term again—an anxiety expressed by states over the questions of national identity and survival that found expression in concerns over the creation and protection of national boundaries. This anxiety comes to life when a gap exists between state representations and the imaginaries held by citizens of the state, particularly between states and the people who inhabit the frontier and the borderlands. Policies towards the northeast demonstrate the anxiety of the state, whose concern is predominantly directed towards securing the frontier and protecting national integrity. As Krishna (1994, 1999) notes in his work, securing the 'troublesome frontier' was one of the first tasks of the national leaders, and, as such, India's northeast occupied centre stage. Securing the frontier trumped all other policies and disregarded the interests and aspirations of the local communities. Affirming this, Baruah (2005) notes that the installing of 'generals as governor' is a manifestation of the security-mindedness of the state towards the region. Furthermore, a mixture of both 'anxiety' and 'insecurity' found expression in the CA debates on the Sixth Schedule for the tribals of the region.

The case of granting autonomy to the tribal communities in the form of the Sixth Schedule of the northeast region provides an interesting account of the integrationist goal of the Indian state (Figure 2.1). The Schedule envisions a form of a decentralized system of governance that recognizes the political and cultural rights of the communities. In the face of the demand for autonomy emerging from the tribal communities, the Schedule acted as an important mechanism to integrate the tribal communities into the Indian Union. Regionally, the Schedule saw opposition

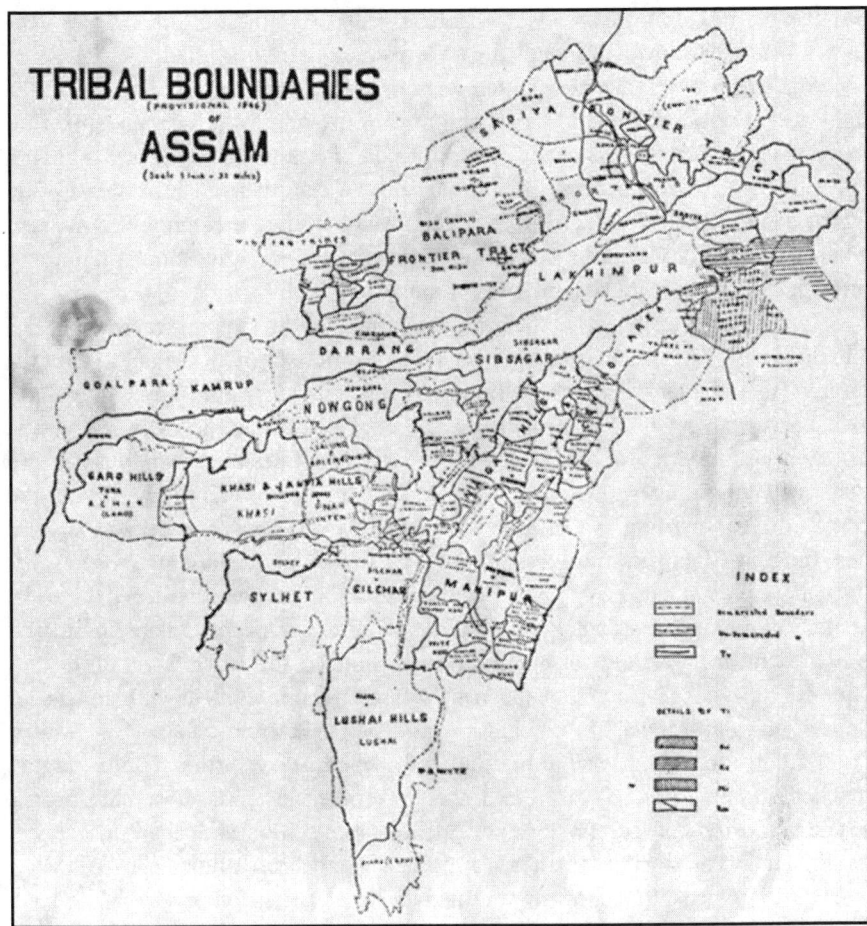

Figure 2.1   Map showing tribal boundaries in northeast India (provisional), 1946
Source: Tarun Bhartiya.
Note: The map was presented before the North-East Frontier (Assam) Tribal and Excluded Areas Sub-Committee of the Constituent Assembly of India in 1946.

from within the region's political elites and communities—mostly the non-tribals—who perceived it as infusing 'separatist' feelings among the tribal communities. There was an expression of 'insecurity' and 'anxiety', stating that these would limit the possibility for 'unity' among the various communities of the 'diverse' region.

Tribal Futures and the Sixth Schedule: The Integration Agenda

The Sixth Schedule was undoubtedly introduced to serve the integrationist purpose of the Indian state (Stuligross 1999: 497; Barbora 2005). To a large extent, it was the promise of autonomy that wooed sections of tribes to join and integrate with the Indian Union. However, not long after its introduction in the region, the provisions could neither protect the tribals' interests nor safeguard their rights. This led to the hill state movements demanding separation from Assam as well as movement for independence. Another issue with the provision of autonomy is the problem with what the political scientist Hausing (2014) calls the 'centralist federalist framework', which allows the central states to overrule, if not override, autonomy provisions when it deemed fit. This produced continued tensions over the question of autonomy, often putting at stake the federal spirit of the Constitution.

Tribes in the northeast led the movement for autonomy to protect both the state and their non-tribal counterparts. Soon, as already noted earlier, the question of the future status of tribes began to be framed within the integration–isolation debate. Tribal leaders who participated in the CA debates did not necessarily envision isolation or integration but asserted protective regimes that would safeguard their rights and interests. Arguably, the CA debates also brought out tensions and contestations regarding the issue of autonomy. At one level, the debates showed how the non-tribal communities and the state shared similar orientations towards the tribals when it came to granting political autonomy. At another level, the tribal communities' assertion depicts that while protection from central state dominance was present, the demand for autonomy was directed towards protection against regional dominance from the non-tribals. This became evident with the major opposition against the Sixth Schedule as was expressed by non-tribal political elites.

Baruah (2003a), in examining the Sixth Schedule in northeast India, argues that autonomous provisions created a regime of exclusion against 'non-tribals', further incentivizing certain forms of identity-recognition as 'tribes'. In areas of its implementation in the northeast, it created what Baruah (2003a: 1624) calls a 'two-tiered citizenship', conferring on the tribal majorities exclusive rights to land, employment, and political representation, as had happened in the states of Mizoram, Nagaland, and Meghalaya. The granting of the Sixth Schedule fomented ethnic strife and violence in the region, creating a crisis over the demand for ethnic homelands. Baruah (2003b: 2), in another instance, argues how the reorganization of the northeast was a 'cosmetic plan' by the Indian state, a top–down affair, a 'hurried exercise' as he calls it. This resulted in the endless demands for ethnic homelands in the region. Since its introduction, the Sixth Schedule has been extended in Tripura and parts of Assam, while multiple new states have been carved out of Assam.

Many tribal communities in the northeast continue to aspire for the Sixth Schedule, such as in Manipur. While the idea of the Schedule was to grant political autonomy to tribes, many felt betrayed by it, which then pushed them towards demanding separate statehood. The hill politics in the 1960s and up to the 1970s saw resentment against the powers conferred on the autonomous District Council under the Sixth Schedule. In the Mizo Hills, in particular, this resentment against the power conferred on the District Council became apparent in 1959, when Assam state leaders ignored the request for precautionary measures by the Mizo leaders in preparation for the oncoming *mautam* (famine caused by bamboo flowering) (Roluahpuia 2021). Up to 1972, tribal political mobilization centred on the demand for separation from Assam, articulating political visions to empower them. More than mere 'cosmetic' posturing, the state reorganization was a response by the central state to the tribal political quest for autonomy. Even today one cannot be dismissive of how the political marginalization of tribes continues to be the precursor to the demands for Sixth Schedule provisions in the region. In short, the mobilization for the Sixth Schedule and statehood was a continuum of tribal politics and aspirations for autonomy and self-rule.

The Bordoloi Committee, as it is commonly known since its formation, was tasked with identifying the future status of the tribals under the new Constitution. Towards this end, its members visited the tribal areas of the region, such as the Lushai Hills and the Khasi Hills, among others. Given its mandate, the committee sought representatives of the tribal leaders and inquired about their aspirations. Nevertheless, the problem remained that it would sideline any voice that opposed the committee's agenda of charting out autonomy provisions. For instance, the Khasi chiefs under the Federation of Khasi States demanded the provision for inclusion of the rights of the chief, even though they were opposed to the proposed Sixth Schedule. Yet this demand was sidelined due to the strong opposition by Nichols Roy, the sole Khasi member of the CA who was a staunch opponent of the chiefs (Nongbri 2003: 102). Likewise, in the Lushai Hills, the committee favoured the MU, whose leaders, consisting of the newly educated elite, were equally opposed to the Lusei chiefs. The committee considered the MU leaders as representing the sole voice and interests of the Mizos.

With this being the case, the context of the introduction of the Sixth Schedule requires its juxtaposition with the political events of the period. One of these was that it came as a response to British withdrawal from India; hence, it had to do with the political future of the tribes in India. Another event was the partition of British India, which was to have a significant impact on the future of Assam. The first case was evident in the CA debates on the future of the 'aborigines' in India. In the debates, what transpired were not merely discussions about the future status of tribes but also the impending fear or grievous consequence of granting self-rule to the tribals. Needless to say, there was both national and regional anxiety. Non-tribal political leaders expressed the fear that the Sixth Schedule would create 'tribalstan' or 'communistan', with some stating that it would end up in 'chaos, anarchy and disorder'. Bordoloi, who headed the Advisory Subcommittee, also reiterated what he called the 'separatist' tendency of the hill areas in the debates on the Sixth Schedule (Syiemlieh 2014: 32). Such fear, as alluded to by Suan (2007), is reflected in how the security-development paradigm remained embedded in granting the Sixth Schedule to the tribals in the northeast. The second factor is that given the Assamese elites' fear of being included in Pakistan, they sought the support of the hill tribals to further their cause to join the Indian Union (Vanlawma 1989).

On 5 September 1949, a lengthy and heated debate took place in the CA on the tribals' future regarding the Fifth and Sixth Schedules for the tribal regions of the country. There was a sharp divide of opinion among the representatives hailing from the region. The exchange between the representatives espoused two polarized positions. For instance, Rohini Kumar Chaudhuri and Kuladhar Chaliha, in expressing their discontent against the creation of autonomous councils, presented a case for an equal relationship between the tribes and the non-tribes of the region. They noted that the creation of autonomous councils would result in the loss of the possibility of the assimilation of the tribals into the mainstream culture. In fact, the report of the Bordoloi Committee on the tribal areas of northeast India also expressed a similar concern—that the hill people had not been assimilated into Assam (Syiemlieh 2014: 32).

On the contrary, Jaipal Singh, a tribal leader from Jharkhand, expressed his optimism about the Sixth Schedule and informed the attending members how it was framed based on consultation with the tribal peoples of the region. In his words,

> Indeed, I am very optimistic about the future of Assam, particularly if the Sixth Schedule, even with all its shortcomings, is operated in the spirit in which it should be operated, in a spirit of accommodation and in the real desire to serve the hill people of Assam, as our compatriots, and as people whom we want to come into our fold, as people we will not let go of our fold and for whom we will make any amount of sacrifice so that they may remain with us. (Constituent Assembly of India 1949)

Nichols Roy, another member who was part of the Advisory Subcommittee, in his response, noted the anxiety of the tribes and the social and political relationships they shared with the *vai*. He noted, 'It is said by one honourable gentleman that the hill tribes have to be brought to the culture which he said "our culture" meaning the culture of the plainsmen' (Constituent Assembly of India 1949). In further responding to the previous speakers, he emphasized why the tribals of the region required autonomous councils:

> There is another point which must be considered in this connection. To keep the frontier areas safe, these people must be kept in a satisfied condition. You cannot use force upon them. Human nature is such that when you use force to make people to do something they run to somebody else. If you want to win them over for the good of India, you will have to create a feeling of friendliness and unity among them so that they may feel that their culture and ways of living have not been abolished and another kind of culture thrust upon them by force. That is why the subcommittee thought that the best way to satisfy these

people is to give them a certain measure of self-government so that they may develop themselves according to their own genius and culture. (Constituent Assembly of India 1949)

At one level, the CA debates echo the isolationist and integrationist divide, but for the tribal leaders, it was an act of self-assertion to claim recognition and constitutional protection. Nevertheless, the provision of autonomy in the form of the Fifth and Sixth Schedules was necessary to reconcile the tribals' quest for autonomy and to act as recognition of their social and cultural rights (Prasad 1994; Xaxa 2008). It was through the recognition of autonomy that tribes participated in the larger democratic process (Dasgupta 1997), and it also worked as a protective mechanism to constrain non-tribal—in this case, the *vai*'s—domination. It is therefore not surprising that the Sixth Schedule continues to be the much-stated goal of autonomy for the tribes even today.

Inclusion or Integration: Contestation and Challenges

We now turn to the more contemporary state of affairs to look at the issue of integration as this is a reminder of how the agenda of integration continues to be the overarching goal of the Indian state. In mainstream society and academia, the general view is that the historiographical exclusion of the northeast region—its history and people—was the cause behind the region being 'unknown' to the rest of the country. One often sees this in the protest of the northeastern communities against racism or by the northeast activists claiming that the history of the region should be included in the school curriculum as a way of integrating the region with the nation's history. One notices the 'lack' of northeastern history in the national curriculum—hence, the need to integrate the region's history. National histories, however, are not merely about accounts of people and past events. As far as the northeastern region is concerned, inclusion also means to 'nationalize' the region's history within mainstream historiography.

The past few years have seen how the state sought to include the region's history as a part of national history. This effort also came as the backdrop to racial profiling and violence against the northeastern communities (McDuie-Ra 2012). Apart from this, tourism and festivals are becoming a bonanza for the state in cities such as New Delhi, which hosts large numbers of northeastern migrants. Such events 'exoticize' and 'ethnicize' the region and its communities as 'timeless' and 'static' communities with tribal dances, dress, and art projected as the essence defining the regional identity. It is within this context that one sees the problem of including the region's history within national history. In studying tourism websites of the northeast, Patil (2011) argues that the history of the region is 'naturalized' and 'depoliticized', obscuring the contested history of the region. In doing so, it ends up advancing the hegemonic narrative of the nation, weaving its history within the Aryan, Hindu, and Vedic heritage.

Since 2014, the BJP coming to the centre coincided with an upsurge of nationalism across the country. The politics of nationalism is seen as a concerted effort towards creating a meta-narrative of 'one nation, one culture'. In regions such as the northeast, the party made gains and advances in erstwhile strongholds of the INC and other regional parties. In line with its ambitions, the BJP has assumed the onus of integrating the regions' histories as well as heroes within national history. One of the attempts came in the form of the agenda to induct various heroes as 'Indian freedom fighters'. It succeeded in its effort in some states, such as Meghalaya and Manipur; however, in other states, such as Mizoram, there was strong opposition, which provided an important clue as to how the communities, such as the Mizos, viewed their relationship with the Indian society and state at large.

The BJP identified a list of 10 forgotten heroes to be named as 'Indian freedom fighters'. The prominent ones among them are Bir Tikendrajit (Manipur), U. Tirot Sing Syiem (Meghalaya), Hem Barua (Assam), and Khuangchera (Mizoram). Whereas those identified may have had been part of the Indian national movement, one is doubtful of figures such as Bir Tikendrajit and Khuangchera. The majority of them, in fact, opposed and led strong anti-colonial movements against the British. What has become contentious, at least in the case of the Mizos, is the labelling of whom they refer to as *pasaltha* (tribal hero or warrior)—Khuangchera, in this case—as an 'Indian freedom fighter'. The opposition by the Mizo public under the aegis of the MZP and the Mizo Student Union (MSU) requires further context.

The history of colonialization of the northeastern region, such as present-day Mizoram, took place at the close of the nineteenth century. The territory inhabited by the Mizos was put under British rule with the annexation of the Lushai Hills after the second military expedition known as the Chin Lushai Expedition (1890–1891). *Pasaltha*, like Khuangchera, died fighting the incursion of the British into present-day Mizoram. *Pasaltha* in Mizo society are highly revered and respected and are known for their bravery and chivalry—attributes which embody Mizo values such as *tlawmngaihna*.[2] In contemporary Mizo society, organizations such as the YMA play a central role in ensuring their stories are passed on to the younger generations. It is also common to find streets, buildings, or parks named after the *pasaltha*.

The objective of naming Khuangchera in line with other figures was to honour such 'forgotten heroes' as 'Indian freedom fighters'. In doing so, the government planned to organize a ceremony to honour Khuangchera in his native village— Ailawng in Mizoram. Therefore, the intent was to project a unified struggle against the British as a way of nationalizing the history of the Mizos. The attempt did not go down well with the Mizos, who clearly saw it as an attempt to decontextualize and distort Mizo history. The MZP and the MSU led the protest and opposed the honouring attempt, contending that although the Mizo *pasaltha* Khuangchera did resist the British, it was for the Mizos and not for India. Issuing a press release to express their resentment, the student bodies of the state noted that Khuangchera did resist and fight against the British, but not for India. The press release further noted the scepticism about the singling out of Khuangchera when there were so many other *pasaltha* who had died resisting the British. The student bodies considered it a belligerent idea to name Khuangchera or, for that matter, any Mizo *pasaltha*, as an 'Indian freedom fighter'.

The student bodies mobilized the Mizo public to boycott the ceremony that was to be held on 18 August 2016, at Ailawng village, the location of Khuangchera's grave. This was to be done in the presence of Rajen Gohain, the then union minister of state for railways. The students blocked the road in Aizawl leading to Ailawng village and met the minister at Lengpui Airport to register their protest and objection to the said plan. The honouring ceremony was thereby called off, with the minister quoted as saying that he understood the sentiments of the Mizo people and did not want to hurt their sentiments by attending the program at Khuangchera's native village at Ailawng (*Business Standard* 2016). It is, however, interesting to note that the gravesite was constructed with the support of the Assam Rifles (AR) in 2010, with an epitaph which read 'Duty nobly done, famous Mizo patriot, a martyr for his country, Mizo/Indian freedom fighter'. On the other hand, the student placards sent a clear message saying that Khuangchera was not an 'Indian freedom fighter'. With the BJP forced to abort the plan, the villagers of Ailawng and the Khuangchera Memorial Society then considered erecting a new headstone and omitting the words 'Mizo/Indian freedom fighter' (*Frontier Despatch* 2016: 7).

The case of naming certain figures of the northeast is beyond mere saffronization. The majoritarian impulse of defining national identity has been an inherent part of the nationalist imagination in India—a 'dilemma', as Uberoi (2002) has noted. Uberoi illuminates this dilemma by showing how majoritarianism was not the sole preserve of the right-wing groups in India by taking us through the use of calendar art as a medium for visualizing the nation where representations were equally complex and contesting. As such, the case of the Mizo student bodies opposing the attempt to name Khuangchera as a 'freedom fighter' is a response to the effort to override the tension over nationality and nationhood. As the Mizos perceived it, the attempt was a larger part of the integrative goals of the state and an act of rewriting Mizo history and appropriating their past through Khuangchera. As such, what was at stake was also the Mizo existence, both as a distinct identity and the sense of having an autonomous history.

Beyond the student bodies' opposition, there were two issues worthy of mention. First, among the Mizos, there is a strong *hnam* consciousness of being distinct and separate. This idea of being distinct works in ways of 'othering' the self from the *vai* and 'non-Mizo'. The sense of being a *hnam*, or Mizo *hnam*, beyond clan and tribal boundaries, is strongly articulated in the Mizos' interactions and negotiations with the colonial and post-colonial state. The second aspect is *ram*—the territory in question—is closely intertwined with *hnam* consciousness. Even as Mizo-*ram* is part of the body politic of the Indian nation-state, the Mizos' sense of attachment is rooted in their *ram*. The case of Khuangchera was a case of the *ram leh hnam* issue that further reinvigorates the presence of *hnam* consciousness. Throughout this book, I have traced and examined how this sense of *ram leh hnam* has had been articulated over time in Mizo political history. From projecting a pan-Mizo identity in place of specific clan and tribal identities, I have placed the Mizos' articulation of their collective self and interrogated how the project of identity formation and political aspirations influences and continues to underpin politics in contemporary Mizo society.

Conclusion

Ever since India's independence, the integration of the northeastern region has been a policy and political priority. This integrationist discourse insists that the lack of integration has caused alienation among the people of the region. Such a view has become entrenched, as can be seen with the demand for secessionist movements in Manipur, Mizoram, Nagaland, and Assam. As noted earlier, there are two caveats to this. First, it purportedly ignores the contested history of the integration of the major parts of the region. Second, it overlooks the political aspirations that began to take shape during the period of colonialism. If one is to accept the political integration of the region, one would have to share the view that the state is successful. This is because political integration can be either voluntary or coerced. Where opposition to it was strong, large-scale militarization ensued, with power concentrated in the hands of the military.

What has remained unresolved is the incorporation of the people that engendered the ideas and imaginations of Indian nationalism, or the 'nationalist thought' (P. Chatterjee 1986). Yet, in so far as inclusionary attempts are considered, they are framed within the goal of integration, in the state's own terms, even today. For instance, the Bezbaruah Committee, in its recommendation to control racial violence against northeastern communities, concluded:

> All our recommendations for increasing two-way exchange and understanding of the people of the northeast and the rest of India has one primary objective, i.e., the ethnic and cultural difference of the northeast should be a cause for celebration and not for raising barriers. They are meant to integrate the northeast with the rest of India and not to segregate it. (Bezbaruah Committee 2014: 5)

The notion of integration continues to be proposed as a solution to India's northeastern problem. Furthermore, it resonates with the larger discourse of Indian nationhood because integration and diversity are central to the national imagining and even in the construction of Indian nationhood. They further affirm the legitimacy of the Indian state and its claims over the region and the people (McDuie-Ra 2017: 28).

This book takes a different view of nationalist politics in northeast India. It moves away from the state-centric narrative of integration and instead examines how communities, such as the Mizos, imagine the nation differently and in their own terms. Unlike existing scholarly studies on Mizo politics and the MNF movement specifically, the book engages with the question of politics in the vernacular, examining the critical and crucial role of the 'oral culture' as a distinctive form of political expression.

Notes

1   The partially excluded areas included the Garo Hills district, the Mikir Hills in the Nowgong and Sibsagar districts, the British portion of the Khasi and Jaintia Hills districts, other than Shillong Municipality and Cantonment. The excluded areas included the Northeast Frontier, including Sadiya, Balipara, and Lakhimpur, the Naga Hills district, the Lushai Hills district, and the North Cachar Hills subdivision of the Cachar district.

2   *Tlawmngaihna* is a Mizo social code of conduct used to refer to altruistic behaviour and conduct.

3 The Emergence of Mizo Nationalism

The Formative Phase

The year 1954 was a turning point in Mizo history for two reasons. First, the Lushai Hills were renamed as Mizo Hills, following the replacement of 'Lushai' with 'Mizo' by an Act of the parliament. Second, the traditional institution of chieftainship was abolished through an Act passed in the Assam assembly. The focus of this chapter is the event that led to the recognition of the *hnam*—herein 'Mizo'—and the movement against the institution of chiefs that led to the eventual abolishing of chieftainship. In the case of the latter, given the support of the chiefs by the British, the movement for the abolishing of chieftainship was enmeshed with a strong anti-colonial fervour. Protests and mobilization against colonial rule were intertwined with resentment against the continuation of chiefs' rule. Furthermore, the role of the MU has largely been overlooked, if not undermined, when it comes to Mizo political history in general and Mizo nationalism in particular. The idea of 'Mizo' and the promise of a new future in the post-British-rule era articulated by the MU were to shape and define the future political contour.

Often, tribes are assumed as apolitical subjects lacking any form of political consciousness and resistance against the British. Such readings are done against the larger anti-colonial movement, which saw minimal participation from tribal communities. It is true that many tribes distanced themselves from the anti-colonial movement. This is also because there were no genuine efforts to ensure the participation of the tribes, and tribes were rarely, if not never, inducted as leaders in the nationalist movement. However, the larger problem remains that many non-tribals, including leaders of the INC in the anti-colonial movement, were responsible for the exploitation of tribes. The class of moneylenders and landlords, for instance, belonged to the INC loyalists against which tribes launched several protest movements (Bates 1988). Hence, the condition of the tribes was complex by this experience of a colonial-like rule from their own brethren. In another instance, Xaxa (2008), for example, notes how tribes have faced double colonialism—one by the British and the other by the Indians themselves.

In northeast India, even as the nationalist movement did not have much presence, political consciousness in the form of demands for autonomy and self-rule began to take shape from the early twentieth century. In the Lushai Hills, one finds that when the Mizo commoners protested against the chiefs' taxation and their autocratic rule, it further pitted the commoners against the British, leading to a strong anti-colonial sentiment among the masses. Similarly, one finds political mobilization taking shape among the Nagas, Bodos, and other tribal communities across the region. This goes against the assumption that tribal communities and the regions they inhabited were intransigent to any form of political mobilization against colonial rule, lacking political consciousness. In this chapter, we trace the political mobilization of the Mizos from the colonial period, showing how rather than being 'passive' subjects, Mizos articulate and assert themselves, questioning colonial authority and claiming rights through the demand for recognition of Mizo *hnam* and autonomy in independent India.

The last two decades of colonial rule in Lushai Hills were marked by resistance and confrontation between Mizo commoners and the British. The Mizos challenged the colonial policy of 'exclusion' on the ground that it denied them political rights and participation. This mood gained much traction, with the Mizos beginning to politically organize themselves, the outcome of which was the formation of the MU. Since its very inception, the political language of the MU was defined by its 'cultural embeddedness', and as soon as modern electoral politics was taking root, it was reworked in such a manner to suit the emerging contexts (Wouters 2014). The culture of what is known as *party hla* began to gain root, acting as an essential medium to disseminate party ideologies and manifestos. It follows what Michelutti (2008), in another context, has termed the 'vernacularization of democracy', where democratic politics became entrenched in the social and cultural practices of the local people. Michelutti (2008) demonstrates how the Yadavs, a formerly backward caste group in north India, reconfigured the idea of democracy, portraying it as a primordial phenomenon passed in the blood from the glorious Yadav ancestors and the god Krishna to the contemporary Yadavs.

In Mizo society, democratic politics began to take root with the formation of political parties. In fact, much prior to the 'rise of the plebians' (Jaffrelot and Kumar 2009) elsewhere in the country, Mizo society has seen a sociopolitical transformation of the commoners' rise to power, both socially and politically. Put differently, while political parties played a significant role in the vernacularization of democracy, it was a process enabled by the participation of the elites as well as the commoners. As such, democratic politics gets entrenched where both the elites and the commoners participate actively in constructing and shaping the discourse. On the one hand, the elites adopted the language of the masses to connect with the commoners, such as using *hnam* and *ram*, while the commoners immersed themselves by composing songs—*party hla* in this context. The use of *party hla* is significant in how the political parties used local resources to muster public support. *Party hla*, due to their oral form, were penetrating and easily receptible in the Mizo life-world. The link between democracy and politics was made through the 'oral', making political discourse part of the everyday life of the people. In other words, the political culture of the Mizos was established through a vernacular process that continues to find relevance even today. Hence, in Mizo society, democratic politics gets consolidated in a vernacular idiom through *party hla*.

In post-colonial India, *party hla* soon became an integral part of the Mizos' democratic politics. The two-dominant parties of the time, the MU and the United Mizo Freedom Organization (UMFO), used *party hla* to mobilize and rally the public for support. During the election, *party hla* were used to promote and spread political agendas while downplaying the rivals. The use of *party hla* heralded a new political awakening, stirring national imaginations within the newly emerging political set-up. Through songs, such imaginations became an everyday vocabulary. The songs were rooted in the local traditions and easily received by the common people. Political parties used *party hla* to convey messages for mobilization and diffusion of ideas. Its centrality therefore lies in how the Mizo public became part of the political process by engaging in the vernacularization of democratic and nationalist politics. In other words, democratic politics was vernacularized using local idioms and politics, where the Mizos used the democratic space to advance their political interest and assert themselves politically.

The emergent political consciousness among the Mizos was shaped by the ideas and events of the time. The MU idea of autonomy envisioned freedom from colonial rule—hence opposing the much-touted Crown Colony and the continued rule of the traditional chiefs. The MU leaders were able to effectively navigate between the dual aspirations: first, the overthrowing of the chiefs; second, the demand for autonomy provisions under independent India. The resistance against colonial rule upset the British, who always considered the 'tribes' as subjects unable to govern themselves. From 1940 onwards, resentment against the colonial state and the chiefs' rule began to brew, resulting in open confrontation. This continued until the adoption of the Constitution in 1950, which also marked the exit of the last British political superintendent in the Lushai Hills. In post-independent India, the MU emerged as the ruling party under the newly formed District Council under the Sixth Schedule. While in power, the MU took up the case of defining the idea of Mizo *hnam*. With a party led by non-chief clans, the non-Luseis specifically, the act of replacing 'Lusei' or 'Lushai' with 'Mizo' shows how it was a conscious choice despite acting against the wish of the more dominant Lusei tribes. As such, the chapter argues that the demand for autonomy for their *ram* and the demand for the recognition of Mizo *hnam* was a display of the Mizos' agency, thereby centring the Mizo voice.

By centring the focus on the MU, the chapter looks at the content and form of mobilization and how the Mizo public participated in and engaged with politics. The period between 1946 and 1951 was crucial in terms of how the Mizos began to organize themselves and articulate their aspirations politically. It was during this period that one sees the emergent nationalist consciousness among the Mizos that coincided with an exponential growth of new songs articulating the mood. The songs lyricized the aspirations and antagonism, the contestations and negotiations undergirding this emergent consciousness. The broad-based support of the MU spread across Mizo-inhabited areas in Manipur and Tripura, where the anti-chieftainship movement was strong, as was the demand for the territorial integration of the Mizo-inhabited areas. The exploration of these wider political processes is helpful in understanding why ethnic and territorial integration was one of the primary goals of the Mizo nationalist movement under the MNF. The role of the MU in the consolidation of Mizo identity and autonomy remains largely neglected, partly due to the overemphasis given to the anti-chieftainship movement. The demand for autonomy and recognition was instrumental in Mizo political history as they depicted modern Mizo political subjectivities, attesting to how the Mizos were conscious actors in their own social, cultural, and political lives. The chapter interrogates the Mizos' engagement with the colonial and the post-colonial state, the confrontation and contestation, and the mode and medium of the mobilizations that have shaped hill politics in the Mizo-inhabited areas of northeast India.

Indirect Rule, Direct Administration: Paternalism and Patronage

In expanding their conquest into the Lushai Hills, the British administered the area through a form of governance known as indirect rule. This formed the basis of colonial governance until colonial rule ended (Zorema 2007). Indirect rule was approved by various colonial states, whereby the governance of such regions was done through the existing structures of authority. This was in contrast to the usual practice of the colonial state imposing a direct form of governance. Under indirect rule, one of the basic tenets was preserving the existing authority structures and governance. In British India, a large part of its empire was under indirect rule, and no provincial laws and legislature could apply in such specified regions except when they threatened colonial order and authority; only then would the colonial state impose its authority.

Indirect rule was a constitutive element of colonial governmentality, a governance strategy 'actively designed to produce the effects of rule' (Scott 1995: 193). Even as this approach was in contrast to the direct form of governance, it instituted a system of difference where the 'customary' was privileged against 'modern' laws (Mamdani 1996). In the tribal areas of northeast India, indirect rule was the modus operandi of governance for the colonial state. This form of administration, however, allowed direct interference on the part of the colonial state in areas where 'indirect rule' was in operation, such as in the Lushai Hills. First, even as the colonial state claimed non-interference in such societies, in many cases it ended up either intervening or transforming local society, culture, or institutions. For instance, the British introduced *gaonburahs* (village headmen) among the Nagas and *lambus*[1] and circle interpreters (CIs) among the tribes in the Lushai Hills, which were part of the colonial governance system. Second, the colonial state agents, or administrators, were at the top of the hierarchy of the government. This allowed the colonial administrators to alter or introduce changes in the administration and subsequently the people's lives. One of the most visible imprints of colonial intervention in the social and cultural lives of the people in the hills of the northeast region was proselytization (Joshi 2012; J. Pachuau 2014).

In the Lushai Hills, the chiefs who were the pre-existing rulers were integrated into the colonial system of governance. The institution of the chief was kept intact despite the reforms in the sociocultural life of the people. As Reid (1987: 56) notes, the idea was to 'interfere as little as possible between the chiefs and their people and impress upon their chiefs their responsibilities for the maintenance of order in the villages'. The subsequent political superintendent, referred to by the Mizos as *bawrhsap*, noted the primacy of the chiefs. Parry (2009 [1932]: 13) goes as far as saying that 'the greatest of care has been taken to avoid in any way lowering of the position of the chief'. Chieftainship was transformed within the colonial administrative system as an apparatus of colonial governance. The transformation of the institution was immense, and it contributed to the resentment against the rule of the chiefs and, consequently, their overthrow.

There were three major areas where the colonial state intervened in the administration—namely the issuance of *ramrilekha* (boundary paper) to the chiefs; the introduction of the CI; and the conferment of chieftainship status on individuals of their own choice or preference. In the first case, the issuing of *ramrilekha* restricted the mobility and shifting of village sites which was practised by the Mizos. This resulted in the sedentarization of society. Second, the introduction of the CI was a part of the administrative reorganization of the Lushai Hills, dividing it into 18 zones with one CI for each circle. The CIs were intermediaries between the colonial state and the people and were a form of decentralized authority at the local level. Third, the conferment of chieftainship status or denial of chieftainship to existing ones was common throughout the colonial period. This had a deeper impact than imagined— for instance, the British rewarded individuals they favoured with the status of a chief; predictably, there was a staggering rise in the number of chiefs from 60 when the British ruled the Lushai Hills to 400 by the 1940s (McCall 1949). This altered the way the chiefs were perceived and affected their relationship with the people. The chiefs under colonial rule could no longer perform their traditional roles, such as hunting in the plains or conducting warfare; instead, their roles were confined to administration and collecting taxes. In this capacity, the chiefs began to be seen as 'decentralised despots' (Mamdani 1996: 16) as they '[became] purely government servants' (cited in Pels 1996: 743). It was therefore no surprise that taxation was one of the major issues during the anti-chieftainship movement.

Towards the end of British rule, the confrontation between the political superintendents and the Mizo commoners grew ostensibly. Whereas the British devised to keep their rule intact in the hills, the Mizos commoners' immediate goal was to oust the chiefs. This intensified as the British's departure was imminent and the Mizos became more politically organized and vocal. The formation of the MU on 29 April 1946 was a watershed moment for its emergence as the first political party among the Mizos and for articulating their political aspirations (Figure 3.1). Established by educated individuals, these groups were what McCall (1949: 217) describes as the 'articulate Lushai' who wanted to break free of the traditional power structures and replace them with modern governance systems. The background to their rise was the evangelical activity of the missionaries and their modern education that introduced them to the wider political processes of the time. This further enabled them to advance and articulate their political aspirations in the Indian federalist system (Fernandes 2009: 131). Two developments which were central to the emergence of the MU and its consolidation were, first, the British plan to continue its rule over the hill populations and, second, the rising political assertion of the hill tribes against colonial rule.

The emergence of the MU was a testament to the increasing political consciousness of the Mizos. For instance, a group of Mizos led by Telela along with his

Figure 3.1   The first Mizo Union (MU) assembly, 24 September 1946
Source: L. R. Sailo collection.

friends, Thuama, Liansiama, V. C. H. Saikunga, Thanzuala, Chawnghnuaia, and V. Z. Biaka, submitted a memorandum for representation to the political superintendent, N. E. Parry. It questioned the chiefs' authority and demanded representation in the Assam legislature by submitting a memorandum to the governor in 1926 (Zorema 2007: 95). The colonial state's response to such demands was quick, and Telela and his friends were put behind bars and later released after a stern warning that they should not indulge in any such activity in the future. Incipient as it might have been, the signs of political awakening were clear, and even today they are regarded as the first-known Mizos to challenge the colonial rule in the Lushai Hills. A memorial stone erected in their honour in Kulikawn, Aizawl, reads 'Kumpinu rorelna rit tak dova kan hnam chhantu hmahruai, hnam pasalṭhate chu an va hlu em' (We pay our highest tribute to our heroes who led the movement that challenged the tyranny of the British Empire). The opposition was directed against the chiefs and therefore the colonial state, which became the major bone of contention and confrontation between the MU and the British.

By 1946, the contest and confrontation between the British, the chiefs, and the Mizo commoners led by the MU dominated the political scene in the Lushai Hills. This was more of a question about the future political status of the Lushai Hills and the Mizos at large, given that it was only a matter of time before the British would leave India. Towards this end, A. R. H. MacDonald, the then political superintendent, convened what he called the District Conference to take place on 6 January 1946, as a body to represent the Mizos. The conference would have 20 members with equal representation from the chiefs and the commoners, with MacDonald appointing himself as the president of the conference. The MU opposed being part of the conference as they objected to the chiefs having equal representation; the MU demanded twice the number of representatives for the commoners (Chaube 1973; Chaltuahkhuma 2001 [1987]). This was done because equal representation implied the continuation of the chiefs' rule, which the MU rejected. The MU leader Pu Ch. Saprawnga wrote to MacDonald:

> He conference hian mipui ai kan awh lohzia tarik ni 6.11.46 ah khan kan thehlut tawh a. Mizoram aiawh tlak nia kan hriat dan leh kan duh dan chu, Hnamchawm member-te hi Lal aiawh lethnih an ni tur a ni. Chumi a nih loh chuan, he Conference-ah hian, nimin ang bawk khan, ban phara thil titlu turin Hnamchawm aiawhte hi kan kal thei tawh lo vang. (Chaltuahkhuma 2001 [1987]: 69)

We have conveyed our stand on 6.11.46 as to how this conference does not represent the wishes of the people. It can only be the representative for the people of Mizoram when the commoners have two-fold the number of representatives to that of the chieftains. If not, and like the way we did before, our, the commoners', representatives will raise our hands against the conference and refrain from further participation.

Henceforth, the MU organized a boycott against the District Conference as a way to pressure the superintendent, MacDonald, who was developing an increasing distaste for the MU leaders. Alongside this, the MU leaders and members were persistent in their demand for abolishing chieftainship and joining the Indian Union. The interest to join India was made on the basis that a new form of governance would be instituted under democratic India. For the majority of commoners, abolishing chieftainship was the main agenda and hence their primary political objective. The MU took an anti-colonial and anti-chief stance. The popular slogans of the MU of the time reflect this:

What do we want?
To join Indian Union.

Why?
To abolish the chiefs.

Such protests and slogans were becoming common across the Lushai Hills and in areas where the MU had its presence. This irked MacDonald, who attempted to have direct control over the party. On 9 November 1946, as the MU was holding a meeting about its future course of action, MacDonald walked in and took away the party's entire financial donation. The financial donation to the MU drew on a membership fee of 1 rupee for the household head and 50 paise for the wives and children who were registered as associate members. MacDonald subsequently issued an order restricting the MU from collecting any such donation. MacDonald's intervention cut off the financial source for the party and paralysed its functioning. The order read as follows:

THUPEK NO. 9190-413G of 1-11-46

'Mizo Union' hi eng atan mah renga renga tangka khawn belh emaw dawn belh emaw khap a ni. Tangka chu 'Luh man' nge 'Thawhlawm' nge 'khawn' nge hming dang eng pawh pu rawh se a pawi chuang lo: 'Mizo Union' chu khawn emaw dawn emaw khap a ni. Tupawh 'Mizo Union' aiawh ni lema tu hnen atang pawha 'Mizo Union' ta tur a ni tia tangka la reng reng chu bumtu anga hrem a ni ang.[2]

ORDER NO. 9190-413G of 1-11-46

'Mizo Union' is restricted from collecting or receiving any form of donation. The donation may be of any kind, inclusive of 'membership fee' or 'contribution' or 'collection' or whatever name it carries; it does not matter: 'Mizo Union' is restricted from any kind of collection or donation. Any individual who is involved in collecting financial donation for 'Mizo Union' would be considered as a liar and should be punished as such.

Quite clearly, MacDonald was being vindictive because of the MU's opposition to the District Conference. Using his authority, he issued various notifications to undermine the MU. In a letter to the president of the MU on 4 July 1946, MacDonald outlined why he opposed the move of the MU and its politics, which he found was entirely centred on what he called 'to hate chiefs'. He stated in his letter:

> The Mizo race, faced as it is with the near prospect of being thrown entirely on its own resources, needs above all things a Mizo Union, in the only true sense, embracing a real unity between the Mizo chiefs and the Mizo commoners. Anyone, who at a time like this, incites commoners to hate chiefs, or provokes chiefs to hate commoners, is like a drunken man starting a fight in a boat which is just about to shoot over the rapids. What is the meaning of this rant about saving the common people 'from the clutches of their chiefs'?[3]

Furthermore, in his bid to exert control over the MU, MacDonald insinuated:

> I suggest also that in future local Branches of the Mizo Union should be directed to submit their resolutions to the central authority of the Union so that they can be expurgated of undesirable matter before it becomes too public and does irrevocable harm to the name of the Mizo Union and to the unity of the Mizos.[4]

The confrontation between the MU and the political superintendent became more apparent over who had the legitimate authority to represent the Mizos. The question was about who would decide for and represent the Mizos when the British left. While the chiefs, with the support of the political superintendent, continued to stake a claim to do this, the MU as a party was becoming more vocal about its political position. From the time it came into being, its intention was clear, as given in one of its resolutions in the first general assembly held on 24 and 25 September 1946. The MU resolved that 'Mizo Union hi kawng engkimah Mizo aiawhtu kan ni. Kan tum dan leh duh dan ang lo chuan, Mizoramah thil engmah a awm tur a ni lo' (The Mizo Union is the legitimate representative of the Mizos in all aspects. No decision against our wish and consent is to be taken on matters concerning Mizoram) (Vanthuama 2001: 22). This resolution was what prompted MacDonald to act against the MU because it challenged his authority and that of the chiefs. At the District Conference held on 7 November 1946, he stated his objection by proclaiming that the 'Mizo Union does not represent Mizoram, only the District Conference does' (Vanthuama 2001: 26). In one of his letters to R. Vanlawma, who was then the general secretary of the MU, he reiterated his views:

> 'Mizo Union' hi vantlang zinga inlar mai mai pawl, tute emaw ram awp thu sawi khawm nuam tia, thuneihna pek lohva mahnia insiam chawp an ni. He ram mi aiawhtu anga dinna tur engmah thuneihna an nei lo reng reng. He rama mipui aiawhtu a ni ti theite chu Conference memberte chauh an ni. Mi dang reng reng he ram mipui aiawha inngaite chu a tha berah pawh mahni inbum mai an ni a, a chhe berah chuan (fascist) (Hitlera rorel dan awn mi) an

ni. Fascist rorel dan chu mipui aiawhtu thuneite el emaw kalh emawa mahni insiam chawpa thuneihna fawm chawp pawl an ni. A hlawhtlin chuan thil bawhlhlawlh a ni a, tin, a hlawchham chuan a hmusitawm a ni. Nang leh in 'Union' hei hi lo hre turin ka hrilh a che u.[5]

'Mizo Union' is an illegitimate self-appointed organization of people who are habituated of talking about governance and society in public. It does not have any legitimate basis of authority and representation. It is only the Conference members who have the sole authority to proclaim it as being representative of the people. Any other individuals or parties who consider themselves as representing the people are, at best, deceiving themselves, and in the worst case, they are like fascists [ascribing to Hitler's fascist rule]. Fascist governments question democratic governance and challenge them by granting themselves de facto rule. It is deplorable when it succeeds and a matter of shame if it fails. I inform you and your 'Union' to remember this.

While this was a contest of power between the MU and the political superintendent, what was more evident was the patronizing attitude of the British as well as the continual suppression of any kind of political mobilization. In fact, from the 1940s onwards, various British administrators were outlining plans for the future administration of the hill tribes of northeast India. Despite being secretive and confidential, the plans, as deliberated by the British officers, envisioned the continued rule of the hill tribes, both in India and Myanmar, under a single administration. As Syiemlieh (2014) points out, what overrode the plan was the need to preserve and protect the tribals from the domination of the *vai* with whom they shared no sociocultural affinity. The other reason was that the tribes were not in a position to govern themselves. Hence, it was in the best interest of the tribes that such plans were to be conceived and designed. The hill tribes of northeast India rejected any form of protectorate or future colony (Syiemlieh 2014: 12). As in the Lushai Hills and elsewhere, the British did not allow the hill tribes to 'speak'.

Meanwhile, new developments were taking place in the Lushai hills. L. L. Peters replaced MacDonald in 1947, and he continued with the same policy of suppressing the MU. After India attained independence, the District Advisory Council was constituted, with elections conducted for the same on 23 March 1948 (Figure 3.2).

The MU emerged victorious, sweeping all of the 25 seats for the commoners; hence, they formed the majority against the chiefs for whom 10 seats were reserved. Peters, the then political superintendent, on 16 August 1948, summoned the first meeting of the Advisory Council. Having the numbers on its side, the MU claimed that the chairman should be appointed from the MU and not by the superintendent. This resulted in an open confrontation between the MU and Peters and was only settled after the intervention of the Assam government. On the next day—that is, 17 August 1948—Peters chaired the meeting and presented draft regulations for the future political status of Mizoram. The MU members refused to pass the

Figure 3.2 Members of the District Advisory Council with L. L. Peters, 1948
Source: Chaltuahkhuma collection.

draft regulations, citing that they needed to study it in toto by demanding more
time. The relationship with Peters soured as he strived to ensure that the chiefs'
powers remained intact. As such, the MU launched a non-cooperation movement
against him by conducting rallies demanding his removal before 27 December 1948
(Chaltuahkhuma 2001 [1987]: 121; Vanthuama 2001: 144). Peters then sent out
arrest warrants for all the MU leaders, subsequent to which several leaders of the
MU were put behind bars as political prisoners under the Maintenance of Public
Order Act, 1861. Similarly, the public who were also protesting in the villages were
severely repressed, such as by *lathi* charges (Vanthuama 2001: 150). In response to
this, Peters issued an order against any political activity. It read as follows:

> Thupek No. 13038-52-G of 30-12-1948

> Nimin Tarik 29-12-48 a khawpui chhunga political kawngzawhna tel Indian
> Penal Code bung 188 dan anga man tak te'n diklo tak leh mumallo taka thupek
> an hriatloh an chhuanlam avangin Aizawl atanga mel 10 bialvel chhung
> khua zawng zawng hnenah he hriattirna hi ka chhuah a ni; tupawh political
> kawngzawhna tel tura Aizawla lokal chuan ama tana pawi tur thil a ti a ni a,
> thupek awih loh man chu a tuar ang.[6]

> Order No. 13038-52-G of 30-12-1948

> Those arrested for participating in political rallies yesterday, i.e., 29-12-48
> under Indian Penal Code Section 188 feigned innocence of not being properly
> informed about the government's order. I am therefore issuing this order
> for the residents of Aizawl and villages within the perimeter of 10 km that

whosoever is coming to Aizawl for participating in political rally should know that they are harming themselves and whoever disobeys the order should be apprehended and punished.

As planned, the MU party members started their protests and rallies, chanting slogans and singing as a sign of expressing their discontentment against the political superintendent's actions. As reported by the officer in charge of the Lunglei subdivision, the protest slogans were as follows.

(By some men)	(By the crowd)
Mizo Union?	Kan ram tan
Zalenna kan chang tawh em?	Chang lo
Eng nge kan chan?	Bawi rorel
Bawi rorelna?	Bo rawh se
Lal thuneihna?	Bo rawh se
Borsap Petera?	Bo rawh se
A bo loh chuan eng nge kan tih ang	A thu kan awih lovang

(By some men)	(By the crowd)
Mizo Union?	For our nation
Have we got freedom?	No, we haven't
What did we get?	Serf rule
Serf rule?	Let it be gone
Chief's rule?	Let it be gone
Superintendent Peter?	Let him be gone
What should we do if he is not gone?	We will disobey his orders

Party hla of different variants began to surface in the political sphere. Such *hla* represented the political mood of the time. They were directed against the chiefs and the colonial state, challenging their rule and authority. In protest and public gatherings, such *hla* were widely popular and became an important way to express discontent. They were sung in public processions and gatherings. One of which was widely popular during the time goes as:

Pu Khawtinkhuma, Pu Saprawnga,
Pu Dengthuama, Pu Thanhlira,
Pu Lalbuaia, Pu Vanthuama'n,
Union an rel sual ngailo.
Ngurpui leh zalen lungmawl,
Tui ang an la nem love.
Union pheisen chhimtlang thli ang,
An la hrang ngei ngei dawn e.
Nem duai duai se ngur nunrawng zawng,
Nation Council siam turin,
Chung Pathianin min hruai zel se,

Hnamtin remthu leng rawh se,
Chutin Zoram zaleng zawng hian,
Chung Pathian malsawm dilin,
A ngurpui leh zaleng zawng hian,
Par ang lawm ni a thleng ang.[7]

Pu Khawtinkhuma, Pu Saprawnga,
Pu Dengthuama, Pu Thanhlira,
Pu Lalbuaia, Pu Vanthuama'n,
Union never errs in its judgement.
    Even the Chieftains are such dimwits,
    Not knowing when to give in yet.
    The Union army will surely march on,
    Like the southern storm, they'll sweep the hills.
Let all the despotic Chieftains surrender,
For the Nation Council to emerge,
Led by the Almighty God to prosper,
And to spread peace among all the tribes.
And for all the people of the Zo-land,
Let's pray for the blessings of the Almighty,
For the day whence elites and commoners alike,
To rejoice in celebration shall come.

This *hla* captures the imagination of freedom from the yoke of the chiefs' and colonial rule. The MU used songs to mobilize the public as early as the 1940s. Although no real outcome was visible from such protests, it showed the challenge to authority by the Mizos, particularly by the majority of the commoners. The political consciousness and mobilization earmarked a new beginning in Mizo politics, the impact of which was seen in a way that continued to shape the political contours of the Mizos. The MU was persistent in its attempt to abolish chieftainship. At its general assembly held on 9 and 10 February 1951 at Hualtu, it resolved to reaffirm its commitment to the task: '[T]his assembly, hereby, declares that the aim and policy of the Mizo Union for the administration of the District is that of a representative government without the present chief system. Therefore, the government is strongly urged to take immediate steps to implement such administrative machinery without delay' (Chaltuahkhuma 2001 [1987]: 139). In the following section, I will continue to examine how the Mizos engaged and negotiated with the new post-colonial state to seek political autonomy and recognition.

Contested Futures: Fragments or Figments of the Political Imagination

The question of the Mizos' political future dominated the political events in the Lushai Hills at the dawn of India's independence (Figure 3.3). Whereas the political

Figure 3.3   Jawaharlal Nehru with Mizo District Council leaders
Source: L. R. Sailo collection.

contest was largely a bipolar one between the MU and the UMFO, what unfolded through such contests were the different political imaginations of the time. The UMFO was a party supported by the chiefs. Led by one Lalmawia, a former Burmese soldier, he proposed the integration of the Mizos with Burma on the ground that the Mizos have close cultural affinities with the Burmese. The MU, on the other hand, sought political autonomy and integration with the Indian Union. The social base of both parties was a determining factor in their political outlook. For the Mizo commoners, overthrowing the chiefs was their primary goal, while for the chiefs, their goal was to counter the MU and keep their power intact. The contest between the UMFO and the MU continued even after the Mizo integration under the Indian Union. Both parties stuck to the demands of their political constituency representing competing political visions.

In addition, beyond the MU and the UMFO, there were various other voices expressed during the time. These voices, often articulated by different individuals, favoured the independence of the Mizos. Based on the pamphlets they circulated, integration with India would result in a loss of the Mizo culture and religion (S. Nag 2002: 148). Independence was also the goal of some of the leaders led by Lalhema and Vanlawma, who were the first president and general secretary of the MU, respectively. This difference split the MU into two factions, the left wing and the right wing, over the question of leadership, particularly after the ousting of Lalhema and Vanlawma. While the MU's left wing continued with its anti-chieftainship campaign, the right wing aspired towards the independence of the Mizos. Consequently, the District Advisory Council election was a triangular contest between the three parties.

Between the UMFO and the MU, the electoral battle was fought with *party hla*. It was during this time that *party hla* began to take root in Mizo politics. The use of *party hla* was instrumental in spreading the party ideology while also countering rival parties. *Hla* were rooted in the local traditions and easily received by the common people, and shortly thereafter, *party hla* swept across the hills, towns, and villages. This shows how political imaginations were the work of the Mizo elites and the ordinary and common Mizo public who actively participated and involved themselves in the politics concerning their future and fate.

Pu Vawmhleia, a MU supporter and representative of the party, narrated the intensity of the battle using *party hla*. As he puts it, in big villages, both the parties' supporters would come out in the open field to confront each other utilizing the *hla*. Concurring with the narrative of Pu Vawmhleia, a volunteer of the MU expressed in his own words, 'An hla an ruihpui lai chuan nula leh tlangval, pa pawh a peih peih kha an lam tluk tluk mai ani' (When enraptured in chanting the *hla*, maidens and young men alike danced with raging fervour).[8] Using *khuang*s,[9] the volunteers of the political parties pitted themselves against each other, often acrimoniously, in their attempt to undermine one another. The intensity, the antagonistic feelings, and the imagination were altogether embedded in these songs. For instance, the MU volunteers marched with much enthusiasm, anticipating freedom from the yoke of the tyranny of the chiefs by singing:

Vice President Nehru-a chuan,
India ram leh Assam ram;
Zalenna kawng a hawng an ti,
Vantlang kan hlim rual ngei e!
    Zalen Ramhual a ngai tawh lo
    Union in kawngdal a ti che
    Dal a ti che e
    Tun chin ah bang tawh rawh

Thlang Sappuiin Durbar a pe,
Kumin chu ngai hram hram ru,
Zalen awzawng a ni lo,
Mahni hmasialna a ni.
Baithak arva, artui khawn leh,
Lalhnungzui reng ka ning tawh,
Kawltu chawina daltu a ni,
Sa zai lian pui pui a ni.[10]

So we've heard, Vice President Nehru,
Both in India and Assam;
Hast opened the door to freedom,

Much to the elation of all.
　　No more room for the chief's favour
　　Thou have impeded the way Union claimed
　　Ye thou did impede they insist
　　Cease such custom from this day since

White Men from West give Durbar away,
Pleaded to endure just the year,
'Tis no freedom at all,
For selfishness it is.
Sickened of hot dishes, fowls, and eggs,
And shadowing the chief's beckon,
They nought but deter daily chores,
Harsh labour is all they are.

The UMFO, backed by the chiefs, propagated the idea of joining Burma. They sang:

Union leh Union a dang mang e,
Keini Union Mizoram tundin nan maw!
Nangni Union ve chu vai dawrna. (Lalthangliana 2002)

Two unions, but not the same,
Our Union, for Mizoram!
Your Union, to please the *vai*.

The MU countered such claims in their songs:

Duhdan tam ber Sub-Committee ah,
Union hruaituten an hlan e;
Bial pawn Kuki, lui dung rizap zawng nen,
Sawi loh reng reng a awm lo e
　　Burma duh hi beram rual zinga
　　Chinghe-koham ang an ni e;
　　Independent an tlin leh si lo,
　　Pakistan an sawimawi e.[11]

Submit have they, the Union leaders,
The majority's opinion to the sub-committee;
Even about the Kuki, and the reserved outside,
Everything's addressed, nothing's missed out.
　　Foxes among sheep they are.
　　Those who want to join Burma;
　　Failing in their independent attempt,
　　Now preaching Pakistan.

The MU was highly spirited in opposing as it had the support of the majority commoners. This gave it leverage in terms of political mobilization against the UMFO leaders and supporters. This was reflected in the nature of the songs that were composed by the MU party supporters. It was also because the MU leaders and supporters were persistent in their demand for the ousting of chieftainship. For them, a new democratic India meant the dawn of freedom from the tyranny of the chiefs' rule, as reflected in this *hla*:

> Kan tang zel dawn Union hi
> A duh apiang hnar lovin
> Khua tin selloh he pawl hi
> Party sang ber a ni
> Zalen Pu Lalmawia'n Union tihchhiat tum mahse
> Zoram bawi hruai chhuak tura
> Van Lal ruat reng a ni
> > Zoram hlui, nang kal liam tawh la
> > Ramthar par ang lo vul chhuak se
> > Dan sual thim leh atna zawng zawng
> > Tunah zamual ah lo liampui ang che
> Zalen muhil lo tho ru
> Ni a chhuak sang tawh em e
> In kawmawl lal ho reng hi
> A lum lua e ka ti
> Union puanthuah lum tawk
> Tunah hian lo sin ve la
> Leng zawng zawng leh val lungrual
> I dang zo lo ang e.[12]

> Endure and march Union shall
> Opening doors to all shunning none
> Disdained by none this faction
> 'Tis truly the grandest party of all
> Chief's pet Lalmawia may seek to sunder
> But to liberate the thralls of Zoram
> Destined we are by the Father above
> > Old Zoram, the hour of thy passing has arrived
> > May paradise sprout forth to bloom
> > Evil laws and superstitions be made archaic
> > And haul them to the grave with thee
> Chief's favoured, awake from thy slumber
> For the peak of the sun summons
> The chiefs thy blanket becomes
> Awfully humid I dare say
> Union's mantle warm enough
> Enwrap thyself within
> All the masses and men unified
> Thou can halt them not.

What made the song doubly popular was the *kaihlek hla* tune it was set to. While there were also songs that were composed using the tunes of gospel hymns, *kaihlek* means to parody, to burlesque, or to poke fun at, and such songs had emerged as a counter to Christian hymns during the 1920s and the 1930s (Zama and Vanchiau 2016: 40–41). As such, the case of *kaihlek hla* is quite significant as such forms of singing were not endorsed by the church. Yet the church was not in a position to quell the mood and feeling of the time. In fact, many of the prominent church leaders were known to be members and supporters of the MU.

Figure 3.4   Block officers and councillors of the Mizo Union (MU)
Source: Chaltuahkhuma collection.

By and large, the MU enjoyed the support of the majority and had a strong mass base (Figure 3.4). As such, it also claimed to have the majority support and represent the interest of the commoners. In their memorandum to the Bordoloi Committee, the party noted that it had '20,000 enlisted full members and 80,000 associated members. Thus, the total members come to around 100,000— which can well represent the entire Mizo people' (Mizo Memorandum 1947). For a population that was barely 2.5 lakhs[13] at the time, a claim of one lakh members is significant. Furthermore, this claim evokes a majority rule under democracy, challenging the traditional rule of the minority chiefs and their supporters.

The theme of competing aspirations underscored the songs that emerged during these tumultuous times. Composed imaginatively, such songs were political in nature. Most importantly, it was in *party hla* that the Mizos established a political culture whose influence continues even today, providing space to both the elites and the non-elites as makers of modern Mizo politics. As can be seen, the use of songs was not only limited to the electoral contest, but also had multiple uses as a sign of protest, resistance, nationalist mobilizations, and as a counter-narrative to state violence. Songs, as such, were one of the most effective forms of political mobilization. Political parties, irrespective of their agenda, utilized songs to counter their political opponents in as much as they used them to garner political support.

Autonomy, Assertion, and Aspirations: The Self-Rule Agenda

It was in the demand for autonomy that the idea of what constitutes *ram* was articulated. The idea of *ram* becomes embedded in the political consciousness of the people. Up until colonial rule, the notion of *ram* was limited to the village. The village also shaped the individual sense of identity. In short, identity and belonging were limited to the village, as was also the idea of *ram*. In post-colonial India, the idea of *ram* has seen a shift, and this shift is accompanied by a change in the Mizos' understanding of the 'self'. J. Pachuau (2014) demonstrates this process by showing that the shifts in the way the Mizos identify themselves depend on their notions of territory. Their identification with the *ram* shows the changing notion of space and territory from identification with the village to the larger Mizo-*ram*. J. Pachuau (2014: 124–125) observes that 'rather than seeing themselves as the inhabitants of different territories or as the subjects of different and contesting chiefs, Mizos now began seeing themselves as the inhabitants of a common territory that belonged to everyone'. This changing notion of space reflects a change in the way the Mizos began to identify themselves with the *ram*. In politics, the objective involves the demand for the redrawing of the colonial boundaries to achieve territorial unity of Mizo-inhabited areas.

One of the main focal points of tribal politics is autonomy, or self-rule. The conception of autonomy has varied across tribes in the northeast region, and, in most cases, the understanding was based on self-rule in the territory they inhabited. Nongbri (2003) observes that ethnic assertions by the tribals were integrally linked to the sociopolitical processes of the modern state. Xaxa (1999), in fact, notes that the demand for tribal autonomy needs to be seen in the wider sociopolitical transformation the tribes underwent in their interaction with the colonial and post-colonial states. Among the Mizos, too, different forms of aspirations were articulated, and the political party, such as the MU, indicated the Mizo capacity to assert and politically represent their interests. In fact, the MU was one of the most vocal in articulating Mizo political aspirations, at least at the dawn of India's independence. In light of this, this section will examine how the Mizos negotiated their place within the Indian Union and how such aspirations for ethnic and territorial unity continue to be the main focus in Mizo politics.

In 1947, through the Advisory Subcommittee (ASC), or the Bordoloi Committee as it is commonly known, the MU submitted a memorandum known as the Mizo Memorandum, representing the case of the Mizos and their aspirations. Even as other political parties like the UMFO were active, the committee considered that the MU was representative of the Mizos, given that the party had the majority support of the commoners. In this memorandum and others that followed, the MU gave a precondition for integration under the Indian Union. It focused on two themes— one was political autonomy, and the other was the ethnic and territorial unity of all Mizo-inhabited areas under one administrative unit. Whereas ethnic unity would be forged through Mizo identity, territorial integration was to be achieved through a redrawing of the borders and boundaries—in short, *inpumkhatna* (unity) (Roluahpuia 2022b). The opening line of the memorandum reads, 'The memorandum seeks to represent the case of the Mizo people for territorial unity and the integrity of the whole Mizo population and full self-determination within the province of Assam' (Mizo Memorandum 1947).

Pursuant to this, the MU outlined a polity, naming it the National Council (NC), under which the Mizos would govern themselves. The NC was to replace the traditional institutions of chieftainship and follow a franchise system with the legislative, the executive, and the judiciary as its pillars. Apart from the overthrowing of the chiefs, territorial integration of Mizo-inhabited areas was the major political goal of the MU. For this reason, it was able to garner support from the Mizos in Manipur, Tripura, and Assam. Principally, unifying the Mizo tribes was the basic ethos of the party. As noted in the party constitution:

> He Mizo Union hi Mizo zawng zawng, Lushai Hills District a mite leh a pawn a mite inpumkhatna atana siam ani, Thu khat vuaa anmahni chungchang leh ram awm dan tur anmahni ngeiin an siam theih nan theih tawp chhuah a tum fo bawk ang. (Constitution of the Mizo Union)

> The Mizo Union is established for all the Mizos living within Lushai Hills District and outside with unity as the primary goal. It aims to foster unity among the Mizo people and commit itself towards instituting the best form of government.

The territory in question comprised parts of Assam, Manipur, Tripura, and Mizoram within India, parts of the Chin Hills and Sagaing divisions in Myanmar, and the Mizo-inhabited areas of the Chittagong Hill Tracts (CHTs). The memorandum stated that the administrative division of the territories inhabited by the Mizos was an act of injustice as they were 'thrown among peoples with their homeland sliced out and given to others'. The demand therefore was for the 'territorial unity and solidarity of the whole Mizo population, to be known, henceforth, as Mizo and Mizoram for Lushai and the Lushai Hills district, retaining the sole propriety right over the land'. This, as the MU stated, was the 'right to self-determination in its fullest form' (Mizo Memorandum 1947).

We Support

The Movement Of The Mizo People

FOR   UNIFICATION

LET THE GOVERNMENT OF INDIA

DO NOT FORGET THE MIZOS

When They Remember The Nagas

MIZOS: UNITE OR PERISH

Supporters in Manipur

Published by   Haukholal Thangnem &   Paolen Haokip, imphal on behalf of
Supporters in Manipur. — Printed at the Swaraj Press, Uripok, 14.2.65.

Figure 3.5 Banner by the Manipur Mizos extending support to the demand for territorial unification of Mizo-inhabited areas
Source: Mizo People Convention (MPC) Library collection, Churachandpur, Manipur.

Between 1946 and 1951, the movement for territorial integration had swept across the Lushai Hills and the adjoining areas of Manipur, Assam, and Tripura (Figure 3.5). In keeping line with this, a separate memorandum in 1948 detailing the demand for integration was made by H. K. Bawichhuaka and L. Tawna, both leaders representing the Assam and the Manipur regions, respectively. Common to both the memorandums, what ran parallel were the ethnic relations and the affinities of the people whose territory the British had put under different administrations. In his letter, Bawichhuaka commented on this as an 'act of injustice' as the Mizos were 'mercilessly disintegrated and those parts have been merged with peoples quite different in outlook, characteristics, and language, etc'.[14] Tawna was more provocative when making claims citing the historical, political, and sociocultural differences between the Manipuris and the Mizos. His letter stated that the hill areas of Manipur, as it claimed, were independent of the rule of the Maharajah of Manipur and administered separately by a political agent under the British. The conclusion of the memorandum sums this up:

> In the circumstances and with a view to conserving their best social and political developments in the Dominion of India, and in conformity with the desired policy of the Dominion Leaders to consolidate the same stock of people of same language and culture under one administrative unit convenient in geography....[15]

The memorandum by Bawichhuaka echoed a similar sentiment when it notes:

> This Memorandum is placed with the Authorities for setting up of the necessary machinery for the immediate merger of the Mizo Area of Cachar with that of the Lushai Hills (autonomous MIZORAM) and thus substantiate the policy of consolidating the same stock of people under one administrative unit through the readjustments of boundaries on the basis of language, customs and culture being the policy pursued by the present government.[16]

The political developments in Manipur are worthy of attention to examine the hill–plain issue that was much discussed even in the CA debates. The MU had a strong presence in the southern district of Manipur inhabited by the Mizos (Figure 3.6). In support of the movement for territorial integration, the Mizos boycotted the assembly election of 1948 and refused to be part of the election process. Manipur was one of the princely states in northeast India, and it enacted the Manipur State Constitution Act in 1947 under the then king, Bodhchandra Singh. The king constituted a committee to draft the Manipur State Constitution under which two members from the hill areas, Athiko Daiho and T. C. Tiankham, were inducted to

Figure 3.6 Office bearers of the Mizo Union, Manipur: (*left to right*) Pu Chhunngenga, Pu Sabuta, Pu H. Darkhuma, Pu Lalchhawnzova, Pu B. Lalhnuna, and Pu T. L. Sangliana
Source: B. Lalhnuna, Join Street, Churachandpur, Manipur.

represent the tribal communities of the state. During this time, the Nagas, under the leadership of Daiho, were spearheading a similar movement for territorial integration of the Naga-inhabited areas of Manipur. As members of the tribes representing the hill communities, the two leaders demanded the inclusion of a clause stating that the hill tribes would be given the right to secede after five years if they so desired (Shimray 2007: 84). In 1948, in their memorandum submitted to the Ministry of State Department of the Dominion Government of India, the Naga National League (NNL) noted that the Maharajah of Manipur could not legally lay claim to the hills.

The boycott of the election was successful in the hills, while the movement for territorial integration was gaining more support. As such, the MU supporters came into conflict with the chiefs, as the latter feared the threat of losing their power, while the Manipur state feared that it would lose control of the hills. The tribal chiefs and the government colluded to suppress the movement, with the government offering the Regional Council (RC) to the Hmar tribes, who were the main supporters of the movement. The offer of the RC resulted in a split among the Hmar public. This was reflected in the folk songs composed at the time, with the supporters of the proposal singing:

> P. B. Singh a hung inzin,
> Assam Rifles a hung thoui;
> Union han an lo ti,
> Bufai leh belte chawin;
> Tuikhur mawng tieng an tlan hmang.

> Came P. B. Singh for a visit,
> Accompanied by the Assam Rifles;
> Frightened are the Union,
> Holding their rice and pots;
> Ran away down the streams. (Dena 2008)

Those that were opposed, particularly the MU supporters, sang:

> State lalber P.B. Singh-an,
> Union kawng a dal thei lo;
> Authority bawm khaia chuan
> Artui khawm I phu tawk e. (Dena 2008)

> P. B. Singh, the state's supreme leader,
> Cannot block the Union's way;
> You, authorities with basket in hand,
> Are indeed fit only to beg for eggs.

In 1952, when the Sixth Schedule was enforced, it was limited only to the Lushai Hills, leaving out Manipur and Tripura. The first district council elections were held the next year, with the MU winning 17 out of the 18 seats (Figure 3.7). In taking over

Tlar hmasa veilam atangin : 1. Pu.Hrangkhuma 2. Pu.Papuia
3. Pu.Tuikhurliana 4. Pu.Lalsawia 5. Pu.Dr.Roslama
6. Pu.Ch.Saprawnga 7. Pu.Lalbuaia 8. Pu.R.Thanhlira
9. Pi.Lalziki 10. Pu.Pachhunga.

Tlar hnuhnung : 1. Pu.Saitawna 2. Pu.Lalchungnunga
3. Pu.Hrangaia 4. Pu.Khuaimanga 5. Pu.Rotluanga
6. Pu.Vanlalbuka 7. Pu.Lalthawvenga 8. Pu.Chaltuahkhuma
9. Pu.Sangkhuma 10. Pu.Pathala 11. Pu.Taikhuma.

Figure 3.7   The first Mizo District Council members, 1952–1957
Source: Chaltuahkhuma collection.

power, it followed up with its commitment to abolish chieftainship, which the party accomplished with the passing of the Assam Lushai Hills District (Acquisition of Chief's Rights) Act, 1954. In its execution, the Act ended the traditional rights of 259 Lusei chiefs and 50 Lai and Mara chiefs. It further established the Village Councils through the Lushai Hills District (Village Councils) Act, 1953, to fill the vacuum in governance at the village level. More significantly, the MU also passed a resolution to rename Lushai Hill as the Mizo Hills as a recognition of the diverse tribal groups inhabiting the region.

Within the re-christened Lushai Hills, a unique form of autonomous councils was set up through a two-tier structure, a district council, and a regional council. Known as the Pawi-Lakher Regional Council (PLRC), it was established in recognition of the Lai and Mara tribes'[17] aspirations for autonomy. The Lai and Mara tribes' political mobilization happened at the same time as the MU's. Their relative independence from Lusei influence and the different trajectories of the colonial rule upon the tribes played a significant role in the political mobilization of the two communities. In 1949, the leaders of the tribes submitted a memorandum to Nari K. Rustomji, the advisor to the governor of Assam, during his visit to the Lushai Hills, pleading for a separate RC (Doungel 2012). Subsequently, the Pawi-Lakher Tribal

Union (PLTU) came into being in 1949, further pursuing the agenda for a separate RC under the leadership of Z. Hengmanga.

The standpoint of the PLTU leaders had been that the Lai and Mara tribes are ethnically distinct from the dominant Mizo community. The political aspiration for a separate RC was articulated on the rationale of protection from the ethnic domination of the Mizos. This largely shaped the political discourse in the Lai and Mara areas, which maintained a distance from the political mobilization that was taking place in the other parts of the state. Initially, the MU leaders attempted to convince the PLTU leaders to abort the demand and align instead with the MU agenda. The sense of being distinct and different from the Mizos and the perception of the Mizo as being Lusei-centric had taken a foothold, and as such, the PLTU leaders continued to pursue their demand for separate RC. In 1953, a separate RC was granted that came to be known as the PLRC for the Lai and Mara tribes (Figure 3.8).

Territorial unity remained a policy of the MU as the party continued to demand statehood, particularly after the 1960s. This was instigated by the Assam government's apathy towards the famine that affected the Mizo Hills in 1959 and their attempt to impose the Assamese language as the official one. Likewise, the

Figure 3.8   Members of the Pawi-Lakher Regional Council (PLRC), along with other political leaders and officers of the Mizo Hills
Source: Information and Publicity Department, Mara Autonomous District Council, Siaha.

aspirations for a statehood movement vis-à-vis territorial unification continued to be expressed in Manipur and Tripura, especially where the Mizos continued to aspire for integration with their co-ethnics in Mizoram. However, even though the Sixth Schedule was meant for the tribals of the northeast, it did not cover large parts of areas inhabited by them. This was the case with the Mizos of Manipur and Tripura.[18] Since independence, the tribals of these two states were at the receiving end of state policies in terms of rights and autonomy. The case was the same for various tribes in Assam, such as the Bodos, who were excluded from the provision. In areas where the Schedule was implemented, it failed to protect what it was intended to (Barbora 2005: 202), and in the areas outside of the Schedule, the aspiration for the autonomy provisions under the Schedule persisted. Generally, a feeling of being marginalized resulted in the increasing demand for the Schedule, which spawned ethnic confrontations between tribes and non-tribes and increasingly among the tribals (Bhatia 2010).

Choosing a Name: From 'Lusei' to 'Mizo'

Like *ram*, the idea and meaning of *hnam* also began to undergo change. While *hnam* commonly coincided with the clan and tribal nomenclature, the use of 'Mizo' gradually changed that mode of identification. The popularity of the MU further added to the popularity of 'Mizo', and it became more acceptable to the larger public. Politically, the MU took the lead in defining the idea of Mizo—what and who it constitutes. The idea of 'Mizo' as articulated by the MU began to take root in people's consciousness, and in no time, 'Mizo' began to be the adopted and accepted identity. There was a changing *hnam* consciousness that paved the way for a collective 'Mizo' feeling. This led to the demand for a change of name from 'Lusei' to 'Mizo' and its official adoption.

In India, recognition by the state is instrumental in accessing rights and privileges and also for affirming place and belonging (Kapila 2008; Middleton 2015). The MU leaders began to pursue the agenda of renaming 'Lushai' to 'Mizo' and sought official recognition. It spelt out its demand for renaming the same in the Mizo Memorandum of 1947 submitted to the ASC by the MU, which stated:

> It was wrong that the word Lushai should be used as covering all the Mizo tribes since it is a misrendering of the Lusei only as a sub-tribe of the Mizo race. Hence though, perhaps, not originally intended, it has created a division. (Mizo Memorandum 1947)

To identify as Mizo and seek recognition of the same was an attempt to forge an inclusive pan-ethnic identity beyond clans and tribal affiliations. Lusei, in this context, was not merely a 'tribe' but also meant belonging to the dominant ruling chiefs. With the MU leaders and their major supporters hailing from among the *hnamchawm* (commoners), or the non-chief clans, the adoption of 'Mizo' was inevitable in order to construct and create an identity transcending tribal affiliations and forging an identity beyond that of Lusei. Groups belonging to the different clans and tribes began to integrate and embrace a Mizo identity. Hassan (2008) argues that it was the inclusionary appeals by the majority commoners that consolidated the Mizo identity. An important point that he notes is how the MU leaders use 'Mizo' to challenge the existing authority of the chiefs. However, the language of the Lusei tribe, the Duhlian language, and their culture were adopted and remained an essential marker for defining Mizo identity, the retention of which needs to be understood in its historical context.

Up until colonial rule, Lusei chiefs mostly ruled large parts of what is now Mizoram. Even as clan and tribal identifications existed, chiefs and village identity were the more preferred and common way of identification. The encounter with colonialism created a rupture where identity began to take on a homogenous character. Therefore, in colonial accounts, the land and the people came to be recorded as Lushai—and hence Lushai tribes and Lushai Hills—and the Duhlian language began to be used in colonial bureaucracy. Later, this was expanded to include missions and education. Colonial rule propagated the Duhlian language, which significantly contributed to its popularization, and it eventually developed as the common language for the tribes. The close association between missionary activities and educational efforts played a pivotal role in entrenching Mizo identity, further fomenting the link between religion and language (M. Kipgen 1997; L. Pachuau 2002). Under these circumstances, religion and language became essential markers of Mizo identity formation.

At the same time, during their role as chiefs, the Luseis were absorbing smaller clans and tribes into their fold (Nunthara 1996: 235). Even as identity and belonging were fluid and malleable across tribes, the influence of the Lusei language and culture was pronounced even among non-Lusei clans and tribes. In addition to this, the suzerainty of the Lusei chiefs had spread beyond the present territorial borders of Mizoram to states such as Manipur and Tripura. As such, even as 'Mizo' was adopted in the place of 'Lusei', they were more or less receptive in areas and among groups that were influenced by the Luseis. The situatedness of the Mizo identity in terms of its acceptance and rejection clearly demonstrated this fact. In areas where Lusei chiefs held dominance, particularly in the northern areas of Mizoram and in areas such as the Jampui Hills of Tripura, the Mizo identity was readily accepted. In the now southern regions of Mizoram inhabited by the Mara and Lai tribes, the Mizo identity is seen as Lusei-centric, and hence its acceptance is limited. This contest over identity continues to mark the sociopolitical processes in the state of Mizoram.

The gradual shift from 'Lusei' to 'Mizo' was evident with the renaming of various organizations. Prominent among these include the renaming of the Young Lushai Association to the Young Mizo Association (YMA), the Lushai Student

Association (LSA) to Mizo Zirlai Pawl (Mizo Students Federation) (MZP), and the Lushai Commoners Union to the MU. This renaming altogether took place in the same year, 1946. Even prior to this, 'Mizo', as a term, was already in circulation, as demonstrated in its usage in newspapers such as the *Mizo Chanchin Laisuih* (1898) and the *Mizo Leh Vai Chanchinbu* (1903). Similarly, among the Mizo public and in political circles, 'Mizoram' or 'Zoram' was gaining more popular usage than 'Lushai Hills'. Colonial intervention in the form of the standardization of the vernacular language was crucial, but its use remained limited to the colonial agents and the literate circles among the Mizos.

In post-colonial India, the renaming of the Lushai Hills to Mizo Hills was pursued as the agenda of recognition. Recognition of the state therefore was necessary to affirm its legitimacy, and it was against this backdrop that the demand for the recognition of renaming the Lushai Hills was made. The post-colonial state inherited the Lushai Hills as the name of the district. Placed under Assam, the district continued to retain its name. After the extension of the Sixth Schedule and the formal inauguration of the District Councils, the MU, which was in power, did not waste any time by renaming it as the Mizo Hills. A resolution for its renaming was moved on 9 October 1952 by Lalsawia, the then chief executive member of the Mizo District Council, for changing the name of the Lushai Hills to Mizoram (Chaltuahkhuma 2001 [1987]: 147). The same was conveyed through a memorandum when the then home minister, Kailash Nath Katju, visited the Lushai Hills on 2 December 1962 (Lawmzuala 2003: 47). The MU leaders made subsequent efforts with a memorandum submitted to Nehru on his maiden visit to the Lushai Hills district on 2 April 1953.

The appeal for renaming was made through a resolution by R. Thanhlira, who was a member of parliament at the time. In moving his resolution, Thanhlira gave a speech to justify his resolution. He argued:

> While I move this resolution, Sir, I think it is only natural for Hon. Members to be curious to know what is the difference between the existing name of 'Lushai Hills District' and 'Mizo Ram' to which I am trying to change it. Actually, there is not much difference. The word 'Lushai', which is the existing name, is decidedly derived from the world 'Lusei', and this Lusei is one of the Sub-tribes in the Lushai Hills. When the British people first came to that area and conquered that area, this Lusei clan was in power, so to say, and it was with the Lusei clan that the British people had contact in that area. Hence, the name 'Lushai', derived from Lusei, was given to the district. Therefore, I feel that the name 'Lushai Hills' is very exclusive and discriminatory, because the name is taken from one of the many sub-tribes and clans living in the Lushai Hills District itself. But the word 'Mizo' is the common and collective name by which all the tribes and sub-tribes in the Lushai Hills District are known, and they call themselves by this name. Hence the term 'Mizo' is all-embracing and inclusive.[19]

Thanhlira's statement exhibited the position of the MU at the time. He went on to say:

> Apart from this, I would like to mention also that the retention of the present name is very detrimental to the society there. The district is inhabited by many tribes who are now living in harmony. But political consciousness having been aroused in that area, people begin to feel that by calling this area by the name of Lushai Hills, the non-Lusei people are being excluded. Consequently, this creates clan feeling and clan consciousness and it also promotes strife among the various clans, and ultimately it sows the seeds of social disharmony in the district. Hence, I am strongly of the opinion that the sooner the name is changed, the better it will be for all concerned.[20]

As such, the choice of 'Mizo' was a process that accompanied the political consciousness of the larger Mizo public—the commoners in particular. The common feeling was that 'Lusei' was exclusive and non-representative. Even if it had an instrumental purpose, the case for proposing 'Mizo' was an attempt to reconfigure identity and belonging that was inclusive for all. In other words, a new concept of belonging was at the heart of this process enacted through self-definition and self-representation.

The Lushai Chiefs Federation opposed the attempt at this renaming. It had become a matter of political contest between the chiefs and the MU supporters. In opposing the resolution, the federation conveyed its opposition to the MU leaders, the chief minister, and other concerned officials. The federation claimed that 'Mizo', unlike 'Lusei', had no local roots and that the term was devoid of meaning: 'These people quickly introduced the word "Mizo" which has no distinctive affinity or existence. It was loosely applied to the inhabitants of the district and the inhabitants of the surrounding districts.' The federation cited the census of 1951 to show its majority in terms of numbers and the popularity of the Lusei language, even among the non-Lusei tribes. In light of this, the renaming was said to be against the wish of the majority of inhabitants of the district. In writing to the president of the MU, the federation requested the party to 're-consider the matter carefully and withdraw the proposal and avoid unnecessary controversy in the District at this critical moment. Also, to point out that the District will gain nothing by the change of the name.'[21]

The outcome was that this developed into a contest between the MU and the Lushai Federation, and this was unsurprising, given the MU's stance on chieftainship. However, the MU clearly had the advantage as it was a part of the ruling government at the time. The resolution also received support from other members of the cabinet, particularly the home minister, Katju. Aware of the opposition by the Lushai Federation against the proposed resolution, Katju, in referring to Thanhlira in his speech at the cabinet meeting, noted that 'they were the views of a handful of people'. In extending support to the resolution, Katju further opined, 'So far as the people themselves are concerned, when I went there, I met with sign boards everywhere throughout the hills, like Mizo Union, Mizo Association, etc. They call their land Mizo Ram. Mizo is the name of the tribe. "Ram" means place, just like our Khand, Rohilkhand, Bundelkhand, etc.'[22] The resolution received the approval of the Council of States to rename the Lushai Hills as Mizo Hills through an Act of the parliament. Towards this, a Bill was introduced in the parliament under Bill No. 1 of 1954, which came to be known as the Lushai Hills District (Change of Name) Bill, 1954, substituting 'Lushai' for 'Mizo' both officially and administratively. This was officially adopted on 1 September 1954.

In seeking recognition, the MU was also engaged in the process of defining 'Mizo' and what constitutes Mizo *hnam*. In fact, defining Mizo identity and determining who it includes is essentially about delimiting the 'boundaries of identity' (Barth 1969), such as the Mizo and the non-Mizo. Again, in the Mizo Memorandum of 1947, the MU listed a number of tribes to show who were Mizos—namely Lusei, Hmar, Ralte, Paite, Zo, Darlawng, Kawm, Pawi, Thado, Chiru, Aimoul, Khawl, Tarau, Anal, Purm, Tikhup, Vaiphei, Lakher, Langrawng, Chawrai, Bawng, Biate, Mualthuam, Kaihpen, Pangkhua, Tlanglau, Hrangkhawl, Bawmzo, Miria, Dawn, Khumi, Khianu, Khiangte, Pangte, Khawlhring, Chawngthu, Vanchiau, Chawhte, Ngente, Renthlei, Hnamte, Tlau, Pautu, Pawite, Vangchhia, Zawngte, Fanai, and so on (Mizo Memorandum 1947). The list contained clans and tribes from within and outside Mizoram. Regardless of whether one was unsure of the degree of its acceptance by the individual clans or tribes themselves as being identified as Mizos, the general understanding was the existence of shared cultural affinities that formed the basis for the construction of a Mizo identity.

Ethnic groups, as we can see, are not homogenous entities. The problem lies in the affirming of fixity—in terms of not only identity but also territory. In the Mizo case, it was common to see the equating of Lusei synonymously with Mizo, reinforcing the homogenous view of identity. Yet it was the non-Lusei clans which were at the forefront of replacing 'Lusei' with 'Mizo'. Given the nature of the territorial borders that demarcated ethnic groups across the northeast region and beyond, it was common to see the conflation of ethnic identities and territory. This fixed Mizo identity within the territorial borders of the state of Mizoram. Therefore, what became more central in understanding Mizo identity were the fluid boundaries and attachments and how the tribes and clans navigated these boundaries. This is a very common pattern across the tribes of the northeast region. Tribes such as the Khasis and the Garos live on both sides of the Indian state of Meghalaya and Bangladesh, as do the Kuki tribes, who are spread across multiple states within the northeast and up to Bangladesh and Myanmar. Even when one looks at the state register of tribes, communities identified as Mizo remain heterogeneous and differ across the states in northeast India. This cross-cutting and overlapping of identities is evidence of how the Mizo identity is 'perennially in tension between static and change' (Toffin and

Pfaff-Czarnecka 2014: 3). This is essentially the problem inherent in classification, a process initiated by the colonial state and taken forward by the respective post-colonial successors. With specific reference to the tribes, the situation remained where the colonial mode of classification continued to influence the post-colonial state's classification of them (L. Jenkins 2003).

Kawnpui Convention and After: From Irredentism to Independence

A convention was held in 1965 at Kawnpui village in Manipur, which is now widely known as the Kawnpui Convention or the Mizo People's Convention of 1965. Located in the Churachandpur district of Manipur, Kawnpui is one of the few Mizo villages in Manipur. The convention took place between 15 and 18 January and was attended by 13 tribal representatives, including the MU and the MNF from the Mizo Hills. The remaining 11 were Manipur-based organizations representing various tribal groups.

The convention's main agenda was to outline common political objectives and for unification under a single nomenclature. The delegates of the convention affirmed in their resolution that they belonged to one *hnam*, and that as such, each party should pursue this agenda. In the meeting, however, they could not arrive at a conclusion regarding the nomenclature. While the MU and the MNF advocated for 'Mizo', representatives from Manipur preferred to use their distinct tribal names such as Paite, Hmar, and so on.[23] This, in part, was due to the different trajectories of identity formation and the specific identity politics that define Manipur. In Mizoram, while unity was forged through Mizo as a common identity, in Manipur, tribe-based identity took precedence, preventing broad-based ethnic unity. For instance, during the period, several tribe-based organizations were advocating a different political agenda, putting specific tribal interests at the forefront. The Kuki National Assembly (KNA) favoured the creation of a Kuki state, while the Hmar National Union (HNU) strived for a separate Hmar autonomous council.

The meeting was inconclusive on the question of identity. However, on matters related to political goals, a common political agenda for territorial unification was agreed on to be pursued, irrespective of tribal affiliations. The next meeting was scheduled for April 1966. While a follow-up did not occur, it left a significant mark on Mizo political history because the Kawnpui Convention was the first time in independent India when the different leaders and political party representatives convened a meeting to pursue a common objective. In Mizo politics, this is most commonly expressed as a desire for *inpumkhatna* among the kindred tribes separated and divided by borders. Even today, one finds how this idea of *inpumkhatna* continues to resonate deeply in the political discourse of the Mizos (Roluahpuia 2022b). Political parties, including non-political parties in the past and the present, have put *inpumkhatna* as their primary objective. In fact, when the MNF emerged as a political force in the Mizo Hills, it brought back the question of territorial unification—this time with a nationalist fervour. The movement primarily focused on two things: the imagination of the nation through the *hnam* and the territorial unification of Mizo-inhabited areas, herein the *ram*. The next chapter examines this in detail.

Notes

1   *Lambu*s were petty officials introduced by the British to aid the colonial state in dispensing its rule in the hill region of Manipur.
2   File Number CB-53, G-660, Mizoram State Archive (MSA), Aizawl.
3   File Number CB-54, G-675, MSA, Aizawl.
4   File Number CB-54, G-675, MSA, Aizawl.
5   File Number CB-53, G-660, MSA, Aizawl.
6   File Number, CB-12, Pol.-119, MSA, Aizawl.
7   Personal note of Pu Vawmhleia, a volunteer of the MU.
8   Interview with Pu Vawmhleia, 11 September 2021.
9   A *khuang* is a Mizo traditional drum that is used widely in occasions involving a group singing.
10   Personal note of Pu Vawmhleia, a volunteer of the MU.
11   Personal note of Pu Vawmhleia, a volunteer of the MU.
12   Personal communication with Pu Vawmhleia, a volunteer of the MU.
13   The population of the Lushai Hills as per the 1951 and 1961 censuses was 196,202 and 266,063, respectively.
14   Memorandum of the case of the Mizo people of Cachar district (inclusive of the North Cachar Hills) submitted by the Mizo Union (Northern Division), Lakhipur, Cachar, Assam; and Memorandum of the case of the Mizo people of the Manipur state for their right to self-determination and their territorial integrity submitted to the Honourable Minister in charge of the States Department of India Dominion, New Delhi, through the Dominion Agent in Manipur, Imphal, by the Mizo Union which is the only political organization of the Mizos in Manipur, National Archives of India (NAI), File No. 4(16)-P/48.
15   Memorandum of the case of the Mizo people of the Manipur state for their right to self-determination and their territorial integrity submitted to the Honourable Minister in charge of the States Department of India Dominion, New Delhi, through the Dominion Agent in Manipur, Imphal, by the Mizo Union which is the only political organization of the Mizos in Manipur, NAI, File No. 4(16)-P/48.
16   Memorandum of the case of the Mizo people of Cachar district (inclusive of the North Cachar Hills) submitted by the Mizo Union (Northern Division), Lakhipur, Cachar, Assam, NAI, File No. 4(16)-P/48.
17   The Lai and Mara tribes were known as Pawi and Lakher, which were terms used by the Luseis to refer to them. This was subsequently replaced in 1988 to Lai and Mara along with the renaming of their respective autonomous councils as the Lai Autonomous District Council and the Mara Autonomous District Council.

18   In 1985, the state government of Tripura granted autonomous councils under the Sixth
      Schedule known as the Tripura Tribal Autonomous District Council TTADC. It also
      covers the Mizo-inhabited areas of Tripura.

19   Resolution in the Council of States by R. Thanhlira regarding the proposal to change
      the name of Lushai Hills district to Mizo Ram, NAI, File No. 15/200/52-Public.

20   Resolution in the Council of States by R. Thanhlira regarding the proposal to change
      the name of Lushai Hills district to Mizo Ram, NAI, File No. 15/200/52-Public.

21   Resolution in the Council of States by R. Thanhlira regarding the proposal to change
      the name of Lushai Hills district to Mizo Ram, NAI, File No. 15/200/52-Public.

22   Resolution in the Council of States by R. Thanhlira regarding the proposal to change
      the name of Lushai Hills district to Mizo Ram, NAI, File No. 15/200/52-Public.

23   See Minutes of The Mizo People's Convention, Kawnpui, Churachandpur, on 15, 16,
      and 17 January 1965.

4   The Mizo National Front and the Vernacularization of Nationalism

In 1962, the MNF organized a choir competition in Aizawl, drawing participants from various local YMA[1] branches. The song 'Harh La, Harh La' (Awake, Awake), composed by Rokunga, was chosen as the common song for the competition. It reflected the events of the time when it was composed. Between 1959 and 1961, the Mizo Hills and their adjoining areas were hit by a massive famine known as *mautam*.[2] The impact of the famine was severe, with massive loss of food grains that led to mass starvation and the deaths of many across the hills. By 1962, the famine was more or less over, and as normal life began to resume, Mizo politics underwent a whirlwind of change. Under the banner of the MNF, a new political formation began to hold sway in Mizo politics rivalling the MU. This reignited debates about the contested ideas splitting the Mizo public on the issue of independence. Around this time, *hnam hla* took over the political discourse, with many of them harking upon the larger issue of independence.

The chapter focuses on the idea of Mizo nationalism. Scholarly studies on the MNF movement have explored how the Mizos' struggle for independence was an outgrowth of the injustice meted out to the Mizos during the famine of 1959 by the Assam government (U. Phadnis 1989; Lalchungnunga 1994; S. Nag 2002). The wider strand of studies has used the greed or grievance factor to explain the rise of Mizo nationalism or the insurgency movement. Likewise, a common approach is to situate them within the conflict and security perspective that focuses on relative deprivation and rational choice theories (Gurr 1970; Brenner 2018). For instance, Gurr (1970: 24) notes that 'the potential for collective violence varies strongly with the intensity and scope of relative deprivation among members of collectivity'. The merit of Gurr's analysis in terms of adopting a relative deprivation approach becomes useful if one uses the 'famine' as the precursor for the MNF movement or Mizo nationalism (Nag 2001, 2002; Vadlamannati 2011). However, the blind spot of this approach is the ideas and ideologies of nationalism and the intimate aspect and the highly emotional nature of nationalist movements. While the MNF marked its presence with the famine of 1959, the idea of Mizo nationalism predates the emergence of the MNF. In the Mizo Hills, it was the chime of freedom, what the MNF called *zalenna*, which began to capture the imagination of the Mizos.

For five years—that is, from 1961 to 1965—the MNF leaders were engaged in the mobilization of the people. Even as the educated elites were the forerunners of the mobilization, non-MNF members such as Rokunga, as well as 'ordinary' Mizos, not only contributed to the idea of a Mizo nation but also remained pivotal in the shaping and dissemination of nationalist ideas. If the movement was for Zoram[3] *zalenna*, the struggle was for *ram leh hnam*. What such expression did is what I call 'vernacular nationalism', which reframed and reconstructed the nation in local terms, making it distinctively Mizo. This is significant in two ways. First, the use of vernacular nationalism shifts the attention to the intimate relations and social dynamics that inform nationalist movements (Shah 2013; Brenner 2018). Both song composers and writers used the vernacular medium to communicate with the audience, create a sense of national feeling, popularize the nationalist ideology, and keep alive the rebels' morale. Second, the reworking of the nation was undertaken through the adoption of a vernacular mode of mobilization, particularly songs, that 'evoked themes of the celebration of community and citizenship, an evocation of landscape and homeland, the recreation of historic histories, and the commemoration of national sacrifice and destiny' (Riley and Smith 2016: 22).

The use of vernacular nationalism connotes the ways in which the modern ideas of nation, sovereignty, and ethno-history are reframed in the local situation. Through vernacularization, the MNF made nationalist ideas accessible and appealing. The sudden growth and rise of the MNF and the acceptance the party received were immense, much to the surprise of the leaders of the MU. A leader of the MU remarked that Laldenga was able to convince all the young, educated people both at home and outside. The literate and illiterate masses connected to the ideas of nationalism on their own terms as they were expressed in a 'language that everyone understood' (Fahmy 2011: xii).

Terms such as *zalenna* and *ram leh hnam* began to appear in diverse forms such as in print and in speeches, apart from songs. In this way, *zalenna* and *ram leh hnam* became intrinsic to the Mizo national consciousness. Again, the pivotal role of the oral culture of the Mizos proved instrumental. This is significant as Mizo society was still predominantly agrarian. Here, the oral played a significant role in acting as a medium and node to disseminate nationalist ideas. At the same time, there was a production of written works by leaders of the movement that laid the foundation of the Mizo nationalist ideology. Some key texts include *Mizoram Marches towards*

Freedom by Laldenga, *Zoram Zalenna Lungphum* (Foundation of Zoram Freedom) by Zoramthanga, and *Exodus Politics* by Lalhmingthanga. This underlies the interface of print and oral culture that catered to the imagination and the construction of Mizo nationalism. The MNF combined the use of both oral and print to disseminate their ideas of nationalism. While the circulation of print remains limited, the idea of nationalism was absorbed into songs within the oral culture that predates the emergence of print in Mizo society. Moreover, by tapping into the oral culture, the MNF was able to diffuse and disseminate nationalist ideas across borders and regions.

The vast majority of Mizos were both consumers and producers of national ideas. Unlike print media, songs as pliable and portable media were not constrained by the requirements for their production and circulation. The social background of the song composers and rebels is diverse, comprising of both the elite and the ordinary classes. This follows the scholarly trend within nationalism studies that incorporates ordinary people into the historical narratives of the construction of nationalist ideas (Billig 1995; Herzfeld 1997; Brubaker et al. 2006; Fahmy 2011). Culling evidence from diverse sources ranging from colloquial language to everyday acts of reading or seeing, scholars bring to the fore narratives of ordinary people at the centre of focus. Nationalism, Hobsbawm (1990: 10) remarked, 'cannot be understood unless it is also analyzed from below, that is, in terms of the assumption, hopes, needs, longings and interest of the ordinary people, who are not necessarily national and still less nationalist'.

Nationalist historiography in India has been challenged for its elitism—colonial elitism and bourgeoisie–nationalist elitism (R. Guha 1997). The national movement was framed as a project of the educated elite who moulded nationalist ideologies. The concern was to focus on the history of the non-elite and rewrite a new nationalist historiography. More recent work began to focus on how certain social groups and communities in India continued to be excluded in such narratives as they ignored the social differentiation across castes, tribes, classes, and genders (Chaudhuri 1993; Aloysius 1998; Ray 2000; Xaxa 2016; Jangam 2017; Xaxa and Roluahpuia 2021). What the idea of the 'nation' means varies across communities and groups, who challenge, if not contest, the hegemonic and exclusionary idea of nationhood (Guru 2016b; Kipgen and Chowdhury 2016; Roluahpuia 2022a). The question is not merely about how marginalized communities imagine the nation and contribute to the making of the nation, but also about how an alternative 'imagination' of the nation itself is representative of the said communities' political agency. This we try to explore through the vernacularization of nationalism by the MNF.

In vernacular work, both the ordinary and the elites were involved in articulating the 'vision of independence' (Pachuau and van Schendel 2015). In as much as the motivations of the MNF movement were political, they were equally culturally rooted. The construction of a modern political community, Hutchinson (1987) argues, is preceded by emerging cultural nationalist movements. If *zalenna* and *ram leh hnam* were the tenets of Mizo nationalism, they were, by and large, the work of various 'moral innovators' (Hutchinson 1987: 9), such as the songwriter and composer Rokunga whose songs were fundamental in understanding the 'passions aroused by nation and nationalism' (Smith 2009: 9). *Zalenna* and *ram leh hnam* were used as a referent to legitimatize the national struggle, embodying the historical past of the Mizos that had seeped into the popular consciousness of the people. The MNF therefore evoked the nostalgia of a sovereign past, the pre-colonial era, to legitimize its demand for independence. Towards this, the chapter takes a broad historical sweep, looking at the rise of the MNF as a political party, locating it within the larger political changes in the hill areas of northeast India, the growing national consciousness, and the ideas that shaped it.

Statehood, Independence and the Assam Government: The Decline of the MU and the Rise of the MNF

The rise of the MNF and the subsequent armed struggle was seen as a direct outgrowth of the Assam government's indifference towards the famine that coincided with the push for Assamese as the state's official language. The proposal was not well received by the hill tribes, resulting in increasing alienation from Assam. Two important consequences make it evident. First, the Assam Pradesh Congress Committee (APCC) government lost its long-time and faithful ally, the MU. Second, it resulted in the mass political movement among the tribal communities for a separate hill state. This resulted in political realignments in the hills with the emergence of new political parties, such as the All Party Hill Leaders Conference (APHLC), demanding a separate hill state (Figure 4.1), and the MNF, which forwarded the demand for self-determination, meaning independence.

The move for making Assamese the official language stirred unrest and conflict between Assamese and Bengali speakers in the plains, whereas, in the hill districts, the response came in the form of a demand for separation from Assam. The APHLC in particular became widely popular in the present-day state of Meghalaya and was the forerunner in the demand for a separate hill state from Assam. The independence movements in the Naga Hills and later in the Mizo Hills further compounded the language problem in the northeast. In India, the issue of language is indeed a national problem that emerged as a vehicle of regional mobilization in the post-British period. Resolute opposition eventually prevailed on the centre to concede to the demand for state reorganization along linguistic lines in 1956.[4] This was largely aimed at meeting the aspirations of the dominant linguistic communities that otherwise could have posed a possible threat to the unity of the nation-state. Even as state reorganization left out the northeastern region, the push for making Assamese the official language galvanized the hill people, who are predominantly the state's tribal communities towards demanding a separate state. However, the state's reorganization had left out the tribal communities at the national level, bypassing their aspirations, irrespective of region.

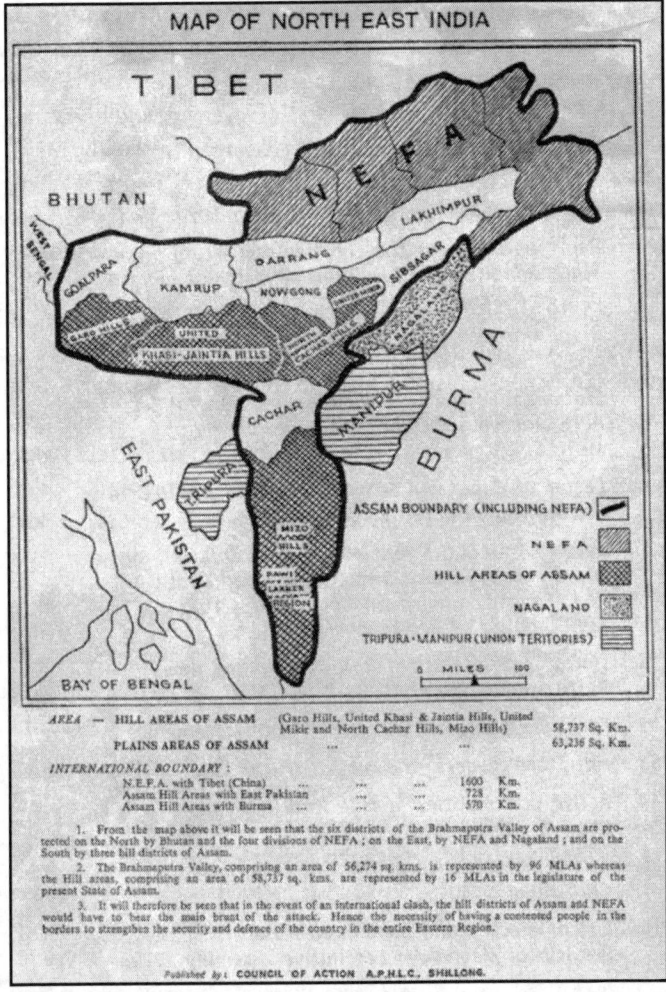

Figure 4.1 Hill and plain areas of Assam showing the areas demanded by the All Party Hill Leaders Conference (APHLC) for the creation of a separate hill state, 1960
Source: Tarun Bhartiya.

In demanding separation from the hills, both 'tribal' and 'hill' identities assumed great significance. This created a rift among the Assam political leaders, with strong opposition against the reorganization of Assam. There was, however, disquiet in the hills, specifically the Mizo Hills, and the contest had become more complex with the MU—the then ruling party and ally of the APCC—being confronted by multiple forces than ever before. However, the demand for separation from Assam received unanimous support from the hill leaders. Seeing the growing movement for a hill state, chief minister Bishnuram Medhi, in one instance, noted that such demands were originally sponsored by a 'reactionary anti-India brain' (*Times of India* 1955). The famine of 1959 in the Mizo Hills only fuelled the discontent. This intensified the movement for separation, not only from Assam but also from India.

As already mentioned, studies on the MNF movement and history have located the famine of 1959 as a starting point in understanding the rise of the MNF. The MNF movement was seen as a direct outgrowth of the government's apathetic response to the famine, which disgruntled the Mizo political leadership and the common people. *Mautam*, or bamboo flowering, is a phenomenon deeply embedded in the oral histories of the Mizos (Aplin and Lalsiamliana 2010). The prediction of the famine was calculated based on their earlier experiences of it. However, it must be noted that it was not only the MNFF that was active in the relief and rehabilitation work; several other organizations were also involved. One such organization was the Tam Do Pawl (Anti-Famine Campaign Organization [AFCO]), which was established in 1951 under the leadership of C. Rokhuma.[5] The AFCO created an awareness campaign and distributed pamphlets such as the 'Tam Do Tlangau' (Anti-Famine Crier), carrying instructions on how to tackle the rat menace and prevent starvation (Rokhuma 2001).

To recount the response of the Assam government, a bamboo expert was sent over to the Mizo Hills to assess the situation. In his report, it appeared that the expert did not see any signs of bamboo flowering in the Mizo Hills. The expert concluded that the fear of the famine was mere tribal superstition. The Assam government also paid no heed to the suggestion and the precautionary steps planned by the AFCO, and so it continued to display open scepticism about the predicted famine (Aplin and Lalsiamliana 2010: 25). Another factor was that the Assam government failed to heed the precautionary advice of the MU to approve 15 lakh rupees as a test relief measure and chose to ignore the latter's warning that the neglect of the request would drive the Mizos towards secessionism. In 1959, the bamboos began to flower, followed by the rapid rise in the rat population that attacked standing crops and storage barns, resulting in mass starvation and deaths. For a population that was barely one lakh at the time of independence, the loss of even a thousand lives was gravely felt (S. Nag 2001).

After a year of the famine, the Assam government sent a four-member team comprising of Ramnath Sharma, Dandeswar Hazarika, Bhuban Chandra Pradhani, and Hareswar Goswami to assess the situation on the ground. From 26 to 29 March 1960, the committee visited villages in and around Aijal (present-day Aizawl) and Lunglei and observed the severity of the situation. While the committee provided many suggestions, it was already too little too late (Aplin and Lalsiamliana 2010: 25). The committee's perception of the problem was striking as the members continued to be sceptical about the Mizos' belief in the cause of the famine. Their report stated:

> It is very difficult to find a causal connection between the flowering of bamboos and an increase in the number of rats. But people seem to believe in this phenomenon so much that no amount of argument will make them change their belief. (Assam Government 1960)

On the political front, to register its protest, the MU withdrew its support of the APCC—hence the resignation of its two incumbent MLAs, A. Thanglura and H. K. Bawichhuaka. During the same time, there was interest among the leaders of the MNFF in establishing a political party, and after several rounds of meetings they formed a new political party that became the MNF in 1961. By this time, the famine had receded, and the MNF and the MU were the two main parties in the race for power and control in the Mizo Hills. However, the famine and its mishandling were costly beyond expectation to the MU. A journalist writing on the period noted, 'The image of the Mizo Union was at an all-time low' (Nibedon 1980: 39). This became clear in the by-election of 1963, where the MNF won the two MLA seats, with its candidates L. H. Lalmawia and J. F. Manliana, defeating two of the most prominent leaders of the MU, Ch. Saprawnga and H. K. Bawichhuaka. With the party openly advocating independence, the success in the by-election gave them the impression that it had the mandate of the people and, hence, the legitimacy to demand independence. As a leader of the movement notes:

> We contested the election in 1962 and there the MNF won 2 seats. The MNF therefore has the majority support or the majority of the Mizo public is supporting the MNF. Therefore, the MNF has the legitimacy to carry forward with the national movement as desired by the party.[6]

The decline of the MU was evident by how it gradually lost its grip over the District Councils as well. In the 1963 Village Council elections, even though the MU was able to win majority seats, the MNF winning 145 seats against the 228 seats of the MU indicated how the MNF could muster popular support despite its recent entry into politics. These factors emboldened the MNF leaders in their demand for independence.

MNF and Nationalist Mobilization: The Early Phase

In 1962, the MNF activated what many scholars refer to as 'sub-national politics' in India. It is notable that in India, sub-national movements are often advanced by political parties, and in such regions, sub-national aspirations remain an undercurrent force, such as in Tamil Nadu, Punjab, Jammu and Kashmir, and in Assam and Mizoram among the northeastern states (J. Pandian 1987; Baruah 1999; Zutshi 2003; Roluahpuia 2021; Singh and Shani 2021). Sub-national movements are marked by mobilizations that utilize local symbols, histories, cultures, religion, and language against the perceived dominance of the central states. In exceptional cases, such as that of the MNF, such mobilizations took a violent form.

National movements have utilized various forms of mobilization for spreading political messages. In the case of armed struggles, it is common to see how various rebel groups engaged in political mobilization for recruitment and support. Armed organizations have adopted creative ways to mobilize the masses, ranging from the use of street theatre by the Maoist rebels in Nepal (Mottin 2010), songs in Palestine (MacDonald 2013), and karaoke music in Myanmar (Brenner 2018). Such mobilization strategies are critical to seeking support and sustaining the movements. In the case of the MNF, the period of 1961–1965 is worth emphasizing to examine its rise more closely. Two significant developments during this period are worth mentioning. First, with the emergence of the MNF, territorial integration was back at the forefront of the political agenda. The MNF gave a nationalist turn by demanding territorial integration along with independence. Second, the social base of the MNF comprised of both the educated elites as well as the common people. From its inception, the MNF undertook a bottom–up mobilization by putting the village as the centre of its mobilization. It enrolled volunteers and established their base in the village. In this way, the MNF nationalist mobilization was characteristic of its broad-based support. It was able to garner and become a formidable political force within a short period of time.

In 1965, the MNF submitted a memorandum making a formal representation of its aspirations to the government of India for the first time. The content of the memorandum was an assertion for independence. The opening line of the memorandum read:

> This memorandum seeks to represent the case of the Mizo people for freedom and independence, for the right of territorial unity and solidarity; and for the realization of which a fervent appeal is submitted to the Government of India. (MNF Memorandum 1965)

In claiming legitimacy for its demand, the memorandum notes that the Mizo nation was historic as it 'stood as a separate nation even before the advent of the British government' and 'lived in complete independence without foreign rule' (MNF Memorandum 1965). It questioned the issue of integration under the MU's leadership as being an act of 'political immaturity, ignorant and lack of consciousness of their fate' (MNF Memorandum 1965). It denounced the British policy of 'divide and rule' that 'arbitrarily carved out and named Lushai Hills (now Mizo District) and the rest of their land being parcelled out to the adjoining people for the sole purpose of administrative convenience without obtaining their will or consent' (MNF Memorandum 1965). The territorial unity of the Mizo-inhabited areas was therefore about the 'recognition of human rights' as 'no one was good enough to govern another man without that man's consent' (MNF Memorandum 1965).

Territorial integration was mooted as an indispensable part of the Mizos' national aspirations. Towards this end, the MNF undertook mobilizations beyond national borders and regions. The MNF leaders reached out to the educated class of the Mizos within and outside of the Mizo Hills. If the famine of 1959 alienated the Mizos, sociocultural differences and discrimination were other factors of discontent. In the words of Pu Hranga:[7]

During our days, to speak the truth, we were highly discriminated. In those days the furthest that we could go for higher study was Shillong or Guwahati. We often got mocked for our food habits as tribals who eat dog meat. This has made us realize that we are not considered as equal citizens and hence not part of them.

We came from Mizoram, and I particularly came from the southern part, near Lunglei. I came to Aizawl about 13 times on truck, which often takes 5 days, to appear for [the] matric exam. From Aizawl and Silchar, we travelled back and forth by truck. The roads were in bad shape as they are not maintained by the government at all. We had a first-hand experience of discrimination from the Assam government. We are looked down upon for being tribals and discriminated against openly for the same, not because of our own inferiority complex.

If we take certain vegetables unknown to them inside the dining hall, they will start accusing us of taking beef inside and surround us. Therefore, we cannot be under one nation as equal citizen[s]. The idea of nationalism therefore is not necessarily a by-product of our own, but it emerges automatically due to such experiences. Mizo nationalism automatically is born out of this. This is particularly true in the case of Mizo. *Vai* in those days were mostly Assamese and Bengali as we hardly see north Indians and knew very less about south Indian[s]. Because of our experience and the mistreatment we faced, it has created alienation among us. Till today, even after introspection about it, I have the feeling that they never treated or considered us as equals. It therefore becomes pertinent to become independent from India and establish a separate Mizo state that we consider as the only possible way out of this mistreatment.[8]

Having felt unheard during the famine and experiencing a sense of being unwanted, the party conveyed this in their memorandum submitted to Lal Bahadur Shastri, the then prime minister of India, in 1965. It read:

During the fifteen years of close contact and association with India, the Mizo people have not been able to feel at home with Indians, or in India, nor have they been able to feel that their joys and sorrows have really ever been shared by India. They do not, therefore, feel Indian. (MNF Memorandum 1965)

It was this feeling of 'difference' that drove the educated Mizo youths towards the MNF. Zamawia, Sangkawia, Lalkhawliana, Bualhranga, Malsawma Colney, and others pursuing their studies in Shillong and Guwahati became active members of the party. The support of the educated class gave strong legitimacy to the party and its objectives as it was then involved in the mobilization of the Mizo public at large. The educated elites played a key role in the 'articulation of the nation' (Suny and Kennedy 1999).

However, the MNF mobilization was not entirely dominated by the elites. In its first general assembly of 1963, it passed a resolution to establish the Mizo National Volunteers (MNVs). The MNVs were then established in villages where MNF units operated. Despite the sociocultural changes during the colonial period, Mizo society was predominantly rural, with villages as the centre of its socio-economic and political life. In fact, during this time, there were only two major towns—Aizawl and Lunglei. The MNF leaders travelled from village to village to undertake mass mobilization campaigns. Its policy of *zalenna* became the rallying point for mobilization and found broad appeal among the youths in particular. The party deployed volunteers in various Mizo-inhabited areas like Manipur, Tripura, and Mizoram.

The MNF recruited both male and female volunteers, who were placed under the command of ex-servicemen. The recruitment was easy as there was no enrolment fee involved. Whereas the male volunteers were trained in military skills, the females were given training in nursing. However, they both took a common oath of allegiance to protect and sacrifice for whatever might come. The oath reads as follows:

> Kei, a hnuaia hming ziaktu hi Mizo National Volunteer ah ka inpe a, Zoram Zalenna tura hna thawk turin tui chungah emaw, boruakah emaw, khawmualah emaw, a tulna hmun apiang ah englai pawha kal turin ka intiam e.[9]

> I, the undersigned, have solemnly agreed to be the volunteer of Mizo National Volunteer and will strive towards the freedom of Zoram, be it in land, air, and sea, and offer unconditional sacrifice for the cause of the nation.

A former youth volunteer opined, 'Tlangval khua a awm mai mai kha a zahthlak' (It was a shame for a young man to be at a village doing nothing.)[10] For others, the feeling of nationalism was homegrown. A former female member of the MNA explained:

> My mother was someone who was really concerned about *ram leh hnam*. She was concerned about *ram leh hnam* much before the emergence of the MNF. We had such orientation from childhood. Although I did not enrol as a volunteer per se, two of my elder sisters enrolled themselves as a volunteer in the MNF. When they established the MNF office, my two sisters were two of the first women who were working as staff in the MNF office.[11]

She continued, 'All of us wanted *zalenna*. Looking at our orientation from childhood and the strong feeling that my mother had imbibed in me, I had a strong desire to fight for the independence of Mizoram.'

Vernacular Nationalism: Songs, Scripts, and Armed Struggle

Songs: The National Voice

Hnam hla were widely popular among the *hnam sipai*[12] during the period of the movement. The theme of *hnam hla* were wide-ranging, covering aspects of the national past, common identity, sacrifice, and struggle. Songs have a unique power of mobilization, and the Mizo case demonstrates the prominent role of *hnam hla* in nationalist politics. Before and after the armed struggle, the *hnam hla* acted as a catalyst for mass mobilization, and due to their oral form, they successfully instilled a strong sense of national consciousness. It were the *hnam hla* that awakened the Mizo national consciousness.

In undertaking nationalist mobilization, the MNF creatively tapped into the oral culture of the Mizos, particularly utilizing songs to disseminate and diffuse nationalist ideas. The songs by Rokunga are worthy of attention as they were the ones that captured the imagination of the Mizos.[13] In fact, the songs he composed mirrored the political background of the time. On the cultural front, for many decades, the only songs that were commonly sung were Christian hymns, and the church welcomed no other genre, particularly in the decades before and after India's independence. This was because of the hard-line position of the church to de-link the Mizo public from their pre-Christian past and practices that they deemed were un-Christian, particularly the consumption of *zu* (rice beer) and traditional rites and songs associated with the worshipping of spirits. In politics, Rokunga's intervention was crucial as he was able to integrate the Mizos' past life within the realm of the Christian outlook. He embraced the various cultural attributes of the Mizos, such as *tlawmngaihna, thian chhan thih ngam,* and *nula tlangval inlawm,*[14] as a way to express Mizo-ness. His songs, therefore, soon became popular and filled the vacuum, giving songs a new lease on life in modern Mizo society. It was in this context that the songs composed by Rokunga need to be understood.

In 1947, being a witness to the events that were unfolding before him, Rokunga began to write and express himself through songs. With the British departure becoming imminent, the opinions of the Mizos were divided over the question of their political future. While there are various pro-integration groups, there were sections that supported independence. It was in this moment of political uncertainty that Rokunga's song 'Harh La, Harh La' sounded the clarion call to awaken the Mizos from their slumber. The lines in the song reflect how Rokunga desired the Mizos to be awaken. In the first four lines, he put it this way:

Harh la, harh la, Zoram, i tlai ang e,
Harh la, harh la, hun ṭha a liam ang e.
Tho la, tho la, ke-in lo ding ta che,
Ngai teh, ri chu, Zalenna dâr ri,
Tho rawh hun ṭha a liam hma hian.

Hei hi kan tum ber lo ni tawh se
Mahni ram puanzâr hnuaia ding tur leh
Rinawmna leh huainaa lo inthuam fo hi.

Awake, Zoram, lest you should be late,
Make haste, make haste, ere the time shall pass,
Arise, Arise, get up on your feet,
Hark! Hark the chime of Freedom bell,
Rise up and shine, make no delay.

Let this our one endeavour be
To stand firm 'neath our nation's banner
In robes of loyalty and courage array.[15]

Soon, this song became widely popular, arousing feelings of nationalism. It had a major influence and spread throughout the length and breadth of the areas where Mizos lived. Another key composer was Laltanpuia, whose songs echoed the same sentiment. His song 'Rorelna Hmaa Zam Lo Nang Kan Vote Ang Che' (We Will Vote You for You Who Do Not Fear the Ruler) was especially seen as referring to the MNF, which was contesting the election in 1963. However, in his song, the affective bond with the *ram* is more pronounced and is expressed this way:

Aw Zoram, aw kan Zoram,
Aw Zoram ka ngaihlu che;
I chhunga hnamze tinreng te,
Lungruala kan insuihkhawm hian,
Finna kulhpui, hriatlohna thim hi chhem kiang la,
Lungrualna hi ram leh hnam tan
Hlimna kulhpui ber a lo ni e. (C. Zama 2005)

O Zoram, our own Zoram,
How precious you are to me,
As all the tribes that reside in you,
Unite and bond with each other,
We pray the ignorance be done and all be enlightened,
That unity is our refuge,
For our land and our community.

Rokunga remained observant of the changes and challenges facing the Mizos. The political fate of the Mizos continued to baffle many of them. For instance, in 1947, the CYMA organized a song-writing competition with the best one to be chosen as the Mizo national anthem. Rokunga's song 'Ro Min Rel Sak Ang Che' (Be Thou Our Counsellor) was chosen as the best and subsequently adopted as the Mizo national anthem. Rokunga himself was part of the MU for a brief period, but his songs tell a story of his nationalist outlook. The MNF in no time adopted it as its anthem too. This further popularized the MNF agenda of *zalenna* among the non-MNF members.

The choice of selecting Rokunga's song as the national anthem needs to be understood against the critical backdrop of national anthems. National anthems have a strong unifying force apart from stirring public emotion. One key aspect of national anthems is their ability and power to arouse emotion. They also popularize the nationalist ideals of the national community, associating themselves with it. Most importantly, they legitimize the existence of the nation—in other words, they are sine qua non of national identity. Anthems are sung in state-sponsored events, official ceremonies, wartime, and sporting events. Irrespective of the occasions, they create what Anderson (1983: 145) refers to as 'unisonance' among people, even wholly unknown to one another when performed and sung. 'Ro Min Rel Sak Ang Che', like many national anthems, is devotional in nature. A devotion to the nation calls for sacrifice while at the same time motivating people to action (Schultz 2013: 4). It was sung in public gatherings, churches, and political campaigns. The first and third stanzas of the song go as follows:

Aw nang kan Lal kan Pathian,
I hming ropui ber se,
I hma a kan lo kun hian,
Kan dil ngaithla ang che,
Kan awmdan tur ngaihtuaha,
Mipui kan inkhawm in,
Finna ropui min pe la,
Ro min rel sak ang che.

Chuvangin aw kan Pathian
Hei hi kan dil ber che,
Kan ram kan hnam min hruaia'n,
Nang chauh kan thlang ber a che.
Chhung lam leh pawn lam hmelma,
Indona thleng mahse,
Hneh zel turin min pui la,
Ro Min Rel sak ang che.

O Thou, Our God, Our Ruler,
Thy name exalted be,
As we bow down before Thee,
Lend Thine ears to our prayer,
As we the host foregather
To plan our future course,
Impart Thy divine wisdom,
Be Thou our counsellor.
Without Thy might and guidance,
Without Thine auspices,
The glories of earthly throne
Oft fade and soon decline;
But Thou eternal stronghold
Of every nation art!

King of kings and Lord of lords,
Be Thou our counsellor.

This, above all, O our God,
Grant us, we beseech Thee.
To lead and guide our nation,
In Thee alone we trust.
Though foes—within and without
Should rage war against us,
Assist us to triumph o'er them,
Be Thou our counsellor.[16]

There was a strong religious overtone in the song. By the 1960s, the Mizos were predominantly Christian, and Christianity had already gained significant influence in the Mizo life-world. Political freedom in the form of independence to the Mizos also implied freedom of religion in a country they perceived as predominantly Hindu or Hindu India. The MNF sang Rokunga's song to mark important occasions such as MNF Raising Day and Independence Day, among others.

It is not surprising that Rokunga and his songs continue to gain attention in Mizo literature even today.[17] His songs continue to be sung with much pride and elation in public gatherings. In his critical study of Rokunga's songs, Vanhnuaithanga (2009) notes that the songs sought to instil a feeling of pride in Mizo identity and the territory the Mizos inhabited. In one of his songs, Rokunga rallies Mizo pride in Zoram with the exhortation:

Kan Zotlang ram nuam hi chhawrpial run I iang e,
Hallo ten lungrual dar ang kan lenna,
Perhkhuang tingtang zai a kan chawi lai i mawi e,
Parmawi tinreng leh thlifim lenna kan Zoram nuam.

The scenic hills of our Zoland feel like Paradise,
Where we live together in perfect harmony,
Harping on our strings we sing your exaltations,
Land of all blossoms and soft breeze, our beautiful Mizoram.[18]

The hill in the colonial imagination is a 'backward' and 'unproductive' space inhabited by 'wild races'. This colonialist perception has been shared by non-tribals and communities living in the plains. Contrary to such representations, Rokunga's idea of *ram* therefore is imbued with an idealized image of the hills as 'paradise' and space of ethnic harmony. The idealized imagination of Zoram captures the popular imagination of the Mizos. This reflects in the increasing centrality of being *tlangmi* (hill people) in their collective consciousness. The attachment to the *ram* and their identity as *tlangmi* shaped their notion of self and differentiated them from the *vai*.

Further, Rokunga laid out the vision by calling upon Mizos to strive for progress and prosperity so that they could be on par with the more advanced communities: 'Raltiang Ram I Kai Ve Ang' (We Shall Go Beyond the Shore). His songs were most popular between the years 1940 and 1966, when the tide of nationalism was on the rise among the Mizos (Chawnghranga 2015: 42). The significance is borne out of the fact that such songs gave rise to a new genre in Mizo literature, which came to be known as *hnam hla*. Indeed, following Rokunga, there was an unprecedented rise in the number of *hnam hla* composed. This skilful use of songs by the MNF can be credited to the pre-existing cultures of the Mizos, whereby songs appeared in various forms as a way of expressing power, authority, defeat, and fear since pre-colonial Mizo society. The effectiveness of *hnam hla* lies in its intention, which is 'to arouse its listeners to political action' (Riley and Smith 2016: 8). As Riley and Smith (2016: 2) further notes, 'The theme of this kind of music echoes those of the project of vernacular mobilization.'

There is a long tradition in nationalism studies that looks at the relationship between songs, their composers, and nationalism (Curtis 2008; Riley and Smith 2016). In colonized countries, songs were a powerful form of expression against colonial rule. In the case of the Mizos, there are two fundamental issues worthy of note. First, unlike other nationalist movements, the composing of songs was not confined to a few persons in the movement. Both renowned composers such as Rokunga and Laltanpuia, along with various lesser-known composers who were part of the movement, composed songs. Second, it was through songs that the nation began to be imagined, constructed, and circulated. The number of *hnam hla* composed demonstrates this significance. One list collected 175 of them, which were composed by MNF and non-MNF members (C. Zama 2005).

With the outbreak of armed conflict, songs continued to play a significant role in the national movement. This time, the tenor of the songs had shifted to that of a call for sacrifice as *zalenna* could be achieved only through this—hence the call upon the Mizos to support the movement. An army leader, Khawlhmingthanga, wrote:

Zofa zaleng kan hlim ve nan,
Zohnahthlak Chhinlung chhuak zawng te;
Mizo hnam run rawn bel ve ru,
Raltiang kai zai kan rel ta e. (C. Zama 2005)

For the sake of our race's contentment,
Come all ye sons of Chhinlung;
Join us in our Mizo nation abode,
Decided have we to cross over to the other side.

The use of 'Chhinlung' (covering rock) in the song is of particular significance. For the Mizos, Chhinlung points towards their shared origin myth[19]—hence their self-identification as Chhinlung *chhuak* (people of Chhinlung origin). Embracing Chhinlung *chhuak* involves constructing a pan-Mizo identity that cut across borders and boundaries. This mythical belief becomes the starting point to understand, if not describe, the origins of the Mizos (Sangkima 1992; M. Zama 2005). The story of their movements and migrations are traced to the cave while at the same time it is utilized to articulate and forge an identity transcending clans and tribal identifications. It underlies how the composer intended specifically to embrace the people's collective history when inviting the masses to join the movement. While the acceptance of such an appeal is still dependent upon the populace, the use of 'Chhinlung' shows the conscious attempt on the part of the composer to make a fervent call for a collective struggle.

In a song he composed, a prominent leader of the movement, K. Vanlalauva, like Rokunga, called to the youth to rise up and protect their *ram*. At the time when the song was composed, the MNF was already in a protracted battle with the Indian security forces. The circumstances and the time when Rokunga composed *hnam hla* differ significantly from those of Vanlalauva. For instance, many of Rokunga's *hnam hla* were composed before the outbreak of the armed conflict which is not the case for Vanlalauva. As such, one could perceive a lyrical change in the *hnam hla* as is reflected in the song composed by Vanlalauva. In the song that he composed, there was a call for sacrifice for the Mizo nation, a call that there is still hope for freedom of their *ram*. In the face of massive counter-insurgency by the Indian state, Vanlalauva makes a clarion call through his song 'Zalenna Kan Tan' (Freedom for Our Nation). A stanza from the song reads:

> Chhan tlak ram I neih hi muang lo la,
> Hnam eiral tum thim lal chuanin;
> I velin kulhbing an siam e,
> Zofa te tho ru a tlai hma hian.

> Late not while you still have a land you can protect,
> Against the dark force threatening the nation,
> That builds a fortress encircling you,
> Make haste Mizos, before it's too late.

Chhawntluanga, a soldier in the movement, joined Vanlalauva in his songs that go like this:

> Sum tamsengah kan sawm lo che,
> Lu chum ban chum tuarah kan sawm bil lo che.
> Kan sawm che ram I hmangaih chhan turin,
> Aw lokal rawh tunah lung I rualza ang. (C. Zama 2005)

> We don't ask for your earnings to be drained,
> We don't ask either that you sacrifice your limbs

We only ask that you save your beloved land,
Come, let's strive together for its betterment.

It was the call for sacrifice that tied such songs together. The composers of the songs note that it was only through sacrifice that the Mizos would achieve their desired goal of *zalenna*. Sacrifice is an integral aspect of nationalist movements, calling on individuals to make a sacrifice for the nation, even if it amounts to sacrificing one's life. Along these lines, Renan (1990) notes that the nation is constituted by the feeling of sacrifices that one has made in the past and those that one is prepared to make in the future. To this date, war commemorations in the form of statues, cemeteries, and annual remembrances restate and underscore the sacrifice made in the past for the nation. The post-World War II period saw the proliferation of war memorials, whereby the sacrifice of heroic soldiers was made central to the national imaginings (Hobsbawm and Ranger 1983; Smith 2001).

The idea of sacrifice has deep cultural significance and symbolic value in Mizo society. Mizo history is replete with stories of *pasaltha* who are predominantly men and widely known for their bravery and courage. In times of war and peace, *pasaltha* act as the guardians of the common people and the safety of the village. They call upon the male members for sacrifice as only the men are entitled to the status of a *pasaltha*, which reinforces the idea of masculinism inherent in Mizo society. For the Mizo armies, sacrifice was about continuing with the past traditions of *hnam pasaltha* like Zampuimanga, Khuangchera, Vanapa, Chawngbawla, and others who in Mizo history were eulogized and emulated as symbols of ethnic pride even today. The *pasaltha* therefore were elevated to the status of 'role models and lessons for the present struggle' (Hutchinson 2005: 15). This is consistent with the narratives of the struggle where 'sacrifice constitutes a powerful social bond' (Riley and Smith 2016: 139), which was also a virtue highly prized by the Mizos.

Each battalion under the MNA was named after a *pasaltha*; special songs valorized the heroics attached to that name as reminders of the values to be emulated in the protection of the *ram leh hnam*. Sung mostly during important occasions such as Raising Day, the battalion songs forged a common feeling among the *hnam sipai*. There was vernacularization at work whereby the idioms of nationalism were expressed using the local repertoires of traditions, cultures, and histories.

Zalenna and *ram leh hnam*, the twin facets of the Mizo nationalist idea, were integrated into the songs. It was the perceptibility of songs, given their 'oral' form, due to which they came to assume a central place in the nationalist narrative. The ideas were internalized in the people's minds, and for those who were participants in the movement, it was a struggle for freedom. Leaders of the MNF infused the idea in their speeches and writings. Of particular importance were Laldenga's *Zoram Marches towards Freedom* and *Zalenna Thuchah*, Zoramthanga's *Zoram Zalenna Lungphum*, and Lalhmingthanga's *Exodus Politics*. They all contained the core of nationalist ideas.

Scripting Zalenna, *The Nationalist Manifesto*

Anderson's (1983) thesis on 'imagined communities' is a familiar theme in nationalism studies affirming the powerful role of the print culture in the emergence of modern nationhood. Following Anderson's thesis, Zou (2010), in detailing the historical emergence of the 'Zo' struggle, examined how at various points in time different Zo leaders and intellectuals had inserted their imagination in print. Zou (2010) argues that such writings had left a strong imprint on the articulation of Zo or Mizo nationality. For the large majority of tribals in northeast India, the emergence of print was closely tied to colonialism. This was significant in two ways. First, there was a reduction of the oral language to a script, mostly under the initiative of Christian missionaries. Second, the print culture was largely confined to the domain of religion, namely the missionaries and the church. The church, for instance, was the first to own a publishing house in Mizoram, known as the Lushai Christian Press in 1911. While this press was started as an individual initiative, the Loch Printing Press began in 1914 and was later renamed the Synod Printing Press in 1973.[20]

The print culture started with the publication of newspapers such as the handwritten *Mizo Chanchin Laisuih* (1898) and the *Mizo Leh Vai Chanchinbu* (1903) published using a cyclostyle stencil brought in from Sylhet (now in Bangladesh). Following this was the publication of the *Kristian Tlangau* (Christian Herald) (1911) by the Presbyterian Church, followed by publications by various other church denominations.[21] The growing print culture signalled the emergence of a literate public among the Mizos. Another impact of the print culture was that it resulted in the consolidation and spread of the Duhlian language adopted by the British as the mode and medium of proselytization and education.

Individuals such as R. Vanlawma and Laldenga, along with the political parties, took advantage of the new technology to disseminate their messages—nationalist and otherwise. For instance, the MU used the *Mizo Arsi* (Mizo Star) as the party's mouthpiece while the MNF published a newsletter under the name *Mizo Aw* (Voice of the Mizo) to propagate its nationalist ideas. With specific reference to the MNF, the prominent leaders of the movement produced various political writings worthy of attention that contained the core ideology of Mizo nationalism. Three key texts will be examined here: Laldenga's *Mizoram Marches towards Freedom*, Zoramthanga's *Zoram Zalenna Lungphum*, and Lalhmingthanga's *Exodus Politics*.[22] The primary focus in these texts was the question of *zalenna*, which was also at the heart of the MNF struggle. This time, the targeted audience and the motivations were different from those of the songwriters and their songs, as the authors wanted more than just the dissemination of their ideas. Their intention was to self-define the struggle, which was filled with 'highly significant and fundamental socio-political discourses' (Narayan 2001: 3923). These texts further reinforced the ideology of the movement and indicated that they were written with these conscious intentions.

In *Mizoram Marches towards Freedom*, Laldenga cogently articulated his understanding of the idea of freedom and what it meant to the Mizos. In spelling out his idea of the nation, Laldenga imagined the Indian nation as a 'house', a symbolic representation of the diverse members that made up the Indian nation-state. The use of the symbolic 'house' also evoked the existing relationship, dominance, and hierarchy among its members. As Laldenga put it,

> In the house of India, their lives an unhappy man. His name is Mizo. He is born of different parents, a descendant of Mongoloid stock. He is blessed with a distinct and separate language, having a different code of social living and cultural practices, worshipping a different God. (Laldenga 2011: 17)

By invoking 'difference', both racial and ethnic, Laldenga noted how this difference between members had caused the tension and contestation of the Indian nation-state. This difference marks out the Mizos from the other members, visible but with 'inassimilable difference' (Pasha 2009: 523). Laldenga doubted whether the Mizos could be considered as equal members in the house of India. The reason he gave is as follows:

> He [the Mizo] is disdainfully looked upon with contemptuous eyes because of his blood, the blood of his ancestors, the blood of Mongolian race by which he was born in this world. He is despised because of his Mongolian facial structure and appearance for which he cannot help himself. Wherever he goes, he is perpetually mocked, ridiculed and made fun of because of his race and religion. (Laldenga 2011: 17)

The suspicion of the loyalty of the tribes of the region has been a well-noted fact in the CA debates. This idea of being framed as 'suspect citizens' still prevails and is embedded in the policies developed for the northeastern region. Yet, for Laldenga, the outcome was a feeling of alienation among the Mizos. For Laldenga, the freedom in question therefore was freedom from alienation, and so for him the MNF movement was a 'liberation movement' (Laldenga 2011: 40).

This idea of the MNF movement as a liberation movement resonates more powerfully in Zoramthanga's *Zoram Zalenna Lungphum*, where he asserts that any nation denied political freedom is in bondage under colonial or alien rule. In this light, political freedom is the highest form of human freedom without which other freedoms are void. Zoramthanga explains:

> Zalenna hi kawng hrang hrangin kan mamawh a. Kan ni tin nun atana hlauhawm thei lak atanga zalenna te, sum leh paia inrahbehna kawnga zalenna te, sakhaw zalenna te, mahni duhzawng sawi chhuak thei tura zalenna te, hriat lohna lak atanga zalenna te leh hnam nunphung rah behna lak atanga zalenna te an ni a. Heng lo pawh hi zalenna kan mamawhna kawng hrang tam tak sawi sen loh an la awm a. Amaherawhchu, heng zawng zawng khai khawmna leh

a bulpui ber chu mihring anga min nuntir theitu tur politics zalenna hi a ni. (Zoramthanga 1980: 45–46)

There are different kinds of freedom that humans need. It can be freedom from the fear of danger, freedom from poverty, religious freedom, freedom of expression, [and] freedom from cultural domination and oppression. There will be an innumerable number of freedoms besides the one named here. However, the basic foundation of all kinds of freedom is political freedom.

The MNF struggle therefore was rooted in this desire for political freedom, which it sought through the unilateral declaration of independence in 1966. Zoramthanga framed the movement's objective within the context of the right to self-determination with the establishment of a separate nation-state as its ultimate destiny. He, however, contended that the right to self-determination was not merely about achieving political independence because independent nations can also live under bondage or their citizens can be denied their rights. For the Mizos, the consciousness of being 'un-free' was the first step towards being free. The achievement of the freedom of Mizoram was possible only through this self-realization, and so it rested with the people. Zoramthanga notes:

Zoram a zalen lohna chhan hi a bul takah chuan Burma Sorkar vang emaw, India Sorkar vang emaw, Bangladesh Sorkar vang emaw a ni lova, Mizoram mipuite vang a ni a…. Chuvangin zalenna nei tur pawh hian ram mipuiten an thawh chhuah a ngai a, a mawhphurhna tawp chu ram mipuiten an pumbil liau liau a ni tih kan hre reng tur a ni. Chutiang bawkin Independence ringawt hian zalenna min thlen theih loh avangin, Independence kan nih hnua zalenna min siam saktu leh kan zalenna venghim zeltu tur pawh ram dang Sorkarte ni lovin keimahni ram mipuite bawk kan ni tih hi zalenna thuthlung dik kumkhua tur leh Mizoramin kan hriat reng tur chu a ni. (Zoramthanga 1980: 57)

The main reason behind Zoram being not an independent state is not because of the Burma government, the Government of India or the Government of Bangladesh, but the people of Mizoram. As such, it is the task and responsibility of the people to struggle to realize freedom. Likewise, independence is not a mere guarantor of freedom. It is thrust upon the people to protect and safeguard their freedom even after the achievement of independence, which the people of Mizoram should be well aware of.

Following Laldenga, Zoramthanga's idea of *zalenna* was the right to live with dignity and respect. As far as the Mizos' relation with the Indian state was concerned, the freedom of the Mizos would remain limited and constrained, for it was determined by ideals that safeguarded the interest of the people who framed it.

In his *Exodus Politics*, Lalhmingthanga takes a more cultural outlook in framing the nationalist ideology. Using the notion of Mizo *saphun*,[23] he notes that the Mizos had two options before them. The first was complete assimilation and the second was to assert self-determination. In the case of assimilation, he identifies two forms—coercive and voluntary. Drawing upon the experience of European nation-states, he observes that the creation of a monocultural and a homogenous national community had resulted in the effacing of minority cultures. Language and education have remained essential to central state policies of building homogeneous national cultures. In India, too, language, particularly the promotion of Hindi, and the nationalization of education play an important role in national integration. This is essentially about promoting the dominant culture by using both language and religion.

Nation-building efforts in India were complemented by the attempt to nationalize the educational curricula. A standardized education was intended to produce a homogenous national community (Gellner 1983). For Lalhmingthanga, this involved a denial of the history of the minority communities, such as the Mizos, since what was essentially taught in schools was about the culture of the dominant groups. In problematizing what constituted 'national history', Lalhmingthanga notes that it resulted in the propagation and celebration of majority cultures in the minds of children at the loss of their own history. He writes:

> Kan sikul zirlaite kan en chuan India rilru (spiritual sentiment) tihsanna leh ngaih ropui theihna tur chanchin a tam em em bawk a ni. Kan sikul bangte chu India thu tha inzirtirna leh hruaitu ropuite lemin kan tikhat a, heihi naupangten an rawn than lenpui chuan an tan chuan a aia thil ropui zawk khawvelah hian a awm thei lo ang tih a rinawm ani. (Lalhmingthanga 2009 [1965]: 41)

> Our school curriculum is all about endorsing and worshipping Indian culture and values. The walls of the school buildings are painted with quotations on Indian philosophy and the images of great leaders of India. Once they are internalized by the students, it is perceivable that there can be no other greater leaders and teachings in the world other than them.

Language and religion have been the two enduring axes of ethno-national mobilizations in India. This was the case in Punjab, Tamil Nadu, and to some extent Jammu and Kashmir. Linguistic and religious dominance imposed the cultural hegemony of the dominant nation-state upon peripheral communities. The themes of domination, language, and religion have also figured prominently in the writings of other leaders. Laldenga, for instance, wrote:

> He [the Mizo] is asked to swallow and follow Indian ways of life with Hindu culture and code of social living and alien (Indian) language imposed upon him. To add to this unbearable pain of his body and soul, he is a lonely Christian, in the vast sea of fanatic Hindus, where abominable practices of caste system are strictly adhered to. Because of his religious belief, he leads the life of an outcast; he is unacceptable in the Indian society so much so that he can share neither

food nor water with them, much less to share happiness and sorrow. To the
Indians he is like a leper, unclean and loathsome. (Laldenga 2011: 18)

Although extraneous to the caste hierarchy, tribes in India occupy a lower status. The
culture, food, and ways of life of the tribes are viewed in caste terms that relegate them
as impure and unequal citizens. Indian nationalist leaders, such as B. R. Ambedkar,
had questioned the promise of equality guaranteed under the Constitution if the
issue of caste was not dealt with. Given their pervasive nature, caste practices affect
even non-caste communities such as the Mizos in that they not only relegate the
Mizos to an 'outcast' status but also describe them as 'backward' and 'primitive'. Such
notions are not merely colonial stereotypes but a viewpoint shared by non-tribal
communities towards tribal communities.

   Zalenna encompasses an imagining that is not only political freedom but
also freedom from social and economic domination. In his own words, Laldenga
(2011: 19) said, '[T]hey want to be themselves, free from any kind of domination
and exploitation.' The writings of the MNF leaders also reflected the influence and
awareness of the larger nationalist ideas that swept the globe. With the modern
nation-state becoming the main political unit of a global organization, it was in
this context that communities such as the Mizos began to articulate and aspire for a
separate Mizo state. For the volunteers and armies, the struggle therefore remained
one of *zalenna*, and many continue to view it as such even today.[24]

Struggling for *Zalenna*: From *Thingfak* to Armed Struggle

On 26 February 1966, a group of MNF leaders met at Zalen Cabin at the residence of
their president, Laldenga, and passed a resolution for the declaration of independence
on the midnight of 28 February 1966. Code-named 'Operation Jericho', the plan had
as its objective the attack of the major security outposts across the districts to take
over civil and military control. The eponym Jericho was derived from the biblical
event of the fall of Jericho, the first city captured by the Israelites led by Joshua in
their conquest of the 'promised land'. Volunteers undertook the task with the same
zeal when 61 signatories of the MNF leaders unanimously declared Mizoram as an
independent nation-state. The declaration of independence read:

   We, therefore, the representatives of Mizo people, meeting on this day, the first
   of March, in the year of our Lord, nineteen sixty six appealing to the supreme
   judge of the world for the rectitude of our intention so, in the name and by
   the authority of the good people of this country solemnly publish and declare,
   that Mizoram is, and of rights ought to be free and independent, that they are
   absolved from all political connections between them and to Government
   of India is and ought to be resolved and that as free and independent state,
   they have full power to levy war, conclude peace, contract alliances, establish

commerce and to do all other Acts and Things which independent state may, of right, do [*sic*]. (MNF Memorandum 1965)

The supply of arms from the then East Pakistan was not sufficient for the volunteers who en masse came to fight for Zoram *zalenna*. Some came with *thingfak*[25] (kindle wood) used while training, and many others had to fight with a *tuboh* (hammer) and a *chempui* (machete). Regardless of this, the volunteers could overrun the major security outposts across the hill districts, except in Aizawl. To the surprise of the Indian central leaders, the Mizo Hills fell into the hands of the rebels rather swiftly. The MNF then established an underground Mizoram *sawrkar* (government) with its base in the CHTs of East Pakistan (now Bangladesh) (Figure 4.2).

Figure 4.2 Mizo National Front (MNF) rebels in their camp in East Pakistan (now Bangladesh), 1970–1980
Source: PAMRA collection.

The response of the government of India was also directed towards controlling and tightening its grip on the Mizo Hills. The first response of the government came in the form of repeated air raids between 5 and 8 March 1966 in areas where the MNF volunteers were in control. This included Aizawl, Champhai, Lunglei, and Tlabung, among others. The air bombings and raids were meant to 'flush out' the MNF rebels from the major towns and villages to make security clearance for the military reinforcements.

By 5 March, the Sikh Regiment made their first entry by reaching Kolasib, the state's northernmost district. They were followed by more reinforcement such as the Bihar and the Gurkha regiments. The Mizo Hills were put under 'Disturbed Areas' under the provision of the Armed Forces (Special Powers) Act (AFSPA), 1958, was enforced.

The most intense battle between the Mizo armies and the Indian security forces occurred between 1966 and 1969. Given the undulating terrain and the vast forested coverage, the government of India started the 'grouping' of villages as a counter-insurgency measure to disrupt the connection between the MNF and the civilians. Knowing the MNF's reliance on the people for food and shelter, the government's strategy worked and the MNF was pushed down to the CHTs, where they established camps and organized planned attacks. In the 20 years (1966–1986) of the armed struggle, the Mizo Hills remained the movement's epicentre. However, the MNF undertook armed operations in Mizo-inhabited areas beyond the Mizo Hills, such as in Manipur and Tripura within northeast India and in the Chin Hills in Myanmar. These regions were part of the MNF's goal, which was to establish a 'sovereign' Mizo state through the ethnic and territorial integration of all Mizo-inhabited areas.

Bayly (1998), in tracing the origin of nationality in South Asia, observes that the idea of nationality was rooted in the indigenous ideas of place, economy, and polity. Such notions of patriotism and nationalism were blended with modern nationalist ideas, and so the concept of nationalism was neither a western import nor colonially induced. As the demand for a sovereign Mizoram took the form of an armed struggle, its idea of sovereignty was shaped by the Mizos' past of living as a free and autonomous people. Until the nineteenth century, the hills of the northeast were an 'anarchist region', which the central states failed to penetrate and with the communities devising strategies to evade any form of direct dominion by external rule (Scott 2009). The aspirations for sovereignty were largely influenced and shaped by this pre-colonial notion of freedom, and, in the context of the MNF struggle, the understanding of *zalenna* was predicated upon the Mizos' past of living as free people.

It is common to see the case for independence being made on this basis, which the MNF also made in its memorandum submitted to Shastri, the then prime minister, in 1965. A line from the memorandum exemplifies this:

> The Mizos, from time immemorial, have lived in complete independence without foreign interference. Chiefs of different clans ruled over separate hills and valleys with supreme authority and their administration was very much like that of the Greek City-State of the past. The territory or any part thereof had never been conquered or subjugated by their neighboring states. (MNF Memorandum 1965)

It is this understanding that was widely in circulation and was integral to the Mizo national consciousness. This evocation of pre-colonial sovereignty reflects how the MNF constructed a 'usable past' (Cockell 2000) to legitimize its struggle. This is an acknowledged fact across scholarly traditions on nationalism studies as to how nation-states 'invent traditions' (Hobsbawm and Ranger 1983) or 'innovatively' construct them, thereby making a fervent appeal for nationalist mobilizations (Hutchinson 2004: 109; Smith 2009). The idea of *zalenna* therefore was both backward- and forward-looking. It was backward-looking as it yearned for the pre-colonial Mizo society when the Mizos were free from external rule. It was forward-looking as it aspired towards a futuristic goal of reinstating freedom with the aspiration to establish a free Mizo state. While the former is about the 'common past', the latter is concerned with a 'common destiny'. As Yuval-Davis (1993: 623) argues, it is not enough to have a common past to arouse nationalist passion; one must also believe there is a shared future.

Within the northeastern region, the movement received extensive support from and participation by the Mizos living in Manipur and Tripura. A large number of volunteers were recruited from these two states. In 1967, operations were carried out in Manipur and Tripura to claim the territory. The operation in Manipur was known as the Manipur Crusade, which was a joint operation undertaken by three battalions of the Mizo *hnam sipai*—namely the Vanapa Battalion (V. Battalion), the Lalvunga Battalion (L. Battalion), and the Chawngbawla Battalion (Ch. Battalion) (C. Zama 2011: 131–132). The targets were the security outposts in the Tadubi and Kangpokpi areas in the Selected Area Development Administrative Region (SADAR) hill district of the state. Two popular leaders of the movement hailing from Manipur were Demkhosiek Gangte and Lalkhohen Kipgen. Under the leadership of Gangte, the MNA made their first journey to China in 1971. The MNA also attacked the Police Armed Constabulary (PAC) in Vanghmun village of the Jampui Hills[26] in Tripura. Whereas the MNA retreated from the Mizo villages in Tripura after the operation, the civilians were under constant threat and surveillance. In many cases, there was a repeated cycle of abuse and violence, physical and sexual. The situation was similar for the Mizos in Manipur.

In the 1970s, the survival of the movement was a big question. There was a series of splits within the movement between the moderate and the extremist leaders. As the liberation of East Pakistan became inevitable, the MNF stood to lose its safe havens in the region along with the support from the Pakistan government. With the Indian state supporting the Bangladesh liberation movement, it was clear that this was an opportunity to defuse the MNF movement too. The moderates within the movement, also known as the Dumpawl (Blue Group), were in favour of negotiation, while the hardliners sided with the president to continue the struggle (Figure 4.3).

Throughout 1971 or until the 'fall of Dhaka', there was a cycle of arrests of the leaders belonging to the Dumpawl, along with the armies suspected of supporting them. Some leaders escaped from jail while others, such as Zamawia and Lalnunmawia, were given free passage to lead groups of men (mostly injured), women, and children to surrender. The rest, mostly the armies, headed towards the Arakan Hills in Myanmar. This restrained the activities of the armies, and armed confrontation between the Indian security forces and the Mizos' soldiers declined considerably.

Figure 4.3   Mizo National Front (MNF) leaders and armies with Laldenga (*second from the left*) and his wife, Biakdiki, 1970–1980
Source: PAMRA collection.

In 1972, the Mizo Hills were elevated to a union territory (UT) status with the second reorganization of Indian states. Another political intervention was the splitting of the PLRC into three different autonomous councils—the Mara Autonomous District Council, the Lai Autonomous District Council, and the Chakma Autonomous District Council. In the areas where the three tribal groups were dominant, the presence and support of the MNF were minimal. Yet there were often clashes in the early years of the movement between the Chin National Front (CNF), led by Lalchunga Chinzah, and the MNF based on the CNF's opposition to the movement. Except for individual participation, there was not much support extended to the MNF by the Mara and the Lai tribes. Relationships with the Chakmas were strained and mutually harboured feelings of suspicion and hostility. Inter-tribal animosity and tribal cleavages worked to the advantage of the government of India in its search for allies and intelligence-gathering efforts from the communities. This only resulted in a hardening of the ethnic boundaries.

During my fieldwork in Siaha,[27] where the Mara tribes are predominant, one observes the consciousness of being Mara over the Mizo identity and the assertion of Mara often being as distinct and different from Mizo. Mizo was often construed as Lusei-centric, and hence the opposition was understood as opposing any Lusei-led movement. Within the district headquarters, the area known as the

'MNF constituency' consists of the locality known as New Saiha, which is largely inhabited by the Duhlian-speaking community belonging to both the Lusei and non-Lusei clans. The area was the bastion of the MNF's base in the region, and hence it has been associated with the MNF party. Language is central to the Mara identity consciousness and serves as the locus of identity assertion. In Lawngtlai, the assertion of identity is based more on 'tribe' and not necessarily on language. Various sub-clans of the Lais are spread throughout Mizoram, including Manipur, and most have accepted Mizo as their preferred self-identification (see also J. Pachuau 2014: 155–156). Yet in Lawngtlai the Lai identity is strongly asserted against not only the perceived Lusei-centric Mizo but also the Mara and other tribal identities.

With the Mizo Hills elevated to a UT status, the central state was able to directly monitor the political developments more closely. The general feeling was that the armed struggle was coming to an end with the dwindling support and the demoralized armies. This perception was shattered when a group of Mizo soldiers struck at the heart of Aizawl, killing the deputy inspector general, the superintendent of police, and the inspector general in broad daylight. Once again the government of India resorted to a counter-insurgency drive, employing targeted manhunts and tactical search operations; a police officer was also appointed as the chief secretary of the UT (Nag 2002: 262). This strike took place against the backdrop of multiple failures of dialogue between the government and Laldenga, who, from the early 1970s, was beginning to shift towards negotiation. Like before, the armies refused to give up the struggle for *zalenna*, and the chief of the army, Biakchhunga, remained adamant in his position.

The persistence of the movement requires a close understanding of the MNF ideology. The armies' commitment and leaders were shaped by the ideology that placed the idea of *ram leh hnam* at the forefront of the struggle. Furthermore, the sacrifice was for *pathian leh kan ram tan* (for god and our country); hence, protecting the *ram* meant protecting the religion. The Mizos were not merely 'Mizo' but 'Mizo Kristian' (Christian) (J. Pachuau 2014), which was an indelible part of the consciousness as a *hnam*. The position of the church, however, remained ambivalent about the movement's objective as the church condemned the use of violence. In the early years of the movement, the relationship between the MNF and the church was under severe strain. While the church condemned the MNF's use of violence, the MNF's position was that the violence was a justifiable means for protecting and safeguarding the religion.

However, the central role of Christianity in the struggle was evident in the way in which the MNF, even in its camps, constructed churches and conducted worship services whenever and wherever possible. It established a separate department known as the Mizoram Evangelical Activity (MEC) to look into worship affairs in the camps and among the members, both in the army and civil wings. Freeing Mizoram therefore implied freedom from what they considered Hindu domination. The Mizos were wary of their right to be Christians in a Hindu-dominated country, and this was compounded by the aversion of the Indian nationalist leaders, including Gandhi, to Christian missions and their activities among the marginalized communities—Dalits and tribals, in particular (J. Pachuau 2014: 160). Laldenga, known for his oratorical skills, in one of his speeches, was noted as saying, 'The time will come when Mizo will be made to worship Krishna in place of *Krista* [Jesus in Mizo]' (Hermana 2015: 20).

Religion indisputably has been part of the nationalist thinking in India. Bose (2017) offers a nuanced analysis of how religion has shaped the understanding of nationhood in India. More importantly, Bose contends that the mistrust of religion by secular intellectuals had given space for majoritarian extremists to further exclusive nationalism. For a long time, in the northeast, Christianity and Christian missions were suspected of instigating secessionist movements in the region. L. Pachuau (1997) cautions against such assumptions and misconceptions by calling for the need to understand why communities such as the Mizos demanded independence. Ethno-national movements by communities such as the Mizos, he argues, represented the challenge against an integration policy that tried to erase and erode their 'differences' (L. Pachuau 1997: 766). As was noted, the Mizos' struggle for *zalenna* was construed as a movement to protect against religious domination.

For many of the leaders and armies, the struggle was not about economic or political interests but a sacrifice for *ram leh hnam*. This was a part of the movement's ideology into which they were indoctrinated. It explains the armies' resilience and readiness to carry forward the struggle and sacrifice for Zoram *zalenna*. Differences over the future of the movement resulted in defection and surrender, which weakened the movement considerably. One was the mass surrender led by Gangte and Biakchhunga in 1977 and 1979, respectively.[28] Even as a power struggle emerged within the movement, Dozinga expressed his feelings in song:

Aw kan Zoram nuam suihlung phang lo la,
Thlang kawrvai bawih atan ka phallo che;
Chung Pathian ruatsa I zalenna tur,
Theihtawpin kan bei zel ang. (C. Zama 2005)

Our beautiful Zoram, may you not worry,
I can't allow you to be subservient to the Vais,
I will strive till the end of your freedom,
Your right divinely ordained.

The armed struggle was also one for survival for the leaders and the armies alike. With limited food supplies and other resources, they recounted how it was very common to go without food for days and weeks. A female rebel narrates:

Our sacrifice was so high. However, we never considered it as difficult. During the movement, surviving one week without food was nothing. The longest one I can remember was when we did not eat food for more than a month almost. We counted till 56 meals. We did not bother to count the rest.[29]

By the 1980s, the MNF leaders forwarded the case for a peaceful resolution through dialogue. Laldenga, along with leaders like Tawnluia and Zoramthanga, was at the forefront of the initiative. Yet there were numerous twists and turns with the agenda for negotiation and dialogue up to signing the Mizo Accord in 1986 between the government of India and the MNF. The peace process was evidence of how it was influenced by political interests beyond the mere restoration of 'normalcy' or 'order'. In other words, there were certain factors of interest and varied agendas that were at work in the peace process or in the making and un-making of peace in Mizoram (discussed in detail in Chapter 5). In 1986, after many trials and tribulations, the Mizo Accord was signed with the MNF armies bidding a 'farewell to arms'.

Conclusion

The chapter demonstrates the effect of vernacular expressions such as *zalenna*, *ram leh hnam*, and *pathian leh kan ram tan* as a pivot in the imaginings of Mizo nationhood and struggle. From 1960 onwards, *hnam hla* emerged as a popular genre, capitalized by the MNF's nationalist mobilizations. Songwriters such as Rokunga and Laltanpuia began to conceive their idea of Mizo *hnam* in tune with the politics that swept the Mizo Hills during those periods. As can be seen, the MNF was able to garner support with songs and diffuse and disseminate nationalist ideas. Notably, the reframing and reworking of nationalist expressions in the local idioms made it effective. The writings of the movement leaders like Laldenga, Zoramthanga, and Lalhmingthanga were examples of this. More than their circulation was the way in which *zalenna* became the core of their thinking and the ideological backbone of the struggle.

The relevance of songs continued to be understudied in research related to politics among the Mizos. Whereas colonial rule introduced the print culture, it is my contention that songs, to the Mizos, continued to appeal and remain a potent force to articulate political aspirations and express dissent and resentment. This is rooted in the Mizo past as well, where songs were used to express pride and love, defame an enemy, contest power, and articulate desires. Even as new technologies are adopted, the basic essence of songs and their cultural meaning in Mizo sociopolitical life continue to remain firm, even today. In the period of heightened counter-insurgency, it was through songs that the Mizos expressed their anguish and sufferings. In the following chapter, I will look at how songs contest the official histories and discourse of counter-insurgency, and, as such, even if they denoted the experience of hardship, they remained a valuable source to put the public voice in the narrative to understand the lives of those under terror and violence.

Notes

1   Established in 1935, the YMA is the largest and most widely accepted non-governmental organization (NGO) of the Mizo people. Headquartered in Aizawl, Mizoram, the organization has the largest number of members among Mizo NGOs and acts as a network among the Mizos from the village to the state levels. It has become central to Mizo public lives in shaping and nurturing community bonds.

2   *Mautam* is a naturally occurring famine that is caused by the flowering of a specific type of bamboo scientifically known as *Melocanna baccifera*. It flowers periodically with a cycle of 50 years, and the bamboo fruits, rich in proteins, stimulate an abnormal increase in the rat population. Such forms of famine are widespread throughout South Asia and South-East Asia.

3   'Zoram' is used interchangeably to denote the present-day territory of Mizoram or the territories inhabited by the Mizos that encompass territories inclusive of Mizo-inhabited areas in Bangladesh and Myanmar.

4   Even as language movements did offset the emergence of new states, various other factors were at play in the creation of new states such as in Punjab and Haryana in 1966 where religion and language were pivotal, whereas it was ethnicity that was the basis of creating a separate state of Nagaland in 1963.

5   The first office bearers of the organization were Lalmawia (secretary), Daha (vice-secretary), C. Rokhuma (organizing secretary and founder), Lalbiaka (assistant secretary), Pachhunga (treasurer), and Lalsiama (financial secretary).

6   Interview with a former MNF leader, 7 March 2015.

7   The name of the narrator has been changed.

8   Interview with a former rebel, 18 March 2015.

9   See MNF Document II, Mizoram State Archives (MSA), Aizawl. There are different formats with regard to the oath of allegiance. For instance, see Zamawia (2012: 238).

10   Interview with a former rebel, 25 March 2015.

11   Interview with a former female member of the MNA, 23 March 2015.

12   *Hnam sipai* is a term used to refer to the MNF armies.

13   Of the 128 songs Rokunga composed, 14 are what came to be known as *hnam hla*.

14   Mizos highly uphold these social values. *Tlawmngaihna* has no exact translation; its closest meanings are altruism, chivalry, and selfless sacrifice. *Thian chhan thih ngam* means ready to put one's life at risk for others. *Nula tlangval inlawm* is mostly practised in times of cultivation where men and women would support each other in the fields on a rotational basis.

15   Translated by Mafaa Haunhnar.

16   Translated by Mafaa Haunhnar.

17   Rokunga was awarded the title of 'Mizo Poet of the Century' in 2001. A separate society known as the Rokunga Memorial Society was established to commemorate and recognize his work and contribution in the year 1999. The society constitutes an award in his name known as the Rokunga Award, which is awarded to individuals with outstanding achievements.

18   The lyrics have been cross-checked against and collated from Mizolyrics.com, https://mizolyrics.com/lyrics/inpui/view/3:1605:kan-zotlang-ram-nuam (accessed in August 2018).

19   According to the myth of origin, the Mizos, along with their cognate tribes, emerged into this world from a cave or a rock called Chhin-lung. This theory of origin continued to resonate in the tales and songs of the Mizos and is the most widely accepted, if not popular, myth of origin. As such, embracing Chhinlung *chhuak* involves constructing a pan-Mizo identity that cuts across borders and boundaries.

20   Synod belongs to the Presbyterian Church, which has the largest number of church members in Mizoram. It is also the first church in Mizoram with a Mizoram Synod as the administrative body of the church headquartered at Aizawl.

21   The other major church denominations are Roman Catholic, Baptist, Salvation Army, and Pentecostal. There are also a few other groups that are outside of these denominations, such as the Pu Ziona Pawl, Pu Biaknunga Pawl, Judaism followers, and so on.

22   After the death of Laldenga in 1990, Zoramthanga took over as president of the MNF, a post which he still holds at the time of writing this. Also, he held the vice-president's post in the underground government in the later years of the movement. Hence, he continues to remain a prominent face of the MNF.

23   *Saphun* is a practice whereby a clan or a tribe adopts another clan or tribe following certain traditional rites.

24   Many of the former leaders and armies of the movement have used *zalenna* in writing about the movement. For examples, Lalrawnliana (1995) and Zamawia (2012).

25   Volunteers of the MNF made guns using wood for military-training purposes.

26   The Jampui Hills comprise 10 villages that are predominantly inhabited by the Mizos. These villages are Phuldungsei, Sabual, Tlangsang, Behliangchhip, Vanghmun, Hmawngchuan, Bangla Zion, Tlaksih, Hmunpui, and Vaisam.

27   Siaha is a district in Mizoram and is located in the southern part of the state.

28   See Nibedon (1980: appendix II) for the details on the surrenders.

29   Interview with a former rebel, 23 March 2015.

5 Violence, Counter-Insurgency, and the Transcript of Resistance

'Successful re-grouping of Mizo villagers, a tribute to the Army,' noted the *Times of India* in its report on village groupings in 1967. The backdrop of this report was the village groupings undertaken in the Mizo Hills as a part of India's counter-insurgency strategy. The grouping was undertaken under Rule 57 of the Defence of India (DoI) Rules, 1962,[1] in the Mizo Hills. The application of the DoI Rules implied the suspension of fundamental rights that further allowed the state to hold any person without explanation. As the rule goes, it was meant to be used against enemy states or threats of external aggression.[2] Implemented in four phases, the grouped villages covered the major parts of the Mizo Hills, except the southern district formerly known as the Chhimtuipui district.[3] The imposition of the DoI Rules also meant that the military was given inordinate powers to undertake counter-insurgency operations.

Village groupings refer to the forcible relocation of the population into larger villages. When used in the case of counter-insurgency, the objective is to isolate civilian populations from the rebels and undertake developmental activities. The *Times of India* report on village groupings (1967) demonstrates this fact when it noted, 'Hundreds of able-bodied Mizos have been employed in road-building. Other avenues of employment are also being found for artisans. Agriculturists are being given the wherewithal to adopt improved practices for raising good crops.' It continued, 'With better economic opportunities and perhaps better water-supply arrangements, the new villages bid fair to prosper in the years to come.'

The use of village groupings as a counter-insurgency strategy has a deeper history and legacy. Inspired by the colonial mode of control, its utility was behind its prominence in counter-insurgency policy, particularly in the post-World War II period. In the global discourse of counter-insurgency, village groupings are mostly referred to as 'camps', and wherever they were implemented, they remade societies and transformed them. More than an 'exception', village groupings were a common and normalized practice in counter-insurgency measures, whereby states continued to confine and incarcerate 'undesirable' populations. Furthermore, its widespread practice across the globe has made it widely popular—ranging from the 'new villages' in Malaya (Hack 2012), the 'strategic hamlets' in the Vietnam War (Cullather 2006), and 'villagization' in Kenya (Whittaker 2012) to 'development poles' in Guatemala (Grandia 2013), 'village evacuation' in Turkey (Jongerden 2010), and 'village grouping' in India (Nunthara 1989). Further, states deploy humanitarian logic to such practices, legitimating other violent acts involving the burning of houses, rice barns, villages, and material assets.

India's peripheral regions such as northeast India and Jammu and Kashmir are marked by a long history of violent counter-insurgency. In fact, it is widely known that violence has been part of the governmentality of the states in such regions (Aggarwal and Bhan 2009; Baruah 2009; Mathur 2012; Deka 2019). It deploys the language of sovereignty as the ultimate justification for its use of force—in other words, in the name of 'national security' (Duschinski 2009: 695). The history of violence is closely associated with nation-building in India, as is evident from the violence against marginalized communities (Butalia 1998; Pandey 2001; Talbot and Singh 2009; Daiya 2011) in the aftermath of the partition. The story of citizens' lives in newly independent states is enmeshed in violence and is integral to the making of the nation (V. Das 2007: 2). Such stories of violence continue to be part of everyday lives in many regions such as Jammu and Kashmir and various states in the northeast that have witnessed counter-insurgency and military occupation (Visweswaran 2013; Sundar and Sundar 2014; Duschinski et al. 2018; Baruah 2020).

Counter-insurgency violence remains an important hallmark of the state in northeast India. A peculiar feature of counter-insurgency violence is that it is legalized violence. This legalization of violence is made possible with the extension of various emergency laws such as the AFSPA.[4] Laws such as the AFSPA produce a regime that renders the population as disposable as they are killable on mere suspicion. The political order in northeast India makes clear that violence continues to shape the everyday life of the people in the region (Kikon 2009; Lokaneeta 2017). Furthermore, the development policies reflect a garrison mentality framed within the logic of securitizing the region from both 'internal' and 'external' threats. This has created a regime of terror marked by impunity and everyday militarization (Mathur 2012). For more than six decades, the imposition of the AFSPA has made the region a 'permanent exception' (Samaddar 2006) mapped into the vocabulary of the state as a 'sensitive space' (Cons 2016).

Numerous scholars have pointed out how violence was a part of the governmentality of the Indian state with regard to the northeast (Baruah 2005; Kshetrimayum 2009; McDuie-Ra 2009). In conflict regions, the logic of nation-making takes a different form, structured around a civil–military nexus with the purpose of integrating the said regions through counter-insurgency efforts. The period of village groupings marks an important event in Mizo history, for there was a combination of both incessant use of violence and force, on the one hand, and massive surveillance of the people, on the other. Violence became 'routinized' (Pandey 2006: 1) and 'ordinary' (V. Das 2007: 7) that expanded the power of the state to regulate and manage the grouped populations. More recent studies on violence moved beyond the state-centric narratives and counter-insurgency by retrieving voices suppressed by official and dominant discourses. One strand of studies looks at oral testimonies to retrieve voices of the ordinary and marginalized communities (Butalia 1998; V. Das 2007; Saikia 2011). The other strand examines the poetry of resistance in situations of violent repression by the state. During the National Emergency of 1975, poems of resistance with their anti-state content challenged the state's repression of freedom and rights of the people (Perry 1983). In conflict regions such as Jammu and Kashmir, poetry continues to serve as an important weapon of resistance against the state (Kak 2011; Kaul 2017).

Such studies centred their focus on the voices of those who are survivors and witnesses of violence. What can be gleaned from them is how the 'oral' served as an important source to retrieve the voice that is invisibilized and suppressed by official and public discourse. The value of oral testimonies lies in the fact that they are direct and personal narratives of accounts of both perpetrators and victims of violence. While the state has been successful in terms of enforcing its rule through punitive measures and the violent suppression of human rights, marginalized communities resort to overt and covert practices to subvert state control. In Mizoram, a new genre of songs known as *rambuai hla* (songs of troubled times) emerged during the time as a way to record life under siege. *Rambuai hla* grew out of this specific experience of violence. The *hla* are significant for understanding how the culture of orality survived and sustained itself even in times of heightened violence and terror. It is the *rambuai hla* that offer the possibility to locate the voice of the people who underwent the grouping.

Further, *rambuai hla* denote what Vizenor (1999) refers to as 'survivance' in the context of Native Americans' history of violent experience and dispossession. The idea of survivance, as Vizenor (1999: iv) notes, 'is an active sense of presence, the continuance of native stories, not a mere reaction or a survivable name. Native survivance stories are renunciations of dominance, tragedy and victory.' Survivance activates the forms of resistance to erasure and makes indigenous people's voices visible in ways counter to dominant cultural narratives. Vizenor's analysis (1999, 2008) underscores Native Americans not as victims or passive recipients of colonial violence and historical traumas but as actively engaged in resistance, demonstrating their resilience throughout history. In this way, *rambuai hla* denote an act of 'survivance' that shows the resilience of the Mizo public against violence and terror rather than portraying them as mere 'silent sufferers' (V. Das 1997). As such, *rambuai hla* are examined in this chapter not only to retrieve the voice of the people but also to refocus our attention on the consequence of counter-insurgency violence. Since the implementation of grouping, the state created a discourse of a successful counter-insurgency strategy around village groupings in official reports and through the media. There was deafening silence on the sufferings of the people and the violence that accompanied the process of conducting village groupings. The grouped populations were relegated as mere silent sufferers. Therefore, this chapter is concerned with how the Mizos lived and survived under such adverse violent conditions—a life that many continue to live in northeast India.

In this way, *rambuai hla* tell the story of the human consequence of lives under violence. They are neither anti-state nor overtly rebellious in content and nature. Rather, *rambuai hla* unravel the wholesale violence and the regime of terror, the dislocation and disruption, the loss and longings, and how the Mizos understand their own condition and speak in their own terms. Beyond this, since the *rambuai hla* are composed in the vernacular, they evaded state censorship even as they were in wide circulation within the grouped centres. Read this way, *rambuai hla* are personal accounts of those who witnessed the violence that unfolded and its consequences on those affected by it. The oral expression became indispensable, where *rambuai hla* became the Mizos' sole medium to express—a testimony of their lives during village groupings.

Counter-Insurgency and the Nation-State

In 1967, the Counter-Insurgency Jungle Warfare (CIJW) was established to deal with the mounting challenges of insurgency in the northeast. It was first established in Shillong and later shifted to Vairengte in the Kolasib district of Mizoram in 1970. Realizing the rugged terrain and the unconventional warfare needed to tackle the insurgency, the CIJW's objective was to train and equip soldiers to 'fight like guerrillas'. The training at the institute included courses in the local languages and adapting to the terrain in order to acculturate the military to the local culture and place (cited in N. Goswami 2009: 76). Over the years, the CIJW has earned a reputation as one of the premier institutions worldwide for hosting various armed forces and conducting military drills with armies from around the world.

A conventional understanding of India's counter-insurgency strategy will lead one to observe that it is guided by the principle that recognizes the involvement of fighting fellow Indians and the avoidance of indiscriminate use of force (Rajagopalan 2000; Ladwig 2009). N. Goswami (2009) advances a similar argument by conceptualizing India's counter-insurgency strategy as one of 'trust and nurture' based on 'a democratic political culture, measured military methods, special counter-insurgency forces, local social and cultural awareness and an integrative nation-building approach' (N. Goswami 2009: 70). Counter-insurgency manuals are not static doctrines, and they are common in countries with a long history of engaging in this strategy. The United States and Britain are known for adapting to changing political circumstances. The strategy of taking a population-centric approach or using less coercive methods is credited to the British model of counter-insurgency in Malaya, which emphasized the use of 'minimum force' with a goal to 'win the hearts and minds' of the people (Dixon 2009: 354). India is known to draw much of its counter-insurgency doctrine from the manuals of other countries.

India's northeast has been a 'laboratory of counter-insurgency' (Khalili 2010). In the eyes of the state, the northeast region has become synonymous with violence, a 'troubled periphery' (Bhaumik 2009). Since independence, the Indian state legitimated the creation of political order, what Pearce (2010) refers to as 'securitized democracy'. In securitized democracies, there is a proliferation of violence alongside democratic transitions. As Pearce (2010) notes, democracy is increasingly subject to the fears and insecurities of the population, enabling the state to build its authority not on the protection of citizens' rights but on its armed encounters and insidious collusions with violent actors in the name of 'security provision'. In northeast India, this securitized democracy comes into existence in the form of various emergency laws, such as the AFSPA, which remain in force in a large part of the region. The AFSPA enabled a regime of rule to provide unrestrained power to the military and a right to kill on mere suspicion. Militarization and security-centric policies continue to guide policies concerning the northeast region (McDuie-Ra 2008).

Emergency laws such as the AFSPA remain key instruments of violence and counter-insurgency policy in northeast India. What the law does is that it implants a model of governance that integrates both civil and military rule, generating a securitizing logic of governance. In fact, what laws such as AFSPA do is not merely create a regime of militarized rule but also create distinct internal space within the nation. As Vajpeyi (2009) puts it, such laws

> effectively create a space within India, a sort of second and shadow nation, that functions as a military state rather than an electoral democracy, and only remains hidden because it is not, at least so far, officially ruled by a general or dictator who presents any sort of overt challenge to the authority of the elected prime minister or chief ministers of different states, including those of the Northeast.

She further notes that this creates two distinct and mutually opposed regimes, a democracy and non-democracy, and two nations, India and not-India (Vajpeyi 2009: 36). Read this way, the northeastern region is outside the realm of national life with a population who are undeserving of the democratic rights offered by the Constitution of India.

Today, India's northeast remains one of the most militarized regions in the world. The story of the militarization of the northeast is connected with the story of counter-insurgency operations in the region. One can recall the counter-insurgency operations that were undertaken in the Naga-inhabited areas, the Mizo-inhabited areas in the early 1950s and the 1960s, and then in Assam and other parts of the region from the 1980s. The intensity of violence differs across states, but the counter-insurgency operations involve the use of brute force, enhanced surveillance, and militarization. Arrest, torture, and disappearance are common and pervade the social existence of the people. Counter-insurgency policy in such a situation entails not merely targeting the insurgent groups but also controlling and regulating the everyday life of the people. This takes place through the installation of check posts, imposition of curfews, regular patrolling, and frisking and searching of vehicles. This everyday militarization of lives becomes deeply entrenched in the people's psyche that produces real social suffering but remains obscured and rendered through the popular rhetoric of protecting national security, promoting national interests, and maintaining law and order (Duschinski 2009).

If the initial impetus of counter-insurgency was to quell the rebellion with brute force, it gradually shifted towards 'winning the hearts and minds', a now popular doctrine of counter-insurgency. Often labelled as the 'carrot and stick policy', there was what Asad (2007: 3) calls a 'combination of cruelty and compassion' when the state engaged in counter-insurgency. This follows the shift of strategies within counter-insurgency by states from the use of force to a focus on 'winning the hearts and minds' of the people. This policy entails adopting multiple strategies in insurgency-affected areas from Jammu and Kashmir, areas affected by left-wing extremism, and the northeastern region. In Kashmir, for instance, Operation Sadbhavana was a counter-insurgency strategy aimed at using developmental efforts. By opening schools and clinics and undertaking infrastructure development, the goal was to attract the civilian population towards the state—that is, the military—in order to transform an 'alienated relationship into one of mutual cooperation and trust' (Aggarwal and Bhan 2009: 527). The thrust of Operation Sadbhavana was what is known as 'perception management' as a counter-insurgency strategy to create a new image—a friendly one of the militaries and, thereby, the state. This shift can be read against an attempt to erase the history of past violence as well as to create a new image of the 'military', which has a long history of engaging in counter-insurgency violence.

In more contemporary times, we witness a different but new strategy crafted to 'Indianize' the minds of the newer generations. This follows the assumption that the geographical isolation of the people has caused alienation from other parts of the country. However, today, national exclusion in the form of racism and the racialization of northeastern bodies are perpetuated in metropolitan centres, where they live among 'mainland Indians' (McDuie-Ra 2012; Gergan and Smith 2021: 365). The exposure tours for students belonging to Kashmir and northeast India sought to achieve this objective. Through the tours, the students were exposed to the rich cultural heritage of India. One of these was the National Integration Tour specially designed for the youths of Jammu and Kashmir and the northeastern region. In the case of Mizoram, 18 students were selected to be part of the National Integration Tour in January 2018 under the aegis of the Assam Rifles (AR), with the students visiting various places of historical importance such as the Lal Qila (Red Fort), Jama Masjid, Parliament House, Connaught Place, Qutub Minar, and the Delhi Metro. The integrationist agenda and the purpose of initiating it demonstrated the political intent of military involvement.

Of course, the counter-insurgency experience has become varied over time, and over the years the state has also adopted new measures and strategies in Mizoram and elsewhere in the country. How far such policies succeed in their agenda remains to be seen. However, by and large, what is etched in the memory of the people is the violent history of subordination and militarization that affected their lives and history. For instance, in the heyday of counter-insurgency in the Mizo Hills, it was not direct violence or physical torture that was the only mode of violence. Rather, the intimate nature of the violence was more palpable and remembered, which, although less visible, was more humiliating. In other words, it was the perpetuation of violence with the intention to desecrate and dehumanize. Therefore, to describe the objective of counter-insurgency as mere tactics for controlling the civilian population and to equate this with minimum use of force ignores and negates the consequence of violence in the lives of the people. In the section that follows, I attempt to examine the different levels of violence and their extremeness, the military excesses and impunity, and how the Indian state, including the MNF, was engaged in perpetuating a regime of violence to control, impose, and contest rule.

Counter-Insurgency: Repression and Violence

Aerial Attack

I spent the month of September 2017 in the Mizoram State Archives (MSA), laboriously reading the archival collections. My regularity in the archives made me develop a cordial relationship with the staff, with whom I shared stories of my field visits across Mizoram. It was during one of these conversations that one member of the staff explained how he had witnessed the aerial attack on Aizawl as a young child. He narrated how his and fellow villagers' families left their homes and witnessed Aizawl being strafed by the jet fighters of the Indian Air Force. As I listened on, I told him that younger generations had been questioning whether or not the bombing had really taken place. He responded assertively that he was a living witness to the aerial bombing. This narrative of the air bombing resurfaced, but this time in a rather different setting; it was at my grandfather's funeral after he had passed away in January 2018. As we were waiting for the body to arrive from Imphal, the state capital of Manipur, the elders present recalled their childhood, and it was a usual *titi*. The period of the *buai* (troubled) years became the subject of the *titi* when one of my uncles said that he and his family had migrated to Manipur as their entire villages were burned down as a result of the jet fighter attacks and bombings. His narrative was a mix of their suffering and struggle to escape the bombing as they had to walk by foot to Manipur to escape the violence. It was a similar experience of *hrehawm* (a very difficult period), as J. Pachuau's (2014: 130) research participants of the *buai* years recorded.

From 5 March 1966, jet fighters flew over the Mizo Hills, strafing the towns and villages for three consecutive days. Dismayed by this response, J. J. Nichols Roy, a prominent politician from Meghalaya, asked Indira Gandhi, the then prime minister, who replied that 'they were dropping rations for the security'. There has been denial about the use of aerial attacks in the Mizo Hills, and this has gradually seeped into the consciousness of most Mizos today. From 5 to 8 March 1966, planes repeatedly flew over the hills, and after circling the hills for a while, the raids ensued in Aizawl and other parts of the Mizo Hills, covering areas such as Tlabung, Lunglei, Champhai, and Kolasib. Like my uncle, many Mizos fled to neighbouring Manipur and Burma; many settled there, never to return.

The aerial attack succeeded in its objective to flush out the MNF rebels and make way for the security reinforcements. Aizawl, the capital of Mizoram, was vacated as inhabitants fled to jungles or migrated to escape the attack. It was only after the arrival of the military reinforcement on 6 March 1966 that an announcement was made on All India Radio (AIR), requesting the people to return (Lalthangliana 2015: 97). Memories of the aerial attacks are scattered, and it was only recently that they have gradually emerged in public discussion. On the one hand, this was a response due to the continuing denial of the act by the Indian state; on the other hand, a feeling of injustice continues to remain strong among the Mizos for being the only community in India upon whom a democratic government has ever used the air force. Writers and journalists have begun to document first-hand accounts of the experience, such as J. V. Hluna's *Zawlkhawpui Senmei Chan Ni* (The Day Aizawl Was in Flames) (2008), C. Zama's *The Untold Atrocity* (2014), and various other personal narratives. Since 2008, the Mizo student body, the MZP, has observed 5 March every year as Zoram Ni (Zoram Day) as a day to mark the bombing of Aizawl.

Village Groupings

The idea of implementing village groupings was discussed as early as October 1966 in a report sent to the army headquarters when Sam Manekshaw, of the Eastern Command, recommended an extensive grouping covering a large area or all of the population for an effective counter-insurgency strategy (Jafa 1999). Village groupings therefore were to be introduced along the lines of spatializing the population into large, grouped centres by isolating them from the MNF rebels while at the same time putting them under easy surveillance and control. The official plan of implementing the policy was announced on the evening of 3 January 1967 by AIR (Jafa 1999). The MNF rebels then shifted their base to the CHTs of East Pakistan (now Bangladesh).

The justification of its introduction was carefully framed within the humanitarian logic of progress and order, a 'discourse of humanitarian intent' in the words of Khalili (2013: 4). Village groupings effectively combined the objective of security and development. The military worked with the civil administration to provide civic and welfare services as a countermeasure to end people's grievances and support the insurgent groups. A development-oriented counter-insurgency policy becomes pertinent, where the military and the state wanted to remake their image and establish trust and cooperation from the people. Bhan (2013), in the context of Kargil in Jammu and Kashmir, noted that the state had utilized humanitarian logic, *aman* (peace), and *insaniyat* (humanism) to exert control over its troubled frontiers and secure the loyalties of the 'alienated hearts'. She further writes that the state reinvented itself through its practices of counter-insurgency by rebuilding its authority and legitimacy. As with the village groupings in the Mizo Hills, this was conceived as having development goals, an objective that tried to accelerate the progress of developmental works and programmes which, hitherto, were impossible due to the scattered nature of the Mizo settlements (Nunthara 1989).

In the Mizo Hills, the grouping was implemented systematically in four phases. The first phase of the grouping was known as the Protected and Progressive Villages (PPVs), which was undertaken along the Silchar–Kolasib–Aizawl–Serchhip–Lunglei Road. Under the scheme, an estimated 52,210 of the population were grouped together during the period between 4 January and 23 February 1967. For the later phases, the DoI Rules were found to be weak, and so a new ordinance known as the Assam Maintenance of Public Order (AMPO), 1968, was passed by the Assam cabinet. This was used as the legal basis for the continued grouping of the villages by force, in preference to the application of the DoI Rules. The second phase, called the New Grouping Centres (NGCs), affected 97,339 of the population; and the third phase, Voluntary Grouping Centres (VGCs), was applied to another estimated 47,156 of the population. The fourth phase, the Extended Loop Areas (ELAs), included another 34,210 persons (Nunthara 1989: 5–6).

It was the scale of the grouping that made the village groupings so central when it came to counter-insurgency in the Mizo Hills. By the time the fourth phase was completed, close to 90 per cent of the entire population of the Mizo Hills had been affected by the village groupings (Nunthara 1989: 7). When one travels around Mizoram today, every village in the Mizo Hills has a story to tell, and when asked about it, the common response is, 'Kan khua hi a tuar nasa ber kan ni ang' (Our village is the worst affected of the grouping scheme). What runs through the narratives of the people's memory of the grouping is the hidden suffering and memory of life under siege (Figure 5.1).

Grouped centres were a 'wartime confinement' (Khalili 2013: 3). It incarcerated the grouped populations as prisoners of the state, characterized by a system of

Evils like drinking, gambling and petty crime took root. People became very lazy. Neighbours became strangers.

—Ralliana *and his father*
Selchhunga, *Saitual, Mizoram*

Figure 5.1   A family in a grouping centre, Saitual, Mizoram, 1970–1980
Source: India Today, 1982.

surveillance. In other words, village groupings were marked by un-freedom and control. The grouping centres conformed to the prison aesthetic commonly described in the context of camps, including watchtowers, barracks, and barbed-wire perimeters. Each grouping centre was an enclosed space and encircled by the use of bamboo spikes with only one or two entry and exit points. Each centre was manned by security officials who controlled the movement of the grouped populations. Everyone within the centre was then issued an identity card (ID) with a pass required for any kind of movement. On the economic front, this made visiting one's *jhum*[5] lands very difficult, resulting in a sharp decline in food production and hence causing starvation and hunger (Nunthara 1989: 1237–1240). The restriction of movement required the routine checking and frisking of bodies, male and female. As some women narrated, 'the *vai sipai*[6] does not care even if you are old'. Others said, 'the prettier you were, the higher the risk of being raped. So we messed up our hair and rubbed charcoal dust on our face and tried to look as shabby as possible'

(Sundar 2011: 54). The body became the site for exerting sovereign control over the population and was routinely violated through an exercise of authority.

House searches and body frisking were used insidiously to hunt for 'MNF volunteers'.[7] Many women were left alone at home because the male members were either held in captivity or directly involved in the movement. In recounting her experience, the wife of the village council president (VCP) in Serchhip town narrated how the security forces, under the pretence of a house search, would barge into their house while her husband was in hiding. She notes, 'My daughters were already in their teens and I knew that they were to violate them, which I was determined not to let happen.' Often many VCPs encountered this difficult situation when commanders or captains demanded women. And sometimes some women gave in to the wishes of the security officers for the safety of fellow villagers or to prevent their village from being burned. As Sundar (2011: 54) reports, 'We could hear the wailing of woman all night long.'

One of the central features of the village groupings was violence. Camps were known for the impunity and punishment and the brutality and terror with which they were imposed. The process of undertaking village groupings involved the burning of villages, the destruction of property and farms, and the killing of livestock. Villagers were herded into specifically identified group centres strategically located near the highway for easy access. In the process, they watched their old village burnt down and left deserted. Within the grouped centres, there was an economic dependency on rations and other supplies. Village groupings as a counter-insurgency strategy 'continually slipped between exemplary or performative forms of violence meant to intimidate, and the more "humane" and developmental warfare intended to persuade' (Khalili 2013: 3).

Each village had an appointed leader who was usually a schoolteacher, a church leader, or the VCP. The leader was commonly summoned and harassed and bore the brunt of violence to ensure the safety of the villagers. As one villager recounts, 'Khang hunlai a VCP kha chu thil nih chakawm lo ber ani' (Being a VCP was one of the most undesirable things during those days). In recounting his experience, Pu Siamhlira, the VCP in Serchhip, recounted how he and other village leaders had greeted the security forces with a white flag[8] as a sign of peace and friendliness. A village elder from Sialsuk recalled this and said, 'Ram a'n buai tak tak chuan flag varte kha kan hmang rimin, a lo tangkai khawp mai' (With the outbreak of the movement, the white flags became very common and they proved to be truly helpful) (Thankima 2014: 4).

Surveillance and suspicion created a psyche of fear, forcing the people to submit and express their loyalty to the nation-state. Rape, torture, and detention were routine, and so was physical exploitation in the form of *puakphurh*,[9] which reminded people of the servitude acts that the Mizos experienced during colonial rule—how they were coerced into carrying loads of the colonial armies, and now it was those of the Indian security forces. These forms of physical coercion were undertaken without much complaint, and their intensity was described by what the common public sardonically called the 'nghawngkawl[10] battalion'. The use of the common people to carry loads meant that these people also served as human shields. With the MNF employing a hit-and-run tactic, the civilians were useful against any such inevitable ambushes.

Village groupings affected all aspects of Mizo social life. The security forces restricted many community practices such as burying the dead, visiting the sick, and church services. For example, it was common to recover the male and female bodies killed either by the security forces or by the MNF soldiers. However, confrontations often ensued when security personnel would not allow the collection of dead bodies or the conducting of the customary rites of burial. Many Mizos died as what is called *arte thih*.[11] The collective existence of the community was reduced to what Agamben (2005: 87) refers to as 'bare life'. The grouping did not merely uproot them from their homes but also dispossessed them of their 'being', which 'constituted a form of suffering for those displaced and colonized' (Butler and Athanasiou 2013; ix). The moral order and fabric of the Mizo society were trampled due to military excesses and violence. As Desjarlais and Kleinman (1994: 10) observe, 'a prolonged intensity of non-repressive violence often leads to a loss of moral bearings at a societal level to such an extent that the society risks losing its very culture'.

Life under Siege: Suspicion and Surveillance in Grouped Villages

It is instructive to think of the grouped centres using Agamben's (2005) idea of the 'state of exception'. The fecundity with which states, totalitarian and democratic, have acted to produce this exception is what Agamben (2005: 2) observes as a 'voluntary creation' that remained an integral part of the state judiciary and politics, and hence the state's existence. What determined life under the grouped villages was how the Mizos had 'lost their legal identity' (Agamben 2005: 4), hence stripping them of their rights under normal civil law. Furthermore, in such spaces, the state utilized exceptional measures to perpetuate a regime of exception through the indiscriminate use of legal excesses to subdue the population. Therefore, what defined life in the grouped villages was the intrusive and intimate nature of control that determined its very 'exceptionalism'.

The case of the 'state of exception', Agamben (2005) shows, is well known through numerous historical examples such as that of the Jews' experience under the Nazi state. The MNF were quick to draw parallels between the two, and so they called the grouped centres 'concentration camps' (Lalrawnliana 1995: 12). Under these grouped villages, the Mizo civilians were kept as captives, both physically and mentally. The former involved controlling their mobility, while the latter was through the inculcation of fear by constant surveillance (Figure 5.2). Holding them captives demonstrated their living in a 'state of exception', where the people's rights were suspended and they were under permanent surveillance (McDuie-Ra 2009: 255).

Figure 5.2   Central Reserve Police Force (CRPF) men arresting a Mizo civilian for violating the curfew rule, 1979
Source: India Today, 1979.

Furthermore, what made this case of the 'state of exception' compelling was how the state constituted itself by institutionalizing its presence through the extension of its sovereign power. This dispersal of sovereign power is achieved through the state's creation of actors and agents to make itself omnipresent. In the grouped centres, the *kawktu* (pointer) served this purpose.

The use of *kawktu* was also one of the most important but unexplored aspects of the counter-insurgency tactics used in the Mizo Hills. The *kawktu* were used as informers whose identities were concealed. Their main task was to identify volunteers and anyone known to provide food or any other form of support to the MNF soldiers. The *kawktu* would inform the security forces about anyone they suspected among the relocated population in the grouped villages. When taken to *kawk* (point out) a suspect, their faces were covered with a cloth with holes for the eyes to keep their identities hidden (Hluna and Tochhawng 2012: 255). In this manner, they were taken around the grouped villages, and whoever they pointed their fingers at was understood to be a rebel or someone sympathetic to the movement. These people were then quickly disposed of (Chhangte 2011: 238). The *kawktu* therefore were greatly feared and, given that they lived among the people, they were considered the pawns of the *vai sipai*. The presence of the *kawktu* to the public meant that they were under constant watch, what Bentham (1995) described as a 'panoptic state'.

The case of the *kawktu* to many remains unresolved but shows the complicated realities of life under a 'state of exception'—unresolved because, to this day, many *kawktu* are still unknown, and complicated because they were often used to advance personal interests. Sainghinga Sailo, a VCP at the time, recalled in his account how the *kawktu* were misused and abused by the security officials and by some from among their own group (S. Sailo 2010). Given that the people lived under duress, it was easy for the security officials to lure them into becoming a *kawktu*. Under such circumstances, a very well-to-do person or a family was highly suspected of being a *kawktu* by the common public because *kawktu* were usually very well rewarded in cash and kind. Therefore, constant suspicion was what characterized everyday life. Furthermore, becoming a *kawktu* also provided an opportunity to avenge personal enmity. For all these reasons, the *kawktu* were a most feared group by the people, as they could identify anyone as a sympathizer or volunteer.

The use of *kawktu* embittered the MNF because being reported by them often led to the arrest of volunteers and soldiers, particularly those stationed within the Mizo Hills. A major under the MNF army whom I interviewed noted how he identified who was the *kawktu* who turned him in. However, without any grudge, he spoke about his life in jail after being arrested and how he rejoined the movement the very day he was released.[12] There were indeed some killings of *kawktu* suspected by the MNF as informers, and this sent the message that no individual would be spared if they were identified (Chhangte 2011: 238). Thus, in as much as becoming a *kawktu* could be used to advance one's personal interests, there was the reality that if anyone was reported as a *kawktu* to the MNF, it would also mean death. The brazen form in which death became easy, 'death certainty' in the words of Appadurai (1998: 245), was the norm within the grouped centres.

Everyday life at grouped centres was characterized by control and subjugation of the population through a perpetual state of terror. Such spaces were marked not by lawlessness but rather by the absence of normal civil and political rights and limits to the juridical order. This was where the state relinquished its obligation to protect or permit the rights of the people. The committing of acts of violence was made permissible by the mapping of the regions and the creation of zones of 'exception'. This became the way in which the sovereign power of the state was manifested in the marginal and borderland regions.

Loyalty in Times of Conflict

The term *dolung leh tuboh* (anvil and hammer) was commonly used to describe civilian life during the period. On one side was the MNF volunteer and armies, often living among the villagers; on the other hand, the security forces who suspected every Mizo as a sympathizer. Even as the security forces had the upper hand in controlling the civilian population, the MNF could undertake armed operations or execute what they called *dahthat*.[13] For the state, supporting the MNF in any way was considered tantamount to being a sympathizer and was seen as treacherous. At the time of the outbreak of the conflict, the chief minister of Assam, B. P. Chaliha, distributed pamphlets all across the Mizo Hills. While denouncing the MNF movement was the main intention, the message also explained why the Mizo public should refuse to support the MNF. A section in the pamphlet reads:

> The first and foremost task for the Government as well as for the people of Mizo District today, therefore, is to liquidate the armed gangs of the Mizo National Front for peace, progress, and prosperity of the people. The people of the Mizo district should refuse to lend any support to these gangs and should help the security forces in liquidating them.14

Notwithstanding the circumstances in which the civilians were put, the question of 'loyalty' was one of life and death (Figure 5.3). Betrayal, treason, and sedition

Figure 5.3   Public rally against the violence in Aizawl, 1980
Source: India Today, 1980.

were the charges levelled at anyone against the nation's cause. While the MNF and the security forces coerced the Mizo civilians to make hard choices, in reality the question of loyalty for them was an ambiguous one. Supporting and aiding the security forces or the MNF was not merely a question of loyalty or treason. 'Treason', Thirangama and Kelly (2010: 1) argue, is the 'grey zones' of political life and a 'product of often contradictory social and political obligations'. The MU leaders and their supporters, the *kawktu*, and the Special Force (SF),[15] all operated within their logic and circumstances, and so did the VCP and the public at large. Nevertheless, being loyal or disloyal caused many deaths as even mere suspicion also made someone liable for arrest or torture.

An order issued to the VCP on 3 March 1966 by the deputy commissioner of the Mizo Hills stated:

> Village Councils which cooperate with the Government in eliminating the MNF goondas will receive Govt. help in various ways. If any village helps the unlawful MNF volunteers it will have to suffer the consequences.[16]

While there was a threatening undertone in the order, it was evident that it demanded loyalty from the Mizo public. Supporting the MNF in any form, such as providing food and shelter, was enough reason to be seen as 'sympathetic' and therefore 'loyal' to them. Likewise, the MNF also issued various orders to the public against supporting the government. There were cases where VCPs suffered capital punishment for supporting the government of India as they were considered *hnam phatsan* (traitors).[17] The MNF *sawrkar* insisted that the VCPs follow their orders as a mark of loyalty, regardless of the fact that they were also being compelled to follow the orders of the Indian government.[18]

In the early years of the movement and the counter-insurgency, a large number of people, men in particular, were arrested and transferred to different jails. In Manipur, for instance, Mizo villages and civilians were the targets of the Home Guard[19] in the Churachandpur district. To be a Mizo was enough to be suspected as a loyalist of the MNF, and villagers of Kawnpui, Thingkangphai, and Nghathal recounted how Mizo men, youth, and adults were tortured and repeatedly abused. Mizos in Manipur often recalled the words of Laldenga who said, 'Mizoramin nghawng chen kan dai chuan nangnin kawng chen in dai ang' (If Mizoram has to tread as neck-deep, then till waist-deep you too shall go). Since being Mizo was seen as being 'loyal' to the MNF, people often concealed their identity to escape torture and violence. The situation was more or less similar in the Jampui Hills in Tripura. One of the common tactics was rounding up villagers and herding them into open fields, irrespective of whether it was day or night. Lianzuala (1998: 43) captures this: 'Mizoram buaina chuan angkhat rengin Zoram dep a Zofate chu min rawn chil chhuak chiang hle mai' (The Zo people inhabiting the territories adjoining Mizoram have all been affected alike by the conflict in Mizoram).

Within the Mizo Hills, the issue of loyalty took on a different dimension with regard to communities such as the Lais, Maras, and Chakmas, which the state saw as being opposed to not only the MNF movement but also being 'loyal' citizens. Noting the uneasy ethnic relationship between the Mizos and the Chakmas, it was proposed to undertake village groupings in Chakma-inhabited areas as a measure to protect them from the MNF rebels. A similar proposal was made in the case of the Lai and Mara tribes in the southern district. Although there was support from some of the Mara leaders, the opposition against grouping was strong, and so the plan was not carried forward. The Lais, Chakmas, and Maras were collectively seen as 'loyalists' or 'patriots' due to their non-participation in the movement. In the Mizo Hills, the area inhabited by them was not covered under the grouping scheme.

The relationship between the Chakmas and the MNF was more uneasy because the MNF was based in the CHTs and had to pass through Chakma villages within Mizoram and in the CHTs. This made the Chakmas vulnerable to the transiting MNF rebels while creating an opportunity for the security forces to use the Chakmas as informers. While this has created ethnic rifts and suspicion, a former Mizo soldier explained how the case of 'loyalty' was determined by the situation of the time. He said:

> I was sent for duty in 1983 with two friends who were in bad health. We did not have any money with us. I then went to Tlabung to find monetary support. While I was away, two of my friends were reported by the Chakma and were arrested by the Indian security force. While I was on my way back, the people nearby told me about the incident and requested me to go to a safer place or out of there. They took everything we had and I was empty-handed. All I had was one knife. I was completely lost and words cannot explain the difficulty. Since I was already in the movement, I did not wish to surrender.[20]

When asked how he was sure that the Chakmas reported them, he further stated:

> We were at Chakma *jhum*-house. Since we asked for and lived on their food, we were somehow a burden to them. In addition, they were scared of the fact that they might face problems due to us. In order to safeguard themselves, they reported us and made the security forces arrest us. From their side, it was entirely true. It was to safeguard and protect themselves for their own security.

The uneasiness of relationships cuts across communities and tribes. For instance, throughout the period of the MNF movement, the MU continued to have a strong influence and support from the people. The relationship between the MNF and the MU volunteers often turned sour, leading to fratricidal killings. This was also the case with the PC led by Brigadier Thenphunga Sailo (famously known as Brig. T. Sailo) who raised the SF by recruiting large numbers from among the surrendered MNF soldiers and the public. Even as the state was able to draw such groups to their side, the soldiers and leaders of the MNF narrated how they tried to un-harm them as much as they could. A former soldier said, 'Anni ai chuan silaite pawh kan nei tha, mahse kan hoututen Mizo leh Mizo thisen in chhuah a tha lo e an tih avang chauhin kan hel kan hel lui thin ani' (We are better equipped with weapons than the SF, and yet we kept avoiding any clash with them only because our leaders did not want Mizos spilling each other's blood).[21]

Securing loyalty was definitely a form of exerting authority and control. In fact, modern nation-states always seek unswerving loyalty from their citizens, which means the feeling of belonging and trust in the state. This becomes one of the ways by which the state distinguishes between 'good and bad' (Mamdani 2005) citizens. The question of being 'good' and 'bad' was not always an easy choice. V. L. Nghaka, a prominent church leader at the time, noted, 'Sipai lamin min chhawr deuhin volunteer lam rinhlelh kai a awl a, volunteer lamin min chhawr deuha a lanin sipai lamin min ringhlel leh a' (If the Indian security forces employed you, the volunteers suspected us which is the same when the volunteer employed us) (Nghaka 2014). Therefore, an exclusive view of the conflict in binary terms, such as the MNF against the Indian security forces, remains incomplete and can lead to a marginalization of the people's experience.

Human Rights Violation

The annual report of the Ministry of Defence, commenting on the arrival of the security forces in the Mizo Hills, reads:

> The army went to the aid of the civil authorities, quickly cleared road blocks, restored communications, and relieved the situation in the administrative centres that were threatened. The besieged posts were supplied with food and ammunition. By the middle of March 1966, the law and order situation had improved considerably and all the main administrative centres and outposts were free from extremist control or threats. (Ministry of Defence 1967: 21)

This was also the beginning of the militarization of the Mizo Hills and the other Mizo-inhabited areas of Manipur and Tripura. 'Militarization,' Anuradha Chenoy notes, 'is not simply the process whereby the military seeks political domination. When civilian leadership put military power to civil use "to save the nation" or to solve political problems, this process itself militarises society' (cited in de Mel 2007: 23). The security forces first marched from Kolasib, the northernmost district, to regain control by establishing camps throughout the Mizo Hills. The abuse of human rights and the news of mass torture and rape began to spread upon their arrival. It was the dreadful mass rape at Kolasib that was the most feared of being repeated and so created a wary feeling among the public. Two noted political leaders from Meghalaya, G. G. Swell and J. J. Nichols Roy, stated in their report of 1966, *Suppression of Mizos in India: An Eye Witness Report*:

In Kolasib, 50 miles of Aizawl, the army rounded up all the men folk of the village, about 500 of them. They were collected, made to lie down on the ground on their stomachs and then were kicked, beaten, trampled upon and confined for the night. At night groups of soldiers moved about the village. They broke into the houses, helped themselves to everything of value—clocks, sewing machines, clothes, etc. … and raped the women. (cited in S. Nag 2002: 249)

The case of Kolasib was not an exception, and it soon became the way by which the state sought to establish its control. The suspension of rights was sanctioned by such emergency laws as the AFSPA that justified violence as a necessity to maintain order and coerce the population into submission. As militarization became more intense, the security forces were able to penetrate and establish control in important towns and villages. The establishment of the military in Mizoram lingers on as the settlement of the military on lands owned by individuals is an ongoing legal case even today. Scores of crimes, including enforced disappearances, bodily torture, and sexual violence became part of everyday life—in fact the face of the 'everyday state' (Fuller and Bénéï 2001)—and the search for those who had 'disappeared', who were often recovered as 'dead' bodies subsequently, was on the rise. The everydayness of militarization affected everyday life, with militaristic terms becoming popular and normalized in everyday conversations, such as *karfiu* (curfew), *chek* (check), bunker, barricade, *kawnvai* (convoy), concentration camp, and *aidi* (ID, or identity card) (Lalrinawma 2014: 1–11).

The pattern of violence and the impunity with which it was done suggested that it was intended to dehumanize and humiliate. The shaming of the women through public molestation and abuse and the arrest of suspected sympathizers and MNF volunteers demonstrated how violence was not a homogenous encounter and experience for everyone. Yet what often compounded the experience was its visceral nature that denied the existence of the victims as 'human'. The regular practice of separating men and women, regardless of the time when conducting search operations, was a regular feature that reinforced the dehumanization of a subject population. The wholesale use of violence against civilians led to tales of endless suffering. The public display of the violence was intended to hurt and further dehumanize by stripping away their existence as people. Furthermore, the attacks on churches and the use of the structures as camps and temporary makeshift dwellings and places for torture were some of the ways the Indian military enforced a regime of impunity. In Lungpher, the VCP of Tualbung village was summoned and arrested on account of supplying food to the MNF volunteers on 26 December 1966 (C. Zama 2008: 12). While torturing him, the post commander had challenged the MNF army to come with Jesus to fight them. However, at the civilians' request, the MNF armies carried out the Tualbung Operation or the Mipuite Chhanchhuahna Operation (Civilian Rescue Operation) in early 1967 by taking over the Tualbung military outpost (Lalrawnliana 1997: 35–43; C. Zama 2008: 11–12).

During this period, there was no human rights watchdog to report on the issue or put the state under any pressure (Hazarika 1996). The media were censored, and there was no reporting about the many cases of human rights abuse. It was only in 1974 that the Human Rights Committee (HRC) was established under the leadership of T. Sailo. Being an army officer and serving the nation, he felt disgusted at the conduct of the armies and wrote to the then prime minister, Indira Gandhi, about it. His letter notes:

> During the years 1966–73 when I was serving in the Indian Army, many instances of atrocities, misbehaviour of the Security Forces towards the people of Mizoram came to my notice through the local newspapers, public conversations and private letters.
>
> The Security Forces have also grossly abused the special powers given to them, mainly, arresting a person on suspicion. In many cases, they would wrongfully detain such persons for long periods of time and torture them. Sometimes they use this method as a weapon of intimidation. If a villager reports to higher civil authorities against the wrong-doing of the Security Forces in his village, the latter will arrest him as being suspected of being an MNF sympathizer and threaten him with dire consequences.
>
> Another instance of bitterness against Security Forces is occasioned by their utter disrespect to the church congregation. If the Security Forces suspect some MNF or their agents being present in the church congregation on a Sunday, they would come and drive the congregation out of the church in a most vulgar manner and herd them together in the open ground outside for a long period in spite of rain or sunshine. (T. Sailo 1981)

In addition to this, the conduct of the security forces began to shape the way the Mizos perceived the Indian state. For the Mizos, as already noted, the security forces were known as *vai sipai*. This had far-reaching consequences in terms of how the Mizos related with the *vai* even in the post-MNF period. T. Sailo captured this feeling in his letter:

> In the course of my meetings with the various sections of the people are the same sorry tales of the excesses committed by the Security Forces on the general population of Mizoram. They have been repeated time and again during conversation, through newspapers and again private letters. I find the people in general utterly disgusted with Indian soldiers. They are bitter to the extreme towards the Security Forces. In almost all the villages, what the villagers see and know of India is the Security Forces stationed on duty in that particular village. It is no wonder, therefore, that the people have been so much antagonized against and alienated from India. To a villager, an Indian soldier is India. (T. Sailo 1981)

In summing up the feeling of the Mizo public, he stated, 'In short, the image of the Indian Army has reached its bottom so far as the general public in Mizoram is concerned.' This image continues to be the case for many. In the Jampui Hills, a local

Figure 5.4 Coffins of the Mizo National Front (MNF) rebels who died during the period of the movement, 1986
Source: PAMRA collection.

leader described how he was tortured by the Indian army on the grounds of mere suspicion and expressed the resentment he harboured towards the *vai sipai* to this day. Such a view of the *vai* as the 'other' is grounded in the historical experience of violence and torture (Figure 5.4).

Telling 'Untold Atrocity': Counter-Discourse and Resistant Voice

In 'Blaming the Victims', Said (1988) argues against the danger of the dominance of a single viewpoint in ideas, representation, rhetoric, and images. Writing in the context of scholarship produced on the Israel–Palestine conflict, he notes how the fate of the victims is being displaced on them when the single narrative becomes part of the official discourse. V. Das (1997), in looking at the Bhopal gas disaster, shows how the state uses the suffering of the victims as a legitimating trope to silence the pains of the disaster victims. She asks, 'How do institutions maintain and signal their legitimacy in the face of massive human suffering?', and she answers this by looking at how different institutions (medical, judicial, and bureaucratic) create a discourse that denies suffering. As such, the victims were not 'sufferers' but instead 'maligners' with their sufferings transformed as their creation, given their pre-existing social (poverty, for instance) and medical problems. What this legitimates is suffering, but, as V. Das (1997) notes, the victims do not submit without any resistance, which is also the key to break sufferers free from their image as mere victims.

In the case of the Mizos' counter-insurgency experience, the discourse of 'successful counter-insurgency' is a trope that legitimizes state actions and violence. There is relatively scant attention paid to the violence and its counter-discourse, thus subduing the Mizos by victimizing and silencing them. Recent studies on violence have increasingly moved away from the 'victim' narrative, particularly when it comes to marginal groups. In the case of the Mizos, too, the impact of violence is framed within the 'victimhood' narrative that foreshadowed the everyday contestation and negotiation of violence undertaken by the security forces and the MNF rebels. The Mizos resort to different ways of escaping state repression and violence, and numerous studies have shown how women, for instance, are more than mere 'victims'. Ségor (2006) provides a description of women's experiences and their struggles to survive and resist violence. The case of the Mizo women's experiences, Ségor notes, signifies the communities' resilience in times of hardship and terror, denoting how the Mizo women were not merely helpless victims.

To take it further, the use of sexual violence has become one of the primary foci in times of war, ethnic violence, and counter-insurgency. There is, however, increasing recognition of how women revolted against the state's sexual violence, challenging their vulnerability to being harassed and abused. In noting this, women like Marini[22] explained how she escaped from prison and joined the movement. She recounted:

> I along with four of my friends were put in jail and tied with ropes all over our bodies. Luck was, however, on our side as there was one Mizo security personnel, seeing our condition, he asked me to call for him in the most desperate situation as he promised to stand by me at any cost. After this experience, I promised myself that I would never be caught and punished by the Indian security personnel.[23]

While one reads this as a way of 'revolting bodies' (Gaikwad 2009), it equally symbolizes an 'active resentment' (Vajpeyi 2009: 32) against violence in the militarized northeast.

Through *rambuai hla*, what I intend to explore here is the language of expression against violence. In other words, what are the forms used to express pain and suffering? What do they say about the lived experiences of the violence of the *buai* years? What are the ways by which we can recover and retrieve those voices? Moreover, how does one retrieve the experiences in a way that preserves the way the people lived through them? In this context, I turn to the Mizo public narratives, particularly the songs, as a medium to unearth the people's experience of the counter-insurgency. Such narratives become an important area of enquiry into the Mizo movement (Chhangte 2011; Hrangbana College 2014). As such, *rambuai hla* can be read both as counter-narratives of the official discourse and as narratives of resistance against state violence.

The Mizos resort to both overt and covert forms of resistance. For instance, in areas under grouping, the Mizos mostly adopted the *vai* way of greeting—namely 'Ram Ram *sap*', a colloquial rendering of 'Ram Ram *sahib*'—whenever they met the security forces. This came after the suggestion by one Kaphrianga, who advised the Mizo civilians to greet the *vai sipai* by saying 'Ram Ram *sap*' in order that they might be less ferocious towards them (Ropianga 2014: 107). They began to greet any *vai sipai* regardless of their ranks whenever and wherever they met them. However, in their absence, they lamented, 'Vai sipai kutthlak a na lua, ram ram sap ka ti e zang dam nan' (The torture of Indian security forces is too agonizing, 'Ram Ram *sap*' I plead to ease my pain) (C. Zama 2008: 170; Ropianga 2014: 107). The peculiar feature of such forms of resistance is that they may not necessarily be recognized by the state or result in any significant outcome or change. However, it does provide avenues to explore and capture the people's narratives about conflict and their experiences. In this way, *rambuai hla* become critical to retrieving and recovering peoples' experience of violence during and after the period of village groupings.

Oral culture, J. Scott (1990) notes, is an important cultural expression of the subordinated group in the face of domination. In India, R. Guha (1983) has persuasively shown how rumour functions as an important medium for 'insurgent communication' in mobilizing peasant rebellion in colonial India. If rumour as an oral form of transmission was key 'to spread the message of revolt' (R. Guha 1983: 254–255), the significance of oral communication in the face of militarized repression lies in the 'irrepressibility of the human voice' (J. Scott 1990: 162). *Rambuai hla*, as they are now known, become a pivotal genre to understand the life-worlds of the Mizos during the period of counter-insurgency. Constrained by surveillance and militarized subordination from above, it is in songs that the Mizos reroute themselves to express their encounter and experience.

In the *hla* composed during the period of counter-insurgency, the period of village groupings was the main theme. The centrality of grouping in such songs reflects how villages were central not as a mere physical space of settlement but as a space where history, culture, and identity are rooted. The burning of villages and the forceful relocation were scarred into their collective memory. As such, Suakliana lamented in a song he composed:

> Kan hun tawn zingah khawkhawm a pawi ber mai
> Zoram hmuntin khawtlang puan ang a chul zo ta;
> Tlangtina mi hruaikhawm nunau mipuiten
> Chhunrawl an van, riakmaw iang in an vai e. (Lalruanga n.d.)

> Grouping, the most atrocious ordeals of our time,
> Leaving the once vibrant hamlets empty and void,
> As the grouped hapless village people gather,
> Clueless, helpless, and left to starve and survive.

Suakliana's song emphasizes how village groupings marked an 'event' in Mizo history. Each stanza in the song has a haunting undertone, from the loss of home to being homeless and the desecration and destruction of one's beloved land. The sheer helplessness expressed in the song made him compare his fellow people with the *riakmaw* (a bird that can never find a tree to stay in) to describe their state of being unable to find a permanent place that they can call home. The song collectivizes the pain of losing the home and the spectre of violence that haunts Mizoram. Laltanpuia joined Suakliana in the same tone, expressing grief about the loss of his village Sialsuk:

Vanhnuai mi hril Siaklhaw zopui khawiah nge maw i awm?
Ka rawn zawng che piallei hawktui, Thlafam dairial maw I chan le!
Lungchimte-a chhung tin par ang vulna kan runnuam,
Hmelma doral darfeng valrualin, Senmenpui hrang an lo ban e.

Aw, tuar a har min hnem zo reng an awm lo,
Chung vankhaw iang kan tawnah Sialkhawpui
Aw I mawi chuang e,
Tunah par ang chul rih mah la dinthar leh na'nge khuanun min hual se,
Ngaihzawng lungduh te an kim nan.[24]

Where have you gone, our famed Sialsuk village once sung into songs?
I keep searching to find your remnants washed away by mud water,
And our sweet cosy homes that were our places of solace,
Burned into ashes by our cruel and heartless uniform-donning foes.

How hard it is to bear such a harsh ordeal,
For us our safe haven,
Our beautiful Sialsuk abode,
We hope to rebuild it again by God's grace even though it's withered now,
For our near and dear ones to live.

Laltanpuia was pained to see his beloved village being ravaged. Hence, the song he composed reverberates with a poignant sense of loss through him being a witness to that loss. This loss, in as much as it is physical and material, has a strong sociocultural and emotional aspect. Villages are imbued with stories and tales that link together the present generation with their past. They are important heritage sites with community values and identity tied to them. On the one hand, the burning of Laltanpuia's village delinked people from this connection by dislocating and uprooting them. On the other hand, the poetics of loss galvanized these dispersed and relocated communities to identify with the village and forge a sense of belonging around it.

In the grouping process, villagers were cut off from their *jhum* fields. The grouped villages were provided with ration supplies to meet the essential needs of each individual and family. There were no reports about the quantity or quality of rations received in government accounts. What was mostly presented was that the grouped populations were supplied with rations for their daily needs. These government-supplied rations barely met the daily requirement of the people living under starvation. In the grouped villages, there was un-freedom from hunger and starvation, which was well captured in a song which goes as follows:

> Lenrualte u tam in ninglo'm ni,
> Chhung tin chawmtu kudam run nuamah sawn,
> Pem mai ka nuam e aw nau ang nuiin, Tam leh AO Sakhming sawi hi a bang mahna. (Vanlallawma 2014)

> Folks everywhere, aren't you tired of this famine?
> I'd like to move into that *kudam* storehouse
> So we may utter no more famine and the AO's name.

There is a strong sense of vulnerability expressed in this song. Within the grouped centres, the grouped populations were made to rely on government rations for their everyday needs. With less possibility for other economic activities, the reliance on the government rations made them subservient to the officers and the security forces. Subjected to dire poverty and starvation, more than PPVs, they were, in the words of Nibedon (1980: 129), 'prohibited poor villages'.

Songs were also about grief, both individual and collective. It was in the songs that the Mizos spoke out about the unspeakable. They grieved the loss of their home, and in Mizo society, the home was the village that embodied collective life. This collective life included social pastime such as *nula rim* (courtship), wherein men go to visit women or their loved ones at night. Social practices such as *lengkhawm zai*[25] were also barred along with various other traditional rites such as the burying of the dead. In Mizo society, social and community gatherings are a privilege that affirms a strong sense of community in times of joy and hardship. The social disruptions caused dislocation within the society, breaking old social norms and community ties. Under curfew and being relocated from their old home, Rammawia poignantly composed:

> Doral lian hrang karah tinkim ka dawn vela,
> Ka ngai em che mi u min hnemtu;
> Nang lo chuan awmkhawhar lunglam vai hrilh ka hai,
> Kei ka tan damnadawi i lo ni.

> Aw, lunglen curfew karah hian,
> Tuar a har hrilh ka thiam zo love,
> Hmanah Zoram nun lehchimloh Thadangi zun,
> Ngaih hian chin lem a neithei dawn lo.

> Tlaikhua a lo ngui zantlai bawhar dungthul in,
> Riahrun an rem curfew hran vang hian;
> Leng zawng hian ngai ve maw hmana kan Zoram nun,
> Kei zawng ka ngai, ka dawnsei ngam lo.

Hmanah sakhmel hriat ngai loh ten leng mah ila,
Tunah min fan thapui i zun hian;
Engtik nge ka nuam ngei hallo ten a leng in,
Ka nghakhlel, aw, ka dawn bang thei lo.

I tiam lo'ng aw Parte, biahthu thamral mai tur,
Khuatlai leh ka tah sei tur dawn hian;
A riang hi lung her a puan ang hnawl leh ai chuan,
Parte, min hrilh rawh i dawn lungruk.[26]

As the mind wanders betwixt foes menace,
I long for thee O wondrous comfort;
None but you soothe my great solitude my heart's turmoil,
Thou art mine sole panacea.

It's hard to bear amidst curfew,
Hard to express the longing I feel;
For our peaceful past lives and my dear beloved,
I'm clinging on to it endlessly.

As the day weakens the night rooster,
Cease and settle for curfew dawns;
Bygone days crave by others too I wonder,
For in me the yearning's deep, I dare not brood.

Though strangers were we in years that passed,
Enthralled me now you have O Gorgeous;
Eagerly for that day of our gallanting,
Restless it made me, my musings cannot rest.

O Parte, let not our vows wither away,
And make me weep in later years;
Lest me lonesome get cast away,
Parte, allow thy heart's secret be known.

There is a deep sense of loneliness and abandonment in the song. Throughout the period of counter-insurgency, curfews were commonly imposed from dusk to dawn, curbing movements. Any movement between towns and villages was restricted and allowed only with due permission. Camps reordered the daily routine of the people; they reorganized space and defined and delimited boundaries under a system of rigorous surveillance (Sofsky 1997: 45–94). As military rule engulfed the hills, people were locked within the grouped centres, limiting their social space. It is this that Rammawia yearned for, the 'peaceful past' and his 'beloved'.

Rambuai hla give a clearer and coherent picture of the counter-insurgency experience and the narratives that are subdued by the discourse of successful counter-insurgency. The *hla*, due to their nature and their vernacular form of expression, escape censorship and hence provide us with counter-narratives. In situations of conflict, they can become tools of resistance to militarism (de Mel 2007: 17). With the media being censored by the state, there was no avenue to raise people's voices against state actions. Hence, *hla* became a viable means and emerged as resistant forces as they were 'crucial in providing alternative narratives to the official historiographies' (de Mel 2007: 17) of militarism and military violence. The 'oral' during and after the period became a valuable source of retelling of the past as it gave 'legitimacy and authority to previously silenced voices' (Becker 2011: 322) that are erased or silenced in the official narrative (Saikia 2011).

Conclusion

In 1971, the Guwahati High Court struck down the plan for further regrouping in the Mizo Hills. This retraction came after the case filed by K. Zahlira, which challenged the orders for grouping as a violation of the fundamental rights guaranteed by the Indian Constitution. However, even today, the narrative on the use of village groupings continues to oscillate between the 'success' and the 'sufferings' of the people (Surahmar, 2010). The case of 'success' has become part of the larger narrative of the state and gradually of academia due to the sustenance of peace in the state of Mizoram. Yet even after the grouping, the MNF movement continued for many more decades, and it was observed that the use of the grouping caused further resentment and alienation among the Mizos. This boosted the MNF support base (Pachuau and van Schendel 2015: 312). In the words of T. Sailo, village groupings were the 'most ruthless measure' that not only embittered the Mizo public but were also 'reminiscent of a concentration camp'. He continued:

> The Security Forces have tried to intimidate the public with all manner of atrocities and ill-treatment. However, this strong-arm method has not brought about any solution. On the contrary, it has driven the solution even further away. It has only engendered bitterness and hatred against the Security Forces and consequently, India. (T. Sailo 1981)

T. Sailo then became one of the first to publicly denounce the atrocities and abuse of power by the security forces in the Mizo Hills. Later, he was active in politics, running for the PC and subsequently becoming the chief minister of the state. However, things turned sour between him and the MNF supremo, Laldenga, and this resulted in bitter rivalries and fratricidal killings. Both leaders began to oppose each other, often putting at stake the peace negotiation between the government of India and the MNF. The peace accord in Mizoram therefore was more than a settlement between the MNF and the government. Despite much jubilance with the accord, the memorandum of settlement is assessed differently and not merely as a political or economic package. It is this differential view that I turn to in the next chapter in trying to understand the question of peace in Mizoram.

Notes

1   The DoI Rules is a legacy of colonial rule, introduced by the British in 1939 at the dawn of World War II.

2   India used the DoI Rules against the Chinese during the Indo-China War, where Chinese populations were put in detention camps in Rajasthan.

3   The district is inhabited by tribal groups belonging to the Lai, Mara, Chakma, and other smaller communities such as the Bawms, Pangs, and so on. The district is now separated into three Autonomous District Councils under two districts—Siaha and Lawngtlai.

4   The AFSPA is an Act of the parliament which grants special powers to the Indian Armed Forces in what is called 'disturbed areas'. Under the Act, members of the armed forces are given sweeping powers to make preventive arrest, search without warrant, and even shoot to kill by a non-commissioned officer.

5   *Jhum* is the local name for slash-and-burn farming, sometimes also referred to as shifting cultivation. It is a form of farming where a variety of crops are planted in cycles of use and fallow.

6   *Vai sipai* is the Mizos' term for the Indian military.

7   The MNF were usually labelled as 'volunteers', and every sympathizer or suspect was labelled as a 'volunteer'.

8   Interview with the VCP of Serchhip, 17 June 2015.

9   *Puakphurh* simply means forced labour, where mostly men were used to carry the goods of the security forces when they relocated or patrolled areas.

10 *Nghawngkawl* is a plaited band of cane that passes over the top of the head and is used by men and women to support a load, light or heavy, when carried on the back.

11 *Arte thih* is a metaphor used by the Mizos when someone who dies has had no one to be looked after by; it is most often used in cases where even the families are unaware of the person's death.

12 Interview with a former rebel, 23 March 2015.

13 *Dahthat* is as a metaphor used by the MNF to indicate those whom they had killed.

14 The pamphlet was dropped using a helicopter and it was entitled 'Mizo National Front Armed Gangs Must Be Liquidated'. CB-115, G-1399, Mizoram State Archive (MSA), Aizawl.

15 The Special Force (SF) was formed to counter the MNF rebels by the People's Conference (PC) government, drawing personnel from MNF returnees and the common public.

16 MNF Document I, Aizawl Theological College (ATC) Archives, Aizawl.

17 MNF Document I, Memo. No. Gx. 11/66/56, date Aijal, 30 June 1966, ATC Archives.

18 MNF Document III, MSA.

19 The Home Guard was established by the state as a counter-insurgence force with recruits mostly drawn from the local community. In Manipur, it was the community known to oppose the MNF movement that comprised the bulk of the recruits.

20 Interview with a former Mizo soldier, 25 March 2015.

21 Interview with a former Mizo soldier, 23 March 2015.

22 The name of the narrator has been changed.

23 Interview with Marini, 29 June 2015.

24   'Vanhnuai Mi Hril (Sialsuk Khaw Kan Hla)', Mizolyrics.com, https://www.mizolyric.
      com/2017/06/vanhnuai-mi-hril-sialsuk-khaw-kan-hla.html (accessed in August 2018).

25   *Lengkhawm zai* is a singing tradition among the Mizos, practised on occasions such as
      festivals, celebrations, and death.

26   'Curfew Kara Lunglen', Mizolyrics.com, https://www.mizolyric.com/2017/06/vanhnuai-
      mi-hril-sialsuk-khaw-kan-hla.html (accessed in August 2018).

6 Discord, Accord, and the Politics for Peace

On 30 June 1986, after numerous attempts and failures in negotiation, the government of India and the MNF signed a memorandum of settlement that put an end to the Mizo struggle for independence. The memorandum contains various safeguards through Article 371(G)[1] of the Indian Constitution while granting statehood status to the erstwhile UT. There was much jubilation across Mizoram as the long-awaited peace finally arrived. For the common people, the accord meant the end of violence and living in perpetual fear. For the Indian state, it was another story of striking an agreement, much like the Punjab and Assam accords signed in 1985. On his return from New Delhi, and with many welcoming him in the AR *lammual* (parade field),[2] Laldenga, the president of the MNF, now revered as Mizo Hnam Pa (Father of the Mizo Nation), gave a speech to the Mizo public. Commenting on the accord, he said that it was neither the end of the struggle nor a complete stop in the quest for independence but a moment to rest and recuperate, and that it was now up to the younger generations to take the struggle forward for ethnic and territorial unity or independence.

However, for others like Raltawna, what was unsettling was that the president did not utter a word about restitution and reconciliation. As he put it, 'In ngaidam tawn tawh ila tih lampang tal pawh hriat tur awm lo kha, engtin emaw rilruah a cham tlat nia!' (There was no mention of mutual forgiveness, to let bygones be bygones, and that to this day still aches the mind!) (Raltawna 2010: 12). This points to the fact that the matter of the violence and injustice meted out to the Mizo civilians during the period of the movement continues to linger, which does not find a mention in the accord.

From the mid-1970s, *remna leh muanna* (settlement and peace) become part of the everyday vocabulary in Mizoram. It was *remna leh muanna* that dominated the political discourse. A vernacularized discourse of peace was created through which the issue of peace took centre stage in the everyday social and political life of the people. In the UT elections of 1977, political parties of all hues and colours promised *muanna* if elected to power. As such, *muanna* became the rallying point during elections to galvanize voters and win the electoral battle. The issue of peace was enmeshed with both national and local politics and the interest in power between both the rebel forces and the government. The MNF began to openly get involved in the electoral process, from fielding candidates to supporting political parties, while the national political parties, such as the INC(I), intended to make peace as a way to consolidate its position in the state.

Within northeast India, the Mizo Accord has received significant attention due to the political stability and peace of the state. Studies on peace-making thus far have been preoccupied with the issue that projects Mizoram as a 'success' and a 'peace model'. Hassan (2008) examined the sustenance of peace in Mizoram and showed how inclusionary identity formation enabled a stable political order. This allowed what Nunthara (2002) calls the 'entrenchment' of the Mizo identity that he argues is 'key to the apparent success of the Mizo Accord' (cited in S. K. Das 2007: 40). For others, the Mizo case is a 'model' or 'success' that can be emulated in other parts of northeast India (Sirnate and Verma 2013), a case of democracy accommodating ethnic nationalism (Kohli 1997). The narrative of 'success' or 'peace model' dominates discussion about issues of peace-making in Mizoram (Roluahpuia 2018b). Both 'success' and 'peace model' are military-centric terminologies underpinned by state-imposed imaginaries of an absence of violence. Peace, according to this, is conceptualized as one that mitigates existing conflict and violence. The interest largely then is in quelling movements that challenge the state's authority. The state projects itself as pro-peace with the agenda of creating 'order' and bringing back 'normalcy'. Interventions by the state are framed as an attempt to accomplish the same.

The chapter shifts our attention to the study of peace-making by examining the political interests and contestation involved in the making of peace in Mizoram. In examining the question of peace, it is argued that a better way to approach peace-making in Mizoram is through what I call the 'politics for peace'. Politics for peace rejects the conceptualization of peace in terms of a one-way understanding that puts the state's role as its focus, thereby turning our attention to the diverse actors and the complexity of social, economic, and political processes involved in it. Neither peace, as the case of the MNF demonstrates, is merely about bringing back 'normalcy' nor was the agenda of settlement determined solely to bring about 'order'. As Nordstrom (2004) has shown, the issue of peace is intertwined with multiple interests and actors. As she puts it, 'people's lives, their careers, their *raison d'être* are staked on peace' (Nordstorm 2004: 170). Hence, the involvement and interests of non-state actors, including the armed groups, in as much as they are important, do not tell the complete story about peace-making. One needs to look at how the interest of the state itself, central and local, and the issue of peace, despite often being derailed, emerged as a site for the contest of power. Even today, political parties in the state of Mizoram compete over the claim as to who actually brought about 'peace' in the state, notably when the then INC(I) chief minister, Pu Lalthanhawla, resigned from his post to give way to Laldenga to establish an interim government.

Furthermore, since the signing of the Mizo Accord in 1986, the MNF has converted into a political party and has been able to emerge as a credible regional political party. This has put many former rebel leaders in the spotlight of state politics as they transform themselves from 'rebels' to 'rulers'. Hence, this chapter will also examine what 'peace' means for the former rebels. Relying on oral testimonies, it shows a differential perception of the idea of peace and what it means to the witnesses. One can discern a multifaceted account of the pre- and post-peace eras in place of a singular narrative of the agreement between the MNF and the government of India.

Since the mid-1970s, Laldenga began to show his inclination towards negotiation and settlement with the government of India, culminating in numerous ceasefire agreements. This was not without opposition. For many leaders, such as Biakchhunga, the struggle for *zalenna* was uncompromising, and hence any settlement without the same was unacceptable. This became more complex in the events that led to the election of a new president during the 1977–1979 period and the arrest of Laldenga by the government of India. The Janata Party (JP) government at the centre also showed no interest in further dialogue by sidelining Laldenga. For some years, the MNF armies struck back by issuing a 'quit order' to the non-Mizos, particularly the *vai*, which was clearly a pressure tactic. By the 1980s, peace had become the dominant political sloganeering, and more than the MNF, it was mainstream political parties that championed the cause for 'peace'. In this way, peace began to be mainstreamed in the political discourse of the state, and it is within this context that I have attempted to locate the politics for peace. As such, the chapter traces the events and processes that led up to the signing of the memorandum of settlement. Even as the accord settled the conflict between the MNF and the government of India, what remained unsettled was how the issue of 'peace' overshadowed the issue of violence and terror that the public experience during the period of the conflict.

Peace and Discords

In 1973, two years before the National Emergency in India, Laldenga wrote a letter from Geneva to Indira Gandhi, the then prime minister. The letter contained Laldenga's proposal for negotiation to be preceded by a ceasefire that would allow the MNF leaders based in Mizoram and the CHTs to deliberate among themselves and put forward proposals for further dialogue with the government of India.

> Since November 1973, my officials have been meeting your representatives to discuss the question of the restoration of peace and normalcy in Mizoram for an ultimate settlement of the political problem. In pursuance of these discussions, I have already written to you a letter mentioning therein about my willingness to discuss the solution of the problem within the Constitution of India. (Zamawia 2012)

The letter further stated:

> In order that I could contact my underground colleagues for injecting into them
> my belief and convictions so that they may come round to my line of thinking,
> I would request for the facility of my coming over to India, which I am prepared
> to do. As I will have to take the greatest risk in coming out of Pakistan once
> again which will be for good, I would need this assurance from your good self.
> I also hope that your government would grant us suitable safe conduct while
> in India and extend facilities to contact my underground colleagues who may
> be in places convenient to you. The underground leaders whom I would like
> to meet first are my Vice President Mr.Tlangchhuaka, MNF party President
> Mr. Chawngzuala, my Army Chief Mr. Biakchhunga and Col. Zamana. Given
> the opportunity to meet them and discuss with them the various aspects of the
> problem, I am confident and can assure you that I will succeed in bringing them
> over to my line of thinking for a settlement of the problem. (Zamawia 2012)

For Laldenga, a dialogue was necessary, taking into consideration the changing
'geopolitical situation and big power attitudes', and hence he saw that the survival of
the Mizos 'will be with Delhi' (Laldenga 1980). He indicated this in his letter to the
prime minister as well when he wrote, 'Those people do not have the opportunity to
appreciate the problem in the wider context of the political developments all over the
world. I would, therefore, have to explain to them all these in detail and give them
some hope'. There were oppositional voices to a dialogue, and this was the main
reason for disagreement, even at the convention. Those who opposed the proposal
objected on two grounds. First, many leaders of the MNF, implying the Dumpawl,
were accused of betraying the cause in trying to negotiate with the government of
India in 1971. However, barely four years after this accusation was made against the
Dumpawl, came the call for this convention. Second, the convention's location was
another reason; the opponents were baffled why it was to be organized in Calcutta
and not in Aizawl or some other area under the MNF's control.

In narrating the event, a leader of the movement, whom Laldenga had chosen,
narrated his meeting with Laldenga in Bonn, West Germany. He said:

> It was the feeling of everyone in the MNF that the suffering of our people is
> immense, and therefore if the Indian government is willing for a dialogue,
> then we should agree. We will have a dialogue, and if we cannot agree, then
> we will go underground again. It was already 1976, and we arrived in Delhi
> in December.[3]

This culminated in what became known as the Calcut (Calcutta, now Kolkata)
Convention, which was held from 24 March to 1 April 1976. The convention took
place in a tense atmosphere as the group that opposed the meeting remained firm in
their stance. Malsawma Colney, one of the senators who later became the president of
the MNF, was one of them. However, since the move by Laldenga, the president had

the support of other members, and the decision for a dialogue was carried forward. An important resolution passed at the convention was the decision to initiate a dialogue within the framework of the Indian Constitution while simultaneously mapping out a strategy for a political settlement. Laldenga, with two of his aides, Rualchhina and Biakvela, flew directly to Delhi for the dialogue and later on came out with a ceasefire agreement that was signed in 1976 and was known as the 1 July Agreement, or simply the July Agreement. The main points of the Agreement as issued in a press release were:

1. The MNF delegation acknowledged that Mizoram was an integral part of India and conveyed to the Government of India their resolve to accept a settlement of all problems in Mizoram within the framework of the Constitution of India.

2. In order to bring about a climate of understanding and an atmosphere of peace and tranquillity in Mizoram at the earliest, the delegation agreed to abjure violence and suspend all such activities. In furtherance of the above objectives, the underground delegation agreed to collect all underground personnel with their arms and ammunition inside mutually agreed camps within one month after their establishment and also agreed to hand over arms and ammunition to the Government of India.

3. The Government of India also decided to suspend all operations thereafter by the security forces. Such suspension, however, would not apply to operation against underground personnel attempting to cross international borders and to the maintenance of law and order. (Zamawia 2012: 1000)

The then chief minister of Mizoram, Ch. Chhunga, issued a public notice requesting every citizen, the security forces, and the MNF to abstain from violence and not to engage in any activities that could abrogate the agreement. A ceasefire ensued between the MNF and the government of India with the signing of this agreement. It was a temporary relief for the civilians, in particular, and for two years there was a cessation of violence both by the Indian security forces and the MNF armies.

By 1978, things began to change as the new JP government at the centre began to sideline Laldenga. The government made a public announcement in 1978 that it was no longer interested in talking to him. The change came as a shock to many observers as 'it is still not clear what exactly went wrong between July 1976 and March 1978 when the Home Minister announced that the government was breaking off talks with Laldenga' (*Economic and Political Weekly* 1978: 786). The regime-change in New Delhi in the post-Emergency period was undoubtedly one reason, while the other was the rise of the PC within Mizoram. An editorial in the *Economic and Political Weekly* (1978) quite startlingly remarked that 'it should be clear that more than Laldenga, Brigadier Sailo, a former officer of the Indian army who, moreover, had a taste of MISA [Maintenance of Internal Security Act] too during the Emergency, would have a better appreciation of the ways of the government of India'. What had become clear, however, was that the question of 'peace' had become a political gamble and not merely an issue between the MNF and the government of India. It was also about regaining power and control in Mizoram.

Peace and the Politics of 'Order'

Order and disorder in the peripheral regions of India, G. Singh (1996) argues, are intimately interwoven; what is fundamental is how people and governments seek to maintain, justify, and, sometimes, legitimize 'order' (G. Singh 1996: 421). If the 1976 agreement gave temporary relief in terms of armed violence in Mizoram, successive political developments were underscored by intermittent power struggles. If the PC, led by Brigadier Thenphunga Sailo, used its position to counter the MNF, political parties such as the INC rallied behind the MNF to support the cause for peace. It is then prudent to understand the rise of the PC in mainstream Mizo politics and its creation of a dystopian order in Mizoram.

On 17 April 1975, Brig. T. Sailo, as he is popularly known, launched the PC as a new political party (T. Sailo 2000: 103). Behind the PC's emergence was the HRC, which gave T. Sailo wide popularity and visibility in Mizoram. Initially, the party's objective was to bring about a peaceful resolution to the conflict between the MNF and the government of India and to continue to pursue the objectives of the HRC. Being non-INC and at the same time popular among the masses, T. Sailo was one of the leaders who was arrested during the National Emergency of 1975. After his release in 1977, the relationship between T. Sailo and Laldenga began to sour, which only soured further with the crisis within the MNF. In explaining the situation, Laldenga wrote:

> He [Sailo] secretly met me and advised me against laying down our arms without first reaching a political settlement. The Government got a hint of this and arrested him during the Emergency. His change of heart occurred in jail. He was shattered by the experience and took to religion. I know that he wrote to the Government pleading for pardon and informing them that he wanted to give up politics. Some sort of an understanding seems to have been reached before his release. (Laldenga 1978)

However, the differences only widened. With the PC in power, the party began to use counter-offensive tactics against the MNF, resulting in numerous internecine killings. The PC was able to penetrate the MNF as well as to give a safe haven to MNF 'returnees'[4] or those who were disgruntled with Laldenga. A prominent face who surrendered was Biakchhunga, the MNF chief of army, who subsequently joined the PC.

In 1978, the PC won the elections, only to be dissolved within a few months due to an internal rebellion. In May 1979, fresh elections were conducted, and the PC won the elections with T. Sailo reinstated as the chief minister. Whereas one could not deny the increasing popularity of the PC and their leaders, T. Sailo received much support from the central leadership of the time—that is, the JP government—which was attempting to 'contain Laldenga'. It was observed:

> In the brief period when Brigadier Sailo was in power, some more progress was made in the continuing task of further splitting and demoralising the insurgent elements among the Mizos and, for a while, it even looked as if the task of finally taking over the political leadership of the insurgency would be achieved under the improbable leadership of Brigadier Sailo himself. The setting up of a rival to the rebel leader Laldenga in the Mizo National Front, the apparent ouster of Laldenga from the post of the president of the MNF, as well as the studied disapproval of attempts by elements within the People's Conference to bring together the warring factions in the MNF—all these can be attributed to Brigadier Sailo's own anxiety to ensure for himself the leadership of not merely the leading parliamentary group in Mizoram, but also, even if indirectly, of an important segment of the Mizo insurgent movement. (*Economic and Political Weekly* 1979: 790)

The strategy did pay off as internal crises beset the MNF for some years. Between 1978 and 1979, the MNF saw three different presidents. This went to the extent of expelling Laldenga from the party, albeit for a short period of time, which was a collective decision taken at the party's assembly in June 1978 (Vanlalauva 2015: 196). Biakchhunga was elected as the new president of the MNF on 3 July 1978, and T. Sailo was able to hold his grip on the internal workings of the MNF. He also successfully persuaded the JP government to arrest Laldenga, which subsequently took place on 8 July 1979 (Jafa 2000).

However, internal problems refused to die down within the MNF. This resulted in the ouster of Biakchhunga, who was replaced by Tlangchhuaka and then Malsawma Colney as the president of the MNF. This new development also indicated the strained relationship between Biakchhuanga and Laldenga, who later led a mass surrender in 1979. His relationship with T. Sailo made it evident as to who had wholeheartedly embraced the dissident leader. In welcoming him, T. Sailo remarked:

> Over the years, difficulties have arisen over the implementation of a commitment to the Calcutta Convention. Mr. Laldenga and some of his followers have been dragging their feet over the matter. On the other hand, Brig. Gen. Biakchhunga, the former Chief of Mizo National Army, his Brigade Commanders and most of the senior officers, took a stand that a commitment once made must be honoured and therefore, the provisions of the Calcutta Convention should be implemented. Accordingly, a group of MNF (both Army Wing and Civil Wing), commonly known as Biakchhunga's group, have decided to surface to join the mainstream of national life. Those of you here today are the second batch coming overground. From today you are opening a new chapter in your life history. We welcome you all with open arms. (T. Sailo 1981: 48)

In the meantime, Laldenga was reinstated as the president in 1979 at the special assembly of the party on 24 April 1979 (Vanlalauva 2015: 249). His reinstatement was followed by a reshuffle within the party's rank and file and the army. The notable changes were Zoramthanga and Tawnluia, who were assigned the new positions of vice-president and chief of army staff, respectively. However, the relationship between T. Sailo and Laldenga continued to deteriorate, with both using their power and position against each other. There was a revival of the infamous SF under T. Sailo's ministry. The SF carried out counter-offensive operations against the MNF. This resulted in fratricidal killings, with a prominent one being the killing of the PC's MLA, Zadinga, who was a former MNF member, in 1982. It soon spilled over into mainstream politics where the MNF began to run a campaign to oust the Sailo ministry. In fact, the MNF leader, Laldenga, was not ready for any kind of settlement with the Sailo ministry in power in Mizoram. Given the strained relationship between the MNF and the PC, the INC sought to leverage the most out of this by campaigning for peace, if voted to power in the upcoming elections.

The differences between the MNF and the PC made way for what became known as the *bengvarna*[5] office managed by individuals who had pro-MNF leanings. The intention of the *bengvarna* office was to act as a link between the MNF and the Mizo public while at the same time trying to bring together the MNF and the government of India for negotiations. Undoubtedly, the office had a pro-Laldenga orientation. The PC soon denounced this as a *bengchhena* (noisy) office. The rivalry between the PC and the MNF continued to widen. In the meantime, other political parties such as the Mizoram Congress (I), the Mizoram Janata, the PC-B,[6] the MDF, and the MU came together to form the Steering Committee for dialogue (Lalrinthanga 1993: 2011). The committee's main goal was to strive for peaceful negotiation between the MNF and the government of India. All political parties, irrespective of their ideology and objectives, projected themselves as seeking 'order' in Mizoram (Figure 6.1).

Political interests were intermingled with the issue of bringing about 'order' in Mizoram. With the ceasefire breaking down, a new wave of violence consumed the hills yet again, with the MNF issuing a 'quit notice' to the *vai*, first in 1975 and later in 1979. There were counter-attacks on the Mizos in the neighbouring states of Assam, particularly in the Cachar region, where the Bengali population was dominant (Jafa 2000). In 1975, many non-Mizos moved away out of fear, leaving the hills and returning to Cachar. The atmosphere was very tense. In 1979, tensions escalated after suspected rebels of the MNF killed R. C. Chowdhury, the sub-divisional officer in Saitual village, Mizoram. In retaliation for his killing, violence was unleashed against the Mizos in Silchar. The Mizo youths flocked to the Lailapur areas of Assam. Amidst all this, Mizo student leaders went down to Assam to mediate the problem and prevent any untoward incidents. They succeeded at defusing the situation by convincing both parties, the Mizos and the Bengalis, as well as the police, to abstain from using force (Lalhmingthanga 2014: 172–174). The state's ruling party, the PC,

Figure 6.1   Rally in demand for the resumption of peace talks
Source: L. R. Sailo collection.

also intervened to bring about an atmosphere of tranquillity. The then chief minister, T. Sailo, in his plea against the violence, said:

> The People's Conference Ministry strongly condemned the fury and carnage let loose by a section of the people of Silchar on all the Mizos they could lay their hands on, on 15 June, 1979, resulting in loss of lives, the exact number of which cannot be ascertained till now, serious physical injuries to several persons, burning of houses, looting of properties, ransacking of Mizoram Government officers, stealing of substantial amount of money (cash and damage to properties). (T. Sailo 1981: 34)

Noting his condemnation and disapproval against such a 'quit notice', he further reiterated:

> Unfortunately, at this juncture, some misguided elements have issued a notice under the caption 'Non-Mizos to quit Mizoram before 1st July 1979' threatening them with dire consequences if they fail to do so. This is politically motivated by self-centered motive and is to prevent peace and prosperity from coming to Mizoram and therefore is not in the interest of Mizoram. (T. Sailo 1981: 37)

The conflict took a complex turn, and every time violence was unleashed, the main casualties were the civilians, whether they were Mizos or non-Mizos. The government at the centre resumed its crackdown on the MNF, leading to a resumption of counter-insurgency measures, while the PC under T. Sailo was also engaged in a manhunt of MNF rebels, all with the objective of creating 'order' in the hills.

The violence of the late 1970s endangered the peace talk between the MNF and the government of India. Local politics and rivalries intensified, blocking the possibility of dialogue. Contrarily, the nature of violence had taken an inward turn, with the MNF targeting local rivals such as the PC and vice versa. It was this shift in the targets of violence that dismayed the Mizo public who had endured most of it, living under perpetual suspicion and fear, not only from the *vai sipai* but also from their own brethren. The yearning for *remna leh muanna*, which began to occupy centre stage, was more of a reaction to the ugly turn of violence in Mizoram with all the political parties, except the PC, using this as bait to contest and hopefully win the elections.

Politics for Peace

'My first priority will be to have talks resumed with Laldenga, and in this I will also seek the help of the church leaders who play a vital role in the social life of Mizoram,' were the words of Lalthanhawla in 1984 before the assembly elections (Sen 1984). He promised—if voted to power—to make way for Laldenga, which the MNF leader had been insisting on for the negotiations to succeed (Figure 6.2). At the centre, the INC(I) replaced the JP government by winning the 1980 general elections. Subsequently, talks resumed between the MNF and the government of India two years later. In this case, the peace process' resumption of talks was not determined by who initiated dialogue or who was in power, be it at the centre or the local level. For instance, the JP government showed no interest in furthering dialogue with MNF leader Laldenga because it was a process initiated by the INC regime under Indira Gandhi. Likewise, the resumption of negotiations after the INC came to power had more to do with Indira Gandhi's interest in her grievance against the leader of the

Figure 6.2 Mizoram Congress leaders meeting Rajiv Gandhi, the then prime minister of India, regarding renewed peace talks, in New Delhi, mid-1980s
Source: L. R. Sailo collection.

PC-A who was supported by the JP government and rose to power on an anti-INC platform (*Economic and Political Weekly* 1982: 130). The peace negotiations therefore were faltering and left to be determined by who was in power in Delhi. Yet, in Mizoram, the public demand was for *remna leh muanna*. The renewed crackdown on the MNF's armies and the resumption of counter-insurgency activities by the security forces furthered the public's desire for it. Jafa (2000) sums up the situation in this way:

> The government responded to the renewed MNF armed activities by inducting an unprecedentedly large body of force in Mizoram. By the middle of 1982, there were four brigades with 12 infantry, 6 Assam Rifles, 2 Border Security Force, and 6 Central Reserve Police Battalions—a total of 26 battalions operating in the State. In fact, every road, town, group centre and village were saturated with troops. By a notification issued on January 20 1982 under the Unlawful Activities Act, the government again banned the MNF and the MNA. Laldenga was asked to leave the country and he left for London on April 21, 1982.

> Such a large concentration of forces, the renewal of restrictions on movement and dusk-to-dawn curfews were a grim reminder of the early days of the war. With many rounds of ceasefire and suspension of operations during the preceding five years, people had become used to this as a normal tenor of life. The renewed restrictions and curtailment of liberties constituted a great psychological pressure on the population. The level of violence did not justify the number of troops in Mizoram, but it had the desired effect. Very soon, nothing was in greater demand than normalcy and a life without security restrictions, so people clamoured for an agreement with the government. (Jafa 2000)

From the public point of view, the settlement represented a 'peace by force' (M. S. S. Pandian 1987). The resumption of counter-insurgency and the military crackdown on the MNF brought back the violent memories of the movement's early years. The quest for a peaceful settlement was evident among the people, regardless of the future political status of Mizoram. As such, the public outcry for *remna leh muanna* and the role of various actors from the church and the student bodies were instrumental in the journey towards a peaceful settlement. Of course, the challenges of convincing the MNF armies were clear to the church and the student leaders, let alone the MNF leaders themselves. Unlike contemporary peace-making efforts, there was no international or third-party involvement in the peace process between the MNF and the government of India. Hence, the voices of the public and the different organizations were fundamental to the peace process. Reflecting on this, Ruata,[7] a former rebel with the MNF, explained why they agreed with the settlement:

> As for someone who had gone out for elephant hunting, it is normal to see him return home with an elephant or with a tusk. The public mood was such that they would agree and settle with anything—be it a deer, antler, or whatever big or small, we decided to accept it for the sake of peace and harmony.[8]

It was clear that the Mizo public was ready to accept a settlement, regardless of the provision or status, leave alone independence. Two leaders, Zoramthanga and Tawnluia, both trusted and close aides of Laldenga, were tasked with convincing the armies towards a peaceful settlement. The most serious challenge came from the armies as one leader stated: 'We were reluctant initially. However, our leader made a number of promises to convince us. They promised us housing facilities, employment opportunities, and special educational facilities for us.'[9]

For many of them, it was also the public outcry for *remna* and the church's plea that convinced them about the settlement. In recalling this, Thanga[10] noted:

> There were many of us who were reluctant to join India again. Apart from this, many of our friends had sacrificed for the cause of the movement. However, since the cry of the people was too immense along with the NGOs, churches, and political parties, and if our leaders were willing for it, we could not do anything much. In addition, since the people for whom we were struggling were requesting us to come overground and find ways for peaceful settlement, we had to go by the voice of the people.[11]

Such narratives were common among the armies, as Kima[12] noted:

> The people for whom we struggled were facing enormous hardships and were calling for peace. Apart from this, the Indian security force raped our women, destroyed rice fields, and burnt down our villages as well as churches. The pain and suffering continued to loom large under such circumstances. The people therefore said that they could no longer bear it. Curfews were imposed regularly, and since we Mizos mostly had a subsistence way of life, the people were in great misery. If we did not find ways for peace, they would not survive for long. Such opinion began to emerge in the difficult circumstances. Subsequently, all the churches, philanthropic organizations, and political parties asked us for a peaceful negotiation, and since the people for whom we fought in the movement could no longer bear the sufferings, we had to climb down from our position. Our leaders therefore began to find ways for peaceful settlement. This was not the best choice. The accord, as Pu Laldenga said, was not the best from our side and nor did the Indian government consider it as the best; we looked for a middle ground, and so the peace accord was signed accordingly.[13]

The renewed negotiation also showed that Laldenga remained critical to any form of a successful agreement. Much to the dismay of the PC-A, the negotiation for settlement proceeded. Two issues of crucial concern in the negotiation were the case of the Chakma Autonomous District Council (CADC), which the MNF proposed to be dissolved, and the other was the case of the territorial integration of the Mizo-inhabited areas under one administrative unit. The two issues were considered to be very serious and sensitive, and the government of India informed the MNF leaders that they could not commit to them. For some time it was feared that, with the two sides not arriving at any agreeable solution, this would sabotage the ongoing peace process. In addition, for the government of India, Laldenga and the MNF were already losing bargaining power, and hence the former was prepared to accept any kind of reasonable settlement. On the issue of the CADC, the MNF found the central leadership sympathetic to them. Back in Mizoram, the PC-A, under T. Sailo, was known to have raised the issue of immigration in his political speech. To this, Nibedon (1980) notes:

> As a soldier, Sailo was, perhaps, the first Mizo leader to have gauged the dangers of 'demographic invasion' from across the borders. All the three countries bordering each other through ambitious, artificial and arbitrary demarcations were engaged in driving minority ethnic groups into each other's territory. Sailo wanted the influx of foreigners—the Chakma tribesmen of Bangladesh—to be stopped forthwith by New Delhi. (Nibedon 1980: 206)

The PC included the case of controlling illegal immigration among its policy priorities. One of the party's objectives since its inception in 1975 was to prevent an uncontrolled influx of non-Mizos into Mizoram—hence the desire to check the influx of the Chakmas into Mizoram (T. Sailo 2000: 104). During the PC ministry, the PC-A was taking up the issue with the government in Delhi, and the MNF considered that this could derail the peace process. As such, it issued an order to the PC-A party not to interfere with or take on the Chakma case. The MNF leadership, and Laldenga in particular, were clear that pushing for territorial integration and the dissolution of the CADC would only prolong the struggle.

With the assembly elections drawing near in the year 1984, *remna* became the dominant political discourse and was part of the main manifesto. It was at this moment that the issue of *remna leh muanna* took centre stage in mainstream electoral politics and shaped the everyday public discourse and conversation. As can be seen, political parties of all hues and colours promised to usher in peace if elected to power. Peace became the rallying point during the elections to galvanize voters. Except for the PC-A led by Sailo, all other political parties rallied around peace in trying to woo voters.

The involvement of other organizations, such as the church, was extremely instrumental in bringing the government of India and MNF for a dialogue (Figure 6.3). From the start of the movement for independence, the church had been vying for a peaceful resolution and negotiations between the MNF and the government of India. As the desire for *remna* was gathering strength, leaders from different church denominations came together and formed the Mizoram Kohhran Hruaitute Committee (Mizoram Church Leaders Committee, MKHC) in 1982. A platform established by church leaders, the committee's agenda was to pursue dialogue and peace in Mizoram collectively. The church leaders were able to meet Laldenga in

Figure 6.3 Mizoram church leaders meeting Rajiv Gandhi, the then prime minister of India, regarding peace talks, in New Delhi, 1982
Source: L. R. Sailo collection.

London in 1982 after they had convinced all political parties in Mizoram to make a joint declaration for peace (MKHC 2012). Similarly, the INC took the extra step of having Lalduhoma fly over to London to meet Laldenga, the MNF president, and the former returned with a tape recording his entire conversation with the president. This recording was distributed across the Mizoram. The MNF then backed the INC to ensure that the latter won the 1984 assembly elections, which it subsequently did.

In 1984, Rajiv Gandhi took over as the new prime minister and appointed R. D. Pradhan as the main interlocutor. The peace process sped up, bringing the MNF and the government of India to the negotiating table, and by the time Pradhan took over, the process was already initiated. In fact, the negotiation had already advanced considerably, with only a few matters still outstanding for consideration. For example, the prime minister objected to amnesty to the MNF armies, the land rights equivalent to Article 371(1) being applied to Nagaland, and statehood for Mizoram, along with a separate high court and a university (Pradhan 1995: 120). In fact, the negotiation had to wait as the 'Punjab problem' was also drawing near its conclusion along with the Assam anti-foreigner campaign. In early 1986, just after the Punjab and Assam accords were finalized, negotiations resumed between the MNF and government of India, where the two parties agreed to sign the agreement on 25 June 1986 (Figure 6.4). One of the crucial agreements was that Laldenga would be instated as the chief minister after the signing of the accord. Only five days later and with Pradhan set to retire, the accord was signed in much haste so as to ensure that the negotiation did not drag on any further. Thus, the memorandum of settlement became a reality on 30 June 1986 (Pradhan 1995: 125) (Figures 6.5 and 6.6).

Figure 6.4   The signing of the Mizo Accord, with (*left to right sitting*) Lalthanhawla,
R. D. Pradhan, and Laldenga, 30 June 1986
Source: L. R. Sailo collection.

Figure 6.5   Mizo National Front (MNF) rebels on their way to peace camps, 1986
Source: L. R. Sailo collection.

Figure 6.6   Rajiv Gandhi (*centre*), the then prime minister of India, inaugurating Mizoram as the 23rd state of the Indian Union, 1987
Source: L. R. Sailo collection.

The Mizoram Congress continued to claim that it had made a huge sacrifice to make peace possible in the state. One of the primary demands of Laldenga was for the setting up of an interim government for six months, after which the MNF would give way to fresh elections. Lalthanhawla, the then Congress president, often made unwarranted claims of making a sacrificial act for peace in Mizoram. The party's election to the state in 1985 was essentially a result of the promise of peace. With the INC in power at the centre, brokering peace with the MNF was in its favour. This became evident in the way in which it destabilized the MNF ministry led by Laldenga, with eight of the MNF MLAs defecting to the INC.

After his induction as the chief minister of the state, Laldenga, speaking to reporters, reiterated his demand for a 'Greater Mizoram' by the inclusion of the Mizo-inhabited areas of the neighbouring states. In his own words, 'I hope the aspiration of these Mizos will be fulfilled within democratic norms.' On the Chakma issue, he commented that 'he would handle the matter in accordance with constitutional procedure', adding that 'the interest of the bonafide Chakmas in Mizoram would be protected as per the existing laws, but the Chakma refugees would have to go back to Bangladesh' (*Times of India* 1986). The position of the government of India was clear in the clause of the accord that said the minority rights of the state would be protected without specifying the communities. On the redrawing of the territorial boundaries, a clause in the accord noted:

... the question of unification of Mizo-inhabited areas of other states to form one administrative unit was raised by the MNF delegation. It was pointed out to them, on behalf of the Government of India, that Article 3 of the Constitution of India describes the procedure in this regard, but that the government cannot make any commitment in this respect. (Memorandum of Settlement [The Mizo Accord] 1986)

Everyday Peace

Peace has stood the test of time in Mizoram. Since the signing of the accord in 1986, there has been no resumption of armed conflict between the government of India and the MNF (Figures 6.7 and 6.8). Mizoram is now associated with *ral muang* (peaceful) or *ral muang ber* (most peaceful) state, which has become part of the official and everyday discourse of the state. The idea of *muanna* has been reproduced by the state and non-state actors and reinforced through various state and cultural events. It is through being *ral muang* that citizens of the state distinguish themselves from other parts of the northeast. In this context, the celebration of Remna Ni (Day of Peace) requires special mention (Figure 6.9).

Figure 6.7 The public welcoming the Mizo National Front (MNF) rebels and the martyrs in Aizawl, 1986
Source: L. R. Sailo collection.

Figure 6.8   Mizo women giving tributes to the coffins of Mizo National Front (MNF) rebels after the signing of the peace accord, 1986
Source: PAMRA collection.

Figure 6.9   Celebration of Remna Ni in Aizawl, 2019
Source: Explore Mizoram, https://www.exploremizoram.com/2019/06/remna-ni-2019.html (accessed in August 2019).

Remna Ni marks the day of the signing of the peace accord between the MNF and the government of India. While the MNF has observed the day since the time of the signing of the settlement, it was elevated to a state-level event in 2006 to commemorate 20 years of successful settlement. This was also the time when the MNF was in power in Mizoram. The event was supported by the North Eastern Council (NEC), too, apart from being granted a peace bonus by the government of India. While Remna Ni commemorates and even celebrates the end of the conflict, it actually celebrates the idea of 'peace'. At important state-led events, the citizens are reminded of the benefits of peace. This narrative has been co-opted by both national- and state-level political leaders, including civil society bodies.

The celebration of Remna Ni is now a part of official and public memory. It is common to see how state leaders and citizens alike proclaim the peacefulness of Mizoram. In fact, the idea of peaceful Mizoram finds mention in events and occasions of the state, both official and non-official. In one of his visits to the state, the former president of India, Ram Nath Kovind, started his speech by acknowledging the peacefulness of Mizoram. He stated, 'The Mizo Accord of 1986 has been honored by all sides, and an insurgency situation ended with all stakeholders agreeing to work peacefully for the greater common good of the state and its people.' He further stated, 'This is a miracle of our times' (Kovind 2017).

To mark 30 years of the settlement, the CYMA took the initiative of commemorating the day, consolidating the event in public memory, and collectivizing its celebration. The celebration saw the participation of civil society groups, student bodies, and church leaders, making the celebration a state-wide event. On the morning of 30 June 2016, at 8 a.m., every YMA branch across Mizoram played the Mizo *hnam hla* (Mizo national anthem), 'Ro Min Rel Sak Ang Che', composed by Rokunga. There was a state-wide commemoration of the day for the first time. In Aizawl, the day was observed at the AR *lammual*, where the then governor, Nirbhay Sharma, hoisted a flag coloured black and white, modified from the traditional Mizo *ngotekherh*,[14] which bears the map of Mizoram and a sketch of two hands intertwined in a handshake while a dove—the universal symbol of peace—hovers over the flag (*Frontier Despatch* 2016). From the idea of *remna leh muanna*, it is the idea of *ral muang* that is now dominating the public discourse. The everyday manifestation of this idea of being a *ral muang ram* (peaceful state) is defined in the way the citizens and state leaders proclaim its benefits. However, this idea of being a peaceful state becomes limited if one examines the continuing tensions over the memory of the MNF movement and the inter-ethnic relationship in contemporary Mizoram (Roluahpuia 2016, 2018a).

Post-Conflict Mizoram

In the last few decades, many of the conflicts that were thought to be intractable have come to an end in South Asia. Noteworthy among them are the Maoist movement in Nepal and the Tamil movement for independence in Sri Lanka. Hence, they are now widely referred to as 'post-conflict' societies. The use of the term 'post-conflict' signifies a break from the past and is referred to as a 'discreet period, marking a break from the history of conflict' (Shneiderman and Snellinger 2014). Shneiderman and Snellinger (2014) further note that the term 'post-conflict' 'frames political history as episodic, rather than as a stream of events that flow into one another in a multi-directional manner'. The problem with such a contextual framework, they contend, lies in the fact that 'such periodization hardly captures the complex temporalities and experiential layers of conflict for those who've lived through the conflict' (Shneiderman and Snellinger 2014).

In Mizoram, there is increasing usage of the term *rambuai* to describe the period of the MNF. This has become part of local expressions and the vocabulary of the common people. *Rambuai*, in its literal meaning, denotes 'troubled land' and hence describes a period of conflict, or what Chawngsailova (2012) calls the 'dark years'. To think of the period of the MNF movement as *rambuai* privileges the state's perception of the northeast region as a 'disturbed area'. On the one hand, the end of the conflict between the MNF and the government of India removed the possibility of restitution and reconciliation. On the other hand, it ignored the experiences of the people who are still suffering the after-effects of the conflict, as seen in the case of the Mizos living in Manipur and Tripura. Hence, there is an increasing territorialization of the term *rambuai* within Mizoram and even the MNF movement itself, as studies remain confined within the borders of the present-day state of Mizoram, leaving out the contribution and suffering of the Mizos of Manipur and Tripura (Figure 6.10).

Memories and memorial sites in relation to the period of the MNF movement are caught in the binary narratives of heroism propagated by the MNF and most former rebel writers on the one hand and of the most peaceful state that projects Mizoram as a case of successful conflict management by the Indian state on the other. The two discourses produce a narrative that erases the violent past and histories, subjugating the terror and silencing the public experience of the conflict. Even within Mizoram, there are neither any public memorial sites that commemorate or signify the village groupings nor any sites to remember the public suffering and loss. Rather, sites that memorialize the armed conflict are constructed by political parties such as the MNF and the INC, with the most visible one being the Martyr Thlanmual (Martyr Cemetery) constructed when the MNF was the ruling party in the state (Roluahpuia 2018b). The cemetery, needless to say, is exclusive as it is only reserved for former rebels who were part of the MNF (Figure 6.11). As such, the everyday peace in Mizoram is marked by this abject silence maintained over past atrocities and violent experiences of the people.

The difference between the other 'post-conflict' regions and Mizoram lies in the fact that there has been no talk about matters of peace and justice or reconciliation and restitution. Chhuanvawra, in a preface of a book, notes, 'Kan dan lam thiam hote

Figure 6.10   Memorial stone of Mizo National Front (MNF) martyrs in Nghathal village, Manipur, 2020
Source: Benjamin V. Jamkhanpau.

Figure 6.11   Martyr Thlanmual (Martyr Cemetery) in Luangmual, Aizawl, 2021
Source: Roluahpuia.

hian tihngaihna an hre hlawl lo anih chuan heti hian kan tuar ral hlen mai dawn chu a ni awm a, thin a na ngawihngawih mai a ni' (It is painful to know that our suffering will be just in vain if those who are law experts are also clueless) (Chhuanvawra 2014: xi). This articulates the unsettled questions and the repressed memories of the people, both issues that were ignored in the accord. It also raises questions about the possibility of talking about justice and restitution for a society and a region enraged by violence and conflict.

Over the years, a significant collection of repressed memories has come into the public domain, which goes beyond the binary narratives of conflict and peace (Pachuau and Sadan 2016; Roluahpuia 2018b). Significant unknown and silenced voices have emerged through such writings. Their significance lies in that they enrich the literature of the MNF period and provide accounts of the people who have lived experiences and encounters. There has been a plethora of writings by former MNF members on the movement that give accounts of the times and provide individual memoirs of that period of struggle and hardships. These are therefore a gradual departure from the dominant MNF account and lean more towards one that focuses on the people's experience. Narrated in the first person, books such as the double-volume *Rambuai Leh Kei* (Troubled Land and I) are significant contributions. The major limitations of these narratives are that most of the contributors are men, so the narratives of women remain locked in silence.

Another fundamental issue that Mizoram faces is the increasingly contentious conflict between the various ethnic communities in the state. Even as one could argue that the accord was between the MNF and the government of India, the absence of 'inter-ethnic peace' (Varshney 2002: 6) is becoming more apparent and serious. The state, over the years, has witnessed massive mobilizations along ethnic lines. Often the state is prone to violence erupting based on a minority–majority conflict (Roluahpuia 2016). While many attribute this to the legacy of the post-conflict Mizo hegemonic politics, mobilizations around tribal lines have an enduring history in the state. The Hmar and Paite struggles, for instance, are a case in point. The Paite demand for an Autonomous Council in the state of Mizoram goes back to the early 1950s. Likewise, the Hmars have demanded recognition of their identity and autonomy in the northern part of the state. The Hmar assertion in the post-MNF period became visible as the movement spearheaded by the Hmar People's Convention (HPC) took up arms to advance their cause. Eventually, in April 2018, the government of Mizoram and the HPC-D signed an agreement that concluded the armed struggle.

The issue is more contentious and complex with communities that are viewed as being outside of the 'Mizo' fold, particularly the Chakmas, the Gorkhas, and the Brus. While the Gorkhas have gradually assimilated into the Mizo culture while retaining their identity, the Chakmas and the Brus have asserted and maintained their difference from the Mizo majority. Moreover, tensions over identity and indigeneity have spilled over into competition for resources and economic opportunities in the state. With the political instability in the neighbouring CHTs of Bangladesh, there has been perpetual displacement and relocation of people across the borders. This was the case with the Kaptai Dam, where thousands of Hajongs and Chakmas who were initially rehabilitated in Mizoram were later relocated to Arunachal Pradesh in the 1960s. The porous border and the presence of shared ethnic groups on both sides have made the issue a sensitive one in Mizoram.

Ethnic issues now dominate politics in Mizoram and the sphere where civil society groups play an active role. Organizations, irrespective of their affiliations, tend to cater to ethnic interests. Ethnic-based organizations remain powerful in all public and political spheres. This is the case with the CYMA and the Central Young Lai Association (CYLA), and the same can be found among other communities such as the Chakmas and the Maras. The case of Mizoram represents what McDuie-Ra (2006: 26) describes as the place where civil society groups are 'driven into a discourse that emphasizes ethnicity and differences rather than shared issues and threats'. Perhaps, the limit of the concept of 'post-conflict' becomes more evident when one examines the political development in the post-MNF period.

Conclusion

In 2006, the state observed a festival known as Peace Fest to mark 20 years of the signing of the accord. The celebration took place under the MNF ministry, and in 2000 the government of India granted a 'peace bonus', valued at 182.45 crore rupees, to the state in recognition of its achievement. Similar events have become a part of the state discourse with non-state actors, such as the CYMA and the church, in furthering the discourse. The recent initiative of the CYMA to mark 30 years of *remna* is a case in point where a state-wide commemoration was observed for the first time. Repeatedly, one is reminded of the peacefulness achieved in Mizoram and the stable order of the state that make it an 'exception' and a 'model'. The accord in this view is the settlement between the MNF and the government of India, which limits an interpretation of it, given that the state continues to be entrapped with contentious and complex questions on the issue of identity, autonomy, and violence in the contemporary period.

Notes

1   The provision states:

Special provision with respect to the State of Mizoram Notwithstanding anything in this Constitution,

(a)   no Act of President in respect of

(i)   religious or social practices of the Mizos,

(ii) Mizo customary law and procedure,

(iii) administration of civil and criminal justice involving decisions according to Mizo customary law,

    (iv) ownership and transfer of land, shall apply to the State of Mizoram unless the Legislative Assembly of the State of Mizoram by a resolution so decides: Provided that nothing in this clause shall apply to any Central Act in force in the union territory of Mizoram immediately before the commencement of the Constitution (Fifty third Amendment) Act, 1986;

   (b) the Legislative Assembly of the State of Mizoram shall consist of not less than forty members.

2 *Lammual* refers to the AR parade field, which is located at the heart of Aizawl city, mostly used for major public gatherings and other recreational activities.

3 Interview with an MNF leader, 23 March 2015.

4 'Returnees' is a term used to refer to surrendered MNF armies and leaders.

5 *Bengvarna* means information.

6 The PC split into two factions—PC-A and PC-B—due to internal differences over cabinet seat-sharing. The PC-A continued to be led by T. Sailo while the discontent MLAs formed the PC-B.

7 The name of the narrator has been changed.

8 Interview with a former rebel, 1 March 2015.

9 Interview with a former rebel, 25 March 2015.

10 The name of the narrator has been changed.

11 Interview with Thanga, 23 March 2015.

12 The name of the narrator has been changed.

13 Interview with a former rebel, 16 March 2015.

14 *Ngotekherh* is s a Mizo traditional shawl.

7   Conclusion

The relevance of nationalism is hard to underestimate. It remains a strong force of political mobilization shaping contemporary society and politics. The past few years have seen the resurgence of what is commonly referred to as right-wing nationalism across the globe. Such movements are characterized by their ideological appeal to exclusive claims on ethnic and racial purity. More so, they envision a homogenous conception of nationhood defined by majoritarian identity and culture. This has brought back the issue of nationalism at the very centre of academic focus. In India, too, the growing force of right-wing nationalism has affected, if not complicated, regional and nationalist politics. However, the focus on this has been largely confined to right-wing forces' ideologies and electoral success. Rarely does one see how this is altering the nationalist politics, such as between the right-wing parties and those that profess a separate, if not strong, sense of nationalism at the sub-state and regional levels.

In India, the discourse of national integration is premised on the idea of anxiety and insecurity. Even after over 70 years of India's independence, the northeast region remains in a state of permanent exception. When it comes to national policies towards the region, one has not seen a shift irrespective of the powers that be at the centre (Baruah 2020). Since 2014, the BJP has succeeded in making inroads in various parts of the region and taking over political power in a majority of the states. With this, there is a renewed push for integration of the region within the national ethos and culture of the country. While one may remain critical of the right-wing agenda, the experience of the northeast region and the tribal communities shows how national integration continued to be opposed in the region, irrespective of the party ruling at the centre. The reason is simple. The national imaginaries are framed from the cultural ethos of the dominant communities, who define what it means to be 'Indian'.

Within northeast India, the Mizos' case is not a unique one. Resistance to integration into the nation-state is particularly evident across the region, and this has inspired various sub-national movements. It has remained one of the core focuses of scholarly research in the region. The majority of the states have witnessed national movements, and there remains a strong identity, if not national consciousness, in the region. Therefore, what this book brings to the fore is not only an issue specific to the Mizos and the region at large but also how communities have imagined and articulated their idea of nation and nationalism. One key aspect of this work is to examine how nationalist ideas are articulated at the 'local' level. The vernacular articulation of nationalist ideas, their reframing, and reworking all combine to make Mizo nationalism appealing.

The book specifically examines *hla* in relation to Mizo nationalism. It interrogates this within the framework of vernacular nationalism and locates the use of *hla* within Mizo oral culture. Scholars of nationalism have long established the importance of print to create a nation. Since Anderson's (1983) publication of *Imagined Communities*, the relationship between print and nationalism has occupied the centre stage in numerous theoretical works on nationalism. However, this relationship has largely been studied in the context of more developed industrial societies—if not society with a 'high culture', as Gellner (1983: 35) has remarked. There is a danger of assuming that nationalism will only emerge in a specific condition such as industrialization, or modernity as commonly put, almost like a 'model' that others will emulate, if not follow suit. Of course, even in the Mizos' case, print media was used to articulate their idea of the nation. However, this articulation and use of the print were to reaffirm the vernacular idea of *zalenna* and *ram leh hnam*. Laldenga, the leader, who at times is elevated as the 'Father of the Mizo Nation', centred his idea on *zalenna* in his book *Mizoram Marches towards Freedom* (2001). Such writings by MNF leaders cannot be understood and read in isolation from the wider nationalist discourses that were produced in the oral.

Broadly, it was in *hla* that the Mizos articulated their aspirations (*party hla* and *hnam hla*) and recorded their experience (*rambuai hla*). While various aspects of Mizo oral culture, *thu leh hla*, are documented, the sociopolitical dimension remains unattended (Chhuanvawra 2011; Lalthangliana 2005). Scholarly studies on the MNF have confined themselves to explaining the rise and emergence of the MNF, linking it with the famine of 1959. There is no attempt at deeper engagement with the idea of Mizo nationalism. This book follows a different approach. Focusing on the oral, it brings forth narratives of the participants of the movement and the way in which ordinary Mizos contributed to the idea of nationalism. The oral is rooted in the sociocultural and political life-worlds of the Mizos. The Mizos' past and present are entangled in the oral, and while print does make its appearance with colonialism, the oral culture of the Mizos remains firm and relevant in contemporary Mizo society. Another aspect of vernacular work is the reframing of nationalist ideas.

Connected to this is how the ideas of nationalism are reframed in the 'local'. This involves how the Mizos and the MNF, in particular, positioned their struggle. For the MNF rebels, the movement for independence was for *zalenna* and *ram leh hnam*. In many of the songs composed by the MNF rebels, the content of *hnam hla* resonate the aspirations of *zalenna* and the struggle for *ram leh hnam*.

Hla made their appearance as soon as modern politics took root in Mizo society. As early as the 1950s, the Mizo political scene was suffused with various *party hla*. Such songs are composed in tune with the political environment of the time and resonate deeply with the people. The period of the 1950s and 1960s saw intense political mobilization across the northeast. A common issue faced by the tribal communities of the region was the question of the political future. While opinion remains divided, there are sections among the Nagas, Khasis, and Mizos who expressed their desire for independence. Others expressed their willingness to integrate with the Indian Union with a precondition for autonomy. Regardless, the newly independent state was persistent to integrate the region, and if and when opposed, it turned to coercive measures to assert its sovereignty and rule (Scott 2009; Leake 2016).

This book reads Mizo politics from the vantage point of the Mizos. This reading offers a new way of looking at tribal politics and nationalist aspirations in northeast India. In India, the dominant assumption remains that tribes are 'isolated' communities, and hence their politics are also 'read' in isolation. Of course, a large part of tribal areas was politically excluded by the colonial state. Mizoram, for instance, is put under the category of 'excluded area' as per the provisions of the Government of India Act, 1935. This has led to the assumption that nationalist feeling is a mere 'separatist' issue whose seeds were sown by colonial agents and missionaries. Such an assumption legitimizes the state agenda of integrating the region, and time and again the call for integration is made as a panacea for the problems of the northeast.

In fact, political events in the hills have shown otherwise. Contrary to the dominant assumption, tribal communities such as the Mizos actively articulate their idea of the nation and assert themselves. Up to India's independence, Mizo society was divided along two classes—the chiefs and the commoners. The chiefs, under the patronage of the colonial state, imposed their authority and rule. Indirect rule, as it was called, was far more direct than imagined. Through the chiefs, the colonial state was able to penetrate and assert its presence. This transformed the chiefs' traditional role as mere agents of the colonial state, a dual autocracy for the commoners as it was called—one under the political superintendent and the other under the chiefs. Dissatisfied and disgruntled by their rule, the new middle class and commoners began to aspire for freedom from the chiefs' rule. For the vast majority of the commoners, the overthrowing of the chieftainship was the immediate concern. Hence, the MU articulated the first idea of political rights by demanding freedom from the rule of the chiefs.

The period between 1946 and 1950 remains critical to understand Mizo politics. The British devised a plan of creating a 'Crown Colony', or future plans, to continue its rule over the hill areas. During this period, the political superintendents exercised their powers 'both autocratically and aristocratically' (Rao, Thansanga, and Hazarika 1987: 136). The period witnessed a new form of identity assertion as Mizo *hnam*. This idea of *hnam* was used in opposition to the more restrictive category such as the 'Lushai' that privileged identity and belonging attached to the chief's clan. The MU led the renaming of 'Lushai' to Mizo and further opposed any form of rule, both by the chiefs and the British. Anti-British sentiments also grew among the people that were largely directed towards the political superintendents. In this, the majority of Mizo commoners were up against the colonial state. The Lushai Hills was unquiet throughout the period with various forms of protest and non-cooperation movement being launched to oust both the chiefs and the colonial superintendent.

What the experience of Mizo nationalism also tells us is how the common people participated in the making and defining of Mizo *hnam*. Even when the movement for independence was led by the MNF, Mizo nationalism was defined and shaped by non-MNF members. Individuals such as Rokunga remain important torchbearers of Mizo nationalism even today. Likewise, MNF members belonging to diverse backgrounds participated in various capacities as *hnam sipai* (MNF armies): volunteers, while some composed songs that became an important medium through which Mizo nationalism was articulated and disseminated. The emphasis of this book therefore is to look at not only the elite character of Mizo nationalism but also to not identify Mizo nationalism exclusively with the MNF as a movement and, at present, a political party. Mizo nationalism is a mass phenomenon. Even today, while many Mizos do not associate themselves with the MNF movement or the party, they strongly identify themselves with Mizo *hnam* and Mizo nationalism. As such, composers of *hnam hla* in the past and present are nationalistic but not necessarily members of the MNF. In short, the idea of the Mizo nation—and, by extension, Mizo nationalism—is a creative process, where a much broader population, if not a cross section of people, play an active part in its construction.

As noted by scholars on nationalism, it is important to underline the social and political context in which musical nationalism emerges (Stokes 1994; Brincker 2014). Likewise, it is the book's contention that the emergence of *hnam hla* needs to be read against the backdrop of Mizo politics and the rise of the MNF. *Hnam hla* represent a specific genre of songs that are now identified with Mizo nationalism, which is intertwined with the idea of *ram leh hnam*. In other words, *hnam hla* are important carriers of Mizo nationalism, and since their emergence *hnam hla* continue to find a place in gatherings as well as in sociocultural and political events. What has changed, however, over the years, is that the *hnam hla* composed during the period of the MNF movement are discouraged from being sung openly in public. Perhaps there is a fear that such songs will re-arouse nationalist feelings among the youth. However, *hnam hla* that refer to the love for Zoram, or Mizoram, continue to be sung in public gatherings and functions. It is a common sight in Mizoram to see singers perform such songs. Singers and composers come from diverse backgrounds, but what remains significant is the continued relevance of *hnam hla* in the sociopolitical life of the Mizos. Further research can illuminate how such performances shape the ideas of Mizo nationalism in the twenty-first century, which is beyond the scope of this book.

By way of conclusion, I wish to return to the introduction. The protest in 2018 demanding the ouster of S. B. Shashank reiterates the persistence of *hnam* consciousness among the Mizos. In the post-MNF movement period, there have been various instances of protest and movements, sometimes even hinging upon exclusive notions of identity and territory. Such instances are determined by the idea of protecting the *ram leh hnam*, and often debates and discussions hark back to the old yet undying issue of political integration of the Mizos with the Indian Union. Protests and demonstrations are emotionally charged with the circulation, if not the singing, of various *hnam hla*. Time and again it is *hnam hla* that Mizos fall back on. As such, understanding the oral is indispensable to explaining Mizo nationalism. As shown in the book, Mizo nationalism is the handiwork of the ordinary Mizos and the elite group who have constructed and defined the contour of Mizo nationalism.

Glossary

bawrhsap	political superintendent
bengvarna	information
chhinlung	covering rock
Chhinlung *chhuak*	people of Chhinlung origin
hla	songs
hnam	clan, tribe, nation
hnam hla	national songs
hnam sipai	Mizo National Front (MNF) armies
hnamchawm	commoners
inpumkhatna	unity
kawktu	pointer
lammual	parade field
lengzem hla	love or romantic songs
mautam	famine caused by a sudden boom in rat population following the flowering of *Melocanna baccifera*, a species of bamboo, every 48–50 years in northeast India
muanna	peace
party hla	songs composed by members of political parties or individuals in support of specific parties
pasaltha	tribal hero, warrior
ral muang	peaceful
ram	land, territory
rambuai	troubled land
rambuai hla	songs of troubled times
ramrilekha	boundary paper

remna	settlement, accord, agreement
Remna Ni	Day of Peace
sawrkar	government
thingfak	kindle wood
tlangmi	hill people
titi	unstructured conversation
vai	a term used by the Mizos to refer to the plains people, which has both racial and religious undertones
veng	locality
zalenna	freedom
zalenna sual	freedom struggle
zo	ethnonym used to refer to the Kuki-Chin-Mizo communities

References

Agamben, G. 2005. *State of Exception*. Chicago and London: University of Chicago Press.

Aggarwal, R., and M. Bhan. 2009. 'Disarming Violence: Development, Democracy, and Security on the Borders of India'. *Journal of Asian Studies* 68(2): 519–542.

Aloysius, G. 1998. *Nationalism without a Nation in India*. Delhi: Oxford University Press.

Anderson, B. 1983. *Imagined Communities: Reflections on the Origin and Spread of Nationalism*. London: Verso Books.

Aplin, K. P., and J. Lalsiamliana. 2010. 'Chronicle and Impacts of the Mautam in Mizoram'. In *Rodent Outbreaks: Ecology and Impacts*, edited by G. R. Singletoin, S. R. Belmain, P. R. Brown, and B. Hardy, 13–48. Los Banos: International Rice Research Institute.

Appadurai, A. 1996. *Modernity at Large: Cultural Dimensions of Globalization*. Minneapolis: University of Minnesota Press.

———. 1998. 'Dead Certainty: Ethnic Violence in an Era of Globalization'. *Public Culture* 10(2): 225–247.

Asad, T. 2007. *On Suicide Bombing*. New York: Columbia University Press.

Assam Government. 1960. *Report of the Committee Appointed by the Assam Legislative Assembly on the Famine Condition of Mizo Hills*. Shillong: Assembly Secretariat.

Barbora, S. 2005. 'Autonomy in the Northeast: The Frontiers of Centralised Politics'. In *The Politics of Autonomy: Indian Experiences*, edited by R. Samaddar, 196–215. New Delhi: SAGE Publications.

Barth, F. 1969. 'Introduction'. In *Ethnic Groups and Boundaries: The Social Organization of Cultural Difference*, edited by F. Barth, 9–38. Boston: Little Brown and Company.

Baruah, S. 1999. *India against Itself: Assam and the Politics of Nationality*. New Delhi: Oxford University Press.

———. 2003a. 'Protective Discrimination and Crisis of Citizenship in North-East India'. *Economic and Political Weekly* 38(17): 1624–1626.

———. 2003b. 'Nationalizing Space: Cosmetic Federalism and the Politics of Development in Northeast India'. *Development and Change* 34(5): 915–939.

———. 2005. *Durable Disorder: Understanding the Politics of Northeast India*. New Delhi: Oxford University Press.

———. (ed.) 2009. *Beyond Counter-Insurgency: Breaking the Impasse in Northeast India*. New Delhi: Oxford University Press.

———. 2020. *In the Name of the Nation: India and Its Northeast*. Redwood City, CA: Stanford University Press.

Bates, C. 1988. 'Congress and the Tribals'. In *The Indian National Congress and the Political Economy of India 1885–1985*, edited by M. Shepperdson and C. Simmons, 231–252. Aldershot and Brookfield: Avebury Publisher.

Bayly, C. A. 1998. *Origins of Nationality in South Asia: Patriotism and Ethical Government in the Making of Modern India*. New Delhi: Oxford University Press.

Becker, H. 2011. 'Beyond Trauma: New Perspectives on the Politics of Memory in East and Southern Africa'. *African Studies* 70(2): 321–335.

Bentham, J. 1995. *The Panopticon Writings*. London: Verso Books.

Bezbaruah Committee. 2014. *Report of the Committee under the Chairmanship of Shri M.P. Bezbaruah to Look into the Concerns of the People of the Northeast Living in Other Parts of the Country*. New Delhi: Ministry of Home Affairs, Government of India.

Bhan, M. 2013. *Counterinsurgency, Democracy and the Politics of Identity in India: From Warfare to Welfare*. Oxon: Routledge.

Bhatia, B. 2010. 'Justice Denied to Tribals in the Hill Districts of Manipur'. *Economic and Political Weekly* 45(31): 38–46.

Bhaumik, S. 2009. *Troubled Periphery: Crisis of India's Northeast*. New Delhi: SAGE Publications.

Bhukya, B. 2017. *The Roots of the Periphery: A History of the Gonds of Deccan India*. New Delhi: Oxford University Press.

———. 2021. 'Featuring Adivasi/Indigenous Studies'. *Economic and Political Weekly* 56(25): 13–17.

Billig, M. 1995. *Banal Nationalism*. London: SAGE Publications.

Bohlman, P. V. 2004. *The Music of European Nationalism: Cultural Identity and Modern History*. Santa Barbara: ABC-CLIO.

———. 2010. *Music, Nationalism, and the Making of the New Europe*. New York: Routledge.

Bose, S. 2017. *The Nation as Mother and Other Visions of Nationhood*. New Delhi: Penguin Random House.

Brass, P. R. 1991. *Ethnicity and Nationalism: Theory and Comparisons*. New Delhi: SAGE Publications.

Brenner, D. 2018. *Rebel Politics: A Political Sociology of Armed Struggle in Myanmar's Borderlands*. Ithaca, NY: Cornell University Press.

Brincker, B. 2014. 'The Role of Classical Music in the Construction of Nationalism: A Cross-National Perspective'. *Nations and Nationalism* 20(4): 664–682.

Brown, D. 1988. *The State and Ethnic Politics in Southeast Asia*. London: Routledge.

Brubaker, R. 1996. *Nationalism Reframed: Nationhood and the National Question in New Europe*. Cambridge, UK: Cambridge University Press.

Brubaker, R., M. Feischmidt, J. Fox, and L. Grancea. 2006. *Nationalist Politics and Everyday Ethnicity in a Transylvanian Town*. Princeton, NJ: Princeton University Press.

Bryman, A. 2012 (2005). *Social Research Methods*. Oxford: Oxford University Press.

Business Standard. 2016. 'Union Min Stays Away from Function to Felicitate Khuangchera'. 18 August. https://www.business-standard.com/article/pti-stories/union-min-stays-away-from-function-to-felicitate-khuangchera-116081801263_1.html. Accessed on 12 August 2017.

Butalia, U. 1998. *The Other Side of Silence: Voices from the Partition of India*. New Delhi: Viking Press.

Butler, J., and A. Athanasiou. 2013. *Dispossession: The Performative in the Political*. Cambridge, UK: Polity Press.

Carye Jr, D. 2017. *Oral History in Latin America: Unlocking the Spoken Archive*. New York and Oxon: Routledge.

Chakrabarty, D. 1999. 'Nation and Imagination: The Training of the Eye in Bengali Modernity'. *Topoi* 18(1): 29–47.

Chaltuahkhuma. 2001 (1987). *Political History of Mizoram*. Aizawl: Vanthangi.

Chandhoke, N. 2006. 'A State of One's Own: Secessionism and Federalism in India'. Working Paper No. 80, Crisis State Programme, London School of Economics and Political Science.

Chatterjee, S. 1994. *The Making of Mizoram: Role of Laldenga*. New Delhi: MD Publications.

Chatterjee, P. 1986. *Nationalist Thought and the Colonial World: A Derivative Discourse?* London: Zed Books.

———. 1993. *The Nation and Its Fragments: Colonial and Postcolonial Histories*. Princeton, NJ: Princeton University Press.

Chaube, S. K. 1973. *Hill Politics in Northeast India*. New Delhi: Orient Longman.

Chaudhuri, M. 1993. 'Gender in the Making of the Indian Nation-State'. *Sociological Bulletin* 48(12): 113–133.

Chaudhury, S. K., and S. M. Patnaik (ed.). 2008. *Indian Tribes and the Mainstream*. New Delhi: Rawat Publications.

Chawngsailova. 2007. *Ethnic National Movement in the Role of the MNF*. Aizawl: Mizoram Publication Board.

———. 2012. *Mizoram during the 20 Dark Years*. Guwahati: Eastern Book House.

Chawnghranga. 2015. *Rokunga Leh A Hlate Par Vul Lai*. Aizawl: Author.

Chhangte, C. L. 2011. 'Loneliness in the Midst of Curfews: The Mizo Insurgency Movement and Terror Lore'. In *The Oxford Anthology of Writings from North-East India*, edited by T. Misra, 237–244. New Delhi: Oxford University Press.

Chhuanvawra, C. 2011. *Hmanlai Leh Tunlai Mizo Hlate*. Aizawl: Author.

———. 2014. 'Editor Thuchang'. In *Rambuai Leh Kei*, vol. 2, edited by C. Chhuanvawra, xi. Aizawl: Mizoram Upa Pawl.

Clifford, J., and G. E. Marcus. 1986. *Writing Culture: The Poetics and Politics of Ethnography*. Berkeley: University of California.

Cockell, J. G. 2000. 'Ethnic Nationalism and Subaltern Political Process: Exploring Autonomous Democratic Action in Kashmir'. *Nations and Nationalism* 6(3): 319–345.

Connor, W. 1972. 'Nation-Building or Nation-Destroying?'. *World Politics* 24(3): 319–355.

———. 1994. *Ethnonationalism: The Quest for Understanding*. Princeton, NJ: Princeton University Press.

Cons, J. 2016. *Sensitive Space: Fragmented Territory at the India–Bangladesh Border*. Seattle: University of Washington Press.

Constituent Assembly of India. 1949. *Constituent Assembly Debates (Proceedings)*, vol. 9. New Delhi: Constituent Assembly of India.

Cullather, N. 2006. '"The Target Is the People": The Representations of the Village in Modernization and U.S. National Security Doctrine'. *Culture Politics* 2(1): 29–48.

Curtis, B. 2008. *Music Makes the Nation: Nationalist Composers and Nation-Building in Nineteenth-Century Europe*. Amherst, NY: Cambria Press.

Daiya, K. 2011. *Violent Belongings: Partition, Gender, and National Culture in Postcolonial India*. Philadelphia: Temple University Press.

Darkhuma, H. 2009. *Manipur Mizo Leh Zo Hnahthlakte Chanchin*. Aizawl: Gilzom Offset.

Das, S. K. 2007. 'Conflict and Peace in North-East: The Role of Civil Society'. Policy Studies, No. 42, East-West Centre, Washington, DC.

———. 2010. 'India: Democracy, Nation, and the Spirals of Insecurity—State Response to Ethnic Separatism in India's Northeast'. In *Fixing Fractured Nations: The Challenge of Ethnic Separation in Asia Pacific*, edited by R. G. Wirsing and E. Ahrari, 116–139. New York: Palgrave Macmillan.

Das, V. 1997. *Critical Events: An Anthropological Perspectives on Contemporary India*. Oxford: Oxford University Press.

———. 2007. *Life and Words: Violence and the Descent into the Ordinary*. California: University of California Press.

Dasgupta, J. 1997. 'Community, Authenticity and Autonomy: Insurgence and Institutional Development in India's Northeast'. *Journal of Asian Studies* 56(2): 345–370.

Datta-Ray, B. 1983. *The Emergence and Role of Middle Class in North-East India*. New Delhi: Uppal Publishing House.

de Mel, N. 2007. *Militarizing Sri Lanka: Popular Culture, Memory and Narrative in the Armed Conflict*. New Delhi: SAGE Publications.

Dejarlais, R., and A. Kleinman. 1994. 'Violence and Demoralization in the New World Disorder'. *Anthropology Today* 10(5): 9–12.

Deka, D. 2019. 'Between Underground and Overground: Narratives on the Identity of Women Insurgents in Assam'. *Asian Ethnicity* 20(4): 469–485.

Dena, L. 2008. *In Search of Identity: Hmars of North-east India*. Delhi: Akansha Publishing House.

Denzin, N. K. 2017. *The Research Act: A Theoretical Introduction to Sociological Methods*. Oxon: Routledge.

Dirks, N. B. 2001. *Castes of Mind: Colonialism and the Making of Modern India*. Princeton, NJ: Princeton University Press.

Dixon, P. 2009. '"Hearts and Minds": British Counter-Insurgency from Malaya to Iraq'. *Journal of Strategic Studies* 32(3): 353–381.

Doungel, J. 2012. *Evolution of District Council Autonomy in Mizoram: A Case Study of the Lai Autonomous District Council*. Guwahati: Spectrum Publications.

Duschinski, H. 2009. 'Destiny Effects: Militarization, State Power, and Punitive Containment in Kashmir Valley'. *Anthropological Quarterly* 82(3): 691–717.

Duschinski, H., M. Bhan, A. Zia, and C. Mahmood (ed.) 2018. *Resisting Occupation in Kashmir*. Philadelphia: University of Pennsylvania Press.

Economic and Political Weekly. 1978. 'The Laldenga Factor'. *Economic and Political Weekly* 13(19): 786.

———. 1979. 'Mizoram: Back to Square One'. *Economic and Political Weekly* 14(18): 790.

———. 1982. 'Mizoram: Not the Whole Story'. *Economic and Political Weekly* 17(5): 130–131.

Edensor, T. 2002. *National Identity, Popular Culture and Everyday Life*. Oxford: Berg Publishers.

Fahmy, Z. 2011. *Ordinary Egyptians: Creating the Modern Nation through Popular Culture*. Redwood City, CA: Stanford University Press.

Fernandes, S. 2009. 'Ethnicity, Civil Society, and the Church: The Politics of Evangelical Christianity in Northeast India'. In *Evangelical Christianity and Democracy in Asia*, edited by D. H. Lumsdaine, 131–155. New York: Oxford University Press.

Frontier Despatch. 2016. 'Waiting at Khuangchera's Grave'. *Frontier Despatch* 1(26): 1–12.

Fuller, C., and V. Bénéï (ed.) 2001. *The Everyday State and Society in Modern India.* London: Hurst & Co.

Gaikwad, N. 2009. 'Revolting Bodies, Hysterical State: Women Protesting the Armed Forces Special Powers Act (1958)'. *Contemporary South Asia* 17(3): 299–311.

Geertz, C. 1973. *The Interpretation of Cultures.* New York: Fontana Press.

Geleta, E. B. 2014. 'The Politics of Identity and Methodology in African Development Ethnography'. *Qualitative Research* 14(1):131–146.

Gellner, E. 1983. *Nations and Nationalism.* Ithaca, NY: Cornell University Press.

Gergan, M. D., and Sara H. Smith. 2021. 'Theorizing Racialization through India's "Mongolian Fringe"'. *Ethnic and Racial Studies* 45(2): 361–382.

Gooptu, S. 2018. *The Music of Nationhood: Dwijendralal Roy of Bengal.* Delhi: Primus Books.

Goswami, B. B. 1979. *The Mizo Unrest: A Study of Politicisation of Culture.* Jaipur: Alakh.

Goswami, N. 2009. 'The Indian Experience of Conflict Resolution in Mizoram'. *Strategic Analysis* 33(4): 579–589.

Grandia, L. 2013. 'Road Mapping: Megaprojects and Land Grabs in the Northern Guatemalan Lowlands'. *Development and Change* 44(2): 233–259.

Guha, A. 1979. 'Great Nationalism, Little Nationalism and Problem of Integration: A Tentative View'. *Economic and Political Weekly* 14(7–8): 455, 457–458.

————. 1982. 'The Indian National Question: A Conceptual Frame'. *Economic and Political Weekly* 17(31): 2–12.

Guha, R. 1983. *Elementary Aspects of Peasant Insurgency in Colonial India.* Delhi: Oxford University Press.

————. 1996. 'Savaging the Civilised: Verrier Elwin and the Tribal Question in Late Colonial India'. *Economic and Political Weekly* 31(35–37): 2375–80, 2382–83, 2385–89.

————. 1997. *Dominance without Hegemony: History and Power in Colonial India.* Cambridge, MA: Harvard University Press.

Gurr, T. R. 1970. *Why Men Rebel.* Princeton, NJ: Princeton University Press.

Guru, G. 2016a. 'The Indian Nation in Its Egalitarian Conception'. In *Dalit Studies,* edited by R. Rawat and K. Satyanarayana, 31–52. Durham, NC: Duke University Press.

————. 2016b. 'Nationalism as the Framework for Dalit Self-Realization'. *Brown Journal of World Affairs* 23(1): 239–252.

Guyot-Réchard, B. 2013. 'Nation-Building or State-Making? India's North-East Frontier and the Ambiguities of Nehruvian Developmentalism, 1950–1959'. *Contemporary South Asia* 21(1): 22–37.

Habermas, J. 1991. *The Structural Transformation of the Public Sphere.* Cambridge, MA: MIT Press.

Hack, Karl. 2012. 'Everyone Lived in Fear: Malaya and the British Way of Counter-Insurgency'. *Small Wars and Insurgencies* 23(4–5): 671–699.

Hassan, S. M. 2008. *Building Legitimacy: Exploring State–Society Relations in Northeast India*. New Delhi: Oxford University Press.

Hausing, K. K. S. 2014. 'Asymmetric Federalism and the Question of Democratic Justice in Northeast India'. *India Review* 13(2): 87–111.

Hazarika, S. 1996. *Strangers of the Mist: Tales of War and Peace in Northeast India*. New Delhi: Penguins Books.

Hechter, M. 1975. *Internal Colonialism: The Celtic Fringe in British National Development*. Berkeley: University of California Press.

Hermana, C. 2015. *Zoram Buai Lai Khan*. Aizawl: Author.

Herzfeld, M. 1997. *Portrait of a Greek imagination: An Ethnographic Biography of Andreas Nenedakis*. Chicago: University of Chicago Press.

Hluna, J. V. 2008. *Zawlkhawpui Senmei Chan Ni*. Aizawl: Zoram Ni Organizing Committee.

Hluna, J. V., and Rini Tochhawng. 2012. *The Mizo Uprising*. Newcastle upon Tyne, UK: Cambridge Scholars Publishing.

Hobsbawm, E. 1990. *Nations and Nationalism since 1780: Programme, Myth, Reality*. Cambridge, UK: Cambridge University Press.

Hobsbawm, E., and T. Ranger (eds.). 1983. *The Invention of Tradition*. Cambridge, UK: Cambridge University Press.

Hrangbana College (ed.). 2014. *Rambuai Literature: Seminar Papers*. Aizawl: Government Hrangbana College.

Hroch, M. 1985. *Social Preconditions of National Revival in Europe*. Cambridge, UK: Cambridge University Press.

Hussain, M. 1993. *The Assam Movement: Class, Ideology, and Identity*. Delhi: Manak Publications.

Hutchinson, J. 1987. *The Dynamics of Cultural Nationalism: The Gaelic Revival and the Creation of the Modern Irish Nation State*. London: George Allen and Unwin.

———. 1994. *Modern Nationalism*. London: Fontana Press.

———. 2004. 'Myth against Myth: The Nation as an Ethnic Overlay'. *Nations and Nationalism* 10(1–2): 109–123.

———. 2005. *Nations as Zones of Conflict*. London, California, and New Delhi: SAGE Publications.

Inoue, K. 2005. 'Integration of the North East: The State Formation Process'. In *Sub-Regional Relations in the Eastern South Asia: With Special Focus on India's North Eastern Region* (Joint Research Program Series No. 133), edited by M. Murayama, K. Inoue, and S. Hazarika, 16–30. Chiba: Institute of Developing Economies.

Ignatieff, M. 1993. *Blood and Belonging: Journeys into the New Nationalism*. Toronto: Viking Press.

Jafa, V. S. 1999. 'Counterinsurgency Warfare: The Use and Abuse of Military Force'. *Faultlines: Writings on Conflict and Conflict Resolution* 3. New Delhi. https://www.satp.org/satporgtp/publication/faultlines/volume3/fault3-jafaf.htm. Accessed on 23 January 2023.

———. 2000. 'Mizoram Contours of Non-Military Intervention'. *Faultlines: Writings on Conflict and Conflict Resolution* 4. New Delhi. https://www.satp.org/satporgtp/publication/faultlines/volume4/Fault4-JafaF1.htm. Accessed on 23 January 2023.

Jaffrelot, C., and S. Kumar (ed.). 2009. *Rise of the Plebeians? The Changing Face of Indian Legislative Assemblies.* New Delhi: Routledge.

Jangam, C. 2017. *Dalits and the Making of Modern India.* Oxford: Oxford University Press.

Jenkins, L. 2003. 'Another "People of India" Project: Colonial and National Anthropology'. *Journal of Asian Studies* 62(4): 1143–1170.

Jenkins, R. 2008 (1997). *Rethinking Ethnicity: Arguments and Explorations.* London: SAGE Publications.

Jongerden, J. 2010. 'Village Evacuation and Reconstruction in Kurdistan (1993–2002)'. *Etudes Rurales* 186: 77–100.

Joshi, V. 2012. *A Matter of Belief: Christian Conversion and Healing in North-East India.* New York: Berghahn Books.

Kak, S. (ed.) 2011. *Until My Freedom Has Come: The New Intifada in Kashmir.* New Delhi: Penguin Books.

Kapila, K. 2008. 'The Measure of a Tribe: The Cultural Politics of Constitutional Reclassification in North India'. *Journal of Royal Anthropological Institute* 14(1): 117–134.

Kaul, S. 2017. *Of Gardens and Graves: Kashmir, Poetry, Politics.* Durham, NC: Duke University Press.

Khai, S. K. 1995. *Zo People and Their Culture.* New Lamka: Khamput Hatzaw.

Khalili, L. 2010. 'The Location of Palestine in Global Counterinsurgencies'. *International Journal of Middle East Studies* 42(3): 413–433.

———. 2013. *Times in the Shadows: Confinement in Counterinsurgencies.* Redwood City, CA: Stanford University Press.

Kikon, D. 2009. 'The Predicament of Justice: Fifty Years of Armed Forces Special Powers Act in India'. *Contemporary South Asia* 17(3): 271–282.

Kipgen, N., and A. R. Chowdhury. 2016. 'Contested State-Craft on the Frontiers of the Indian Nation: "Hills–Valley Divide" and the Genealogy of Kuki Ethnic Nationalism in Manipur'. *Studies in Ethnicity and Nationalism* 16(2): 283–303.

Kipgen, M. 1997. *Christianity and Mizo Culture: The Encounter between Christianity and Zo Culture in Mizoram.* Aizawl: Mizo Theological Conference.

Kohli, A. 1997. 'Can Democracies Accommodate Ethnic Nationalism? Rise and Decline of Self-Determination Movements in India'. *Journal of Asian Studies* 56(2): 325–344.

Kohn, H. 1944. *The Idea of Nationalism: A Study in Its Origins and Background.* New York: Macmillan and Co.

Kovind, R. N. 2017. 'Address by President of India, Shri Ram Nath Kovind, on the Occasion of Inauguration of Housing Complexes for Economically Weaker Sections under BSUP Schemes'. http://presidentofindia.nic.in/writereaddata/Portal/Speech/ Document/397/1_Speechinauguration_of_housing_complexes__Mizoram.pdf. Accessed on 2 March 2018.

Krishna, S. 1994. 'Cartographic Anxiety: Mapping the Body Politic in India'. *Alternatives: Global, Local, Political* 19(4): 507–521.

———. 1999. *Postcolonial Insecurities: India, Sri Lanka and the Question of Nationalism.* Minneapolis: University of Minnesota Press.

Kshetrimayum, J. 2009. 'Shooting the Sun: A Study of Death and Protest in Manipur'. *Economic and Political Weekly* 44(40): 48–54.

Ladwig, W. C. III. 2009. 'Insights from the Northeast: Counterinsurgency in Nagaland and Mizoram'. In *India and Counterinsurgency: Lessons*, edited by D. P. Fidler and S. Ganguly, 45–62. London: Routledge.

Lalchungnunga. 1994. *Mizoram: Politics of Regionalism and National Integration.* New Delhi: Spectrum Publications.

Laldenga. 1978. 'People Will Fight as Long as Their Grievances Are Not Settled: Laldenga'. *India Today*, 30 June. https://www.indiatoday.in/magazine/interview/ story/19780630-people-will-fight-as-long-as-their-grievances-are-not-settled-laldenga-823252-2014-04-04. Accessed on 12 November 2018.

———. 1980. 'We Can Make Ho Chi Minhs in Mizoram Also: Laldenga'. *India Today*, 31 July. https://www.indiatoday.in/magazine/indiascope/story/19800731-we-can-make-ho-chi-minhs-in-mizoram-also-laldenga-821295-2014-01-17. Accessed on 12 November 2018.

———. 2011. *Mizoram Marches towards Freedom.* Aizawl: Lalbiakdiki.

Lalhmingthanga. 2009 (1965). *Exodus Politics.* Aizawl: Christina Zorinliani.

Lalhmingthanga. 2014. 'Buai Laia Zirlai Hruaitu-Silchar Bubai'. In *Rambuai Leh Kei*, vol. 2, edited by C. Chhuanvawra, 168–175. Aizawl: Mizoram Upa Pawl.

Lalrawnliana. 1995. *Zoramin Zalenna A Sual*, vol. 1. Aizawl: Author.

———. 1997. *Zoramin Zalenna A Sual*, vol. IV. Aizawl: Author.

Lalrimawia. 1995. *Mizoram: History and Cultural Identity.* Guwahati: Spectrum Publications.

Lalrinawma. 2014. 'Rambuai Hrin Chhuah Tawngkam'. In 'Rambuai Literature: Seminar Papers', 1–11, Government Hrangbana College, Aizawl.

Lalrinthanga, M. C. 1993. *Zoram Politik (1976–1986).* Aizawl: Author.

Lalruanga. n.d. *Mizo Hla Leh A Phuahtute Chanchin* (Mizo Songs and the Story of Their Composers). Aizawl: Zomi Book Agency.

Lalthangliana, B. 1993. *Mizo Literature*. Aizawl: RTM Press.

———. 2002. *Mizo Hun Hlui Hlate*. Aizawl: Author.

———. 2005. *Culture and Folklore of Mizoram*. New Delhi: Ministry of Information and Broadcasting, Government of India.

———. 2015. *Zawlkhawpui: A Din Kum 125-na Pualin*. Aizawl: Author.

Lawmzuala, K. 2003. *Mizo District Council Kha*. Aizawl: Author.

Leake, E. 2016. 'At the Nation-State's Edge: Centre–Periphery Relations in Post-1947 South Asia'. *Historical Journal* 59(2): 509–539.

Liangkhaia. 1938. *Mizo Chanchin* (Accounts on Mizo). Aizawl: LTL Publications.

Lianzuala, S. 1998. *Kan Ram A Dam Lo*. Jampui: Ngura.

Lokaneeta, J. 2017. 'Sovereignty, Violence and Resistance in North East India: Mapping Political Theory Today'. *Theory and Event* 20(1): 76–86.

Mamdani, M. 1996. *Citizen and Subject: Contemporary Africa and the Legacy of Late Colonialism*. Princeton, NJ: Princeton University Press.

———. 2005. 'Good Muslim, Bad Muslim: America, the Cold War and the Origins of Terror'. *India International Centre Quarterly* 32(1): 1–10.

Mathur. S. 2012. 'Life and Death in the Borderlands: Indian Sovereignty and Military Impunity'. *Race and Class* 54(1): 33–49.

Marcus, G. E. 1995. 'Ethnography in/of the World System: The Emergence of Multi-Sited Ethnography'. *Annual Review of Anthropology* 24: 95–117.

McCall, A. G. 1949. *Lushai Chrysallis*. Aizawl: Tribal Research Institute.

McCracken, G. 1988. *The Long Interview*. Newbury Park, London, and Delhi: SAGE Publications.

McDonald, D. A. 2013. *My Voice Is My Weapon: Music, Nationalism, and the Poetics of Palestinian Resistance*. London and Durham, NC: Duke University Press.

McDuie-Ra, D. 2006. 'Civil Society Organisations and Human Security: Transcending Constricted Space in Meghalaya'. *Contemporary South Asia* 15(1): 35–53.

———. 2008. 'Between National Security and Ethno-Nationalism: The Regional Politics of Development in Northeast India'. *Journal of South Asian Development* 3(2): 185–210.

———. 2009. 'Fifty-year Disturbance: The Armed Forces Special Powers Act and Exceptionalism in a South Asian Periphery'. *Contemporary South Asia* 17(3): 255–270.

———. 2012. *Northeast Migrants in Delhi: Race, Refuge and Retail*. Leiden and Amsterdam: International Institute for Asian Studies and Amsterdam University Press.

———. 2017. 'Solidarity, Visibility and Vulnerability: "Northeast" as a Racial Category in India'. In *Northeast India: A Place of Relations*, edited by Y. Saikia and A. R. Baishya, 27–44. Cambridge, UK: Cambridge University Press.

Michelutti, L. 2008. *The Vernacularisation of Democracy: Politics, Caste and Religion in India*. New Delhi: Routledge.

Middleton, T. 2015. *The Demands of Recognition: State, Anthropology and Ethnopolitics in Darjeeling*. Redwood City, CA: Stanford University Press.

Ministry of Defence. 1967. *Annual Report 1966–67*. New Delhi: Ministry of Defence, Government of India.

Misra, U. 2000. *The Periphery Strikes Back: Challenges to Nation-State in Assam and Nagaland*. Shimla: NIAS.

Mizo Memorandum. 1947. *Mizo Memorandum 1947: Memorandum of the Case of Mizo by Mizo Union (MU) Submitted to the Sub-Committee on North-East India's Excluded and Partially Excluded Areas (Assam), Known as the Bordoloi Committee*. Aizawl: Mizo Union.

Mizo National Front (MNF) Memorandum. 1965. *Memorandum Submitted to the Prime Minister of India by the Mizo National Front General Headquarters*. Aizawl: Mizoram.

Mizoram Kohhran Hruaitute Committee (MKHC). 2012. *History: MKHC Chanchin (1982–2012)*. Aizawl: MKHC.

Mottin, M. 2010. 'Catchy Melodies and Clenched Fists: Performance as Politics in Maoist Cultural Programs'. In *The Maoist Insurgency in Nepal: Revolution in the Twenty-first Century*, edited by M. Lawoti and A. K. Pahari, 52–72. Oxon: Routledge.

Nadai, E., and C. Maeder. 2005. 'Fuzzy Fields: Multi-Sited Ethnography in Sociological Research'. *Forum: Qualitative Social Research* 6(3): art. 28.

Nag, C. 1999. *Post-Colonial Mizo Politics*. New Delhi: Vikas Publishing House.

Nag, S. 2001. 'Tribals, Rats, Famine, State and the Nation'. *Economic and Political Weekly* 36(12): 1029–1033.

———. 2002. *Contesting Marginality: Ethnicity, Insurgency and Sub-Nationalism in North-East India*. New Delhi: Manohar Publications.

Nairn, T. 1977. *The Break-Up of Britain: Crisis and Neo-Nationalism*. London: New Left Books.

Narayan, B. 2001. 'Heroes, Histories and Booklets'. *Economic and Political Weekly* 36(41): 3923–3934.

Nghaka, V. L. 2014. Ram Buai Lai- Kolasib-Ah' (Kolasib during the Troubled Years). In *Ram Buai leh Kei* (Troubled Land and I), edited by Mizoram Upa Pawl (Mizoram Senior Citizens Association), 16-30. Aizawl: Mizoram Upa Pawl.

Nibedon, N. 1980. *Mizoram: The Dagger Brigade*. New Delhi: Lancer.

Nongbri, T. 2003. *Development, Ethnicity and Gender: Select Essays on Tribes in India*. Jaipur: Rawat Publications.

Nordstrom, C. 2004. *Shadows of War: Violence, Power, and International Profiteering in the Twenty-First Century*. Berkeley and Los Angeles: University of California Press.

Nunthara, C. 1989. *Impact of the Introduction of Grouping of Villages in Mizoram*. New Delhi: Omsons.

———. 1996. *Mizoram: Society and Polity*. New Delhi: Indus Publishing.

Oommen, T. K. 1986. 'Insiders and Outsiders in India: Primordial Collectivism and Cultural Pluralism in Nation-building'. *International Sociology* 1(1): 53–74.

Pachuau, J. L. K. 2014. *Being Mizo: Identity and Belonging in Northeast India*. New Delhi: Oxford University Press.

Pachuau, J. L. K., and M. Sadan. 2016. 'The Social Memory of the Mizo Buai: Some Comparisons with the Kachin Conflict'. In *War and Peace in the Borderlands of Myanmar*, edited by M. Sadan, 434–457. Copenhagen: NIAS Press.

Pachuau, J. L. K., and W. van Schendel. 2015. *The Camera as Witness: A Social History of Mizoram, Northeast India*. New Delhi: Cambridge University Press.

Pachuau, L. 1997. 'In Search of a Context for a Contextual Theology: The Socio-Political Realities of "Tribal" Christians in Northeast India'. *National Council of Churches in India Review* 117: 760–772.

———. 2002. *Ethnic Identity and Christianity: A Socio-Historical and Missiological Study of Christianity in Northeast India with Special Reference to Mizoram*. Berlin: Peter Lang.

Pandey, G. 2001. *Remembering Partition: Violence, Nationalism and History in India*. Cambridge, UK: Cambridge University Press.

———. 2006. *Routine Violence: Nations, Fragments, Histories*. London: Routledge.

Pandian, J. 1987. *Caste, Nationalism and Ethnicity: An Interpretation of Tamil Cultural History and Social Order*. Mumbai: Popular Prakashan.

Pandian, M. S. S. 1987. 'Peace by Force: Lankan Tamil's Tragedy'. *Economic and Political Weekly* 22(46): 1950–1951.

———. 2009. 'Nation Impossible'. *Economic and Political Weekly* 44(10): 65–69.

Parry, N. E. 2009 (1932). *The Lakhers*. Aizawl: Tribal Research Institute.

Pasha, M. K. 2009. 'Global Exception and Islamic Exceptionalism'. *International Politics* 46(5): 527–549.

Patil, V. 2011. 'Narrating Political History about Contested Space: Tourism Websites of India's Northeast'. *Annals of Tourism Research* 38(3): 989–1008.

Pearce, J. (2010). 'Perverse State Formation and Securitized Democracy in Latin America'. *Democratization* 17(2): 286–306.

Pels, P. 1996. 'The Pidginization of Luguru Politics: Administrative Ethnography and the Paradoxes of Indirect Rule'. *American Ethnology* 23(4): 738–761.

Perry, J. O. (ed.) 1983. *Voices of Emergency: An All India Anthology of Protest Poetry of the 1975–77 Emergency*. Bombay: Popular Prakashan.

Phadnis, U. 1989. *Ethnicity and Nation Building in South Asia*. New Delhi: SAGE Publications.

Pradhan, R. D. 1995. *Working with Rajiv Gandhi*. New Delhi: Indus Publishing.

Prasad, R. N. (ed.) 1994. *Autonomy Movements in Mizoram*. Delhi: Northern Book Centre.

Raltawna, H. 2010. 'Mizoram Buai Lai Hun (1966–86-?)'. In *Rambuai Leh Kei*, vol. 1, edited by Mizoram Upa Pawl, 1–12. Aizawl: Mizoram Upa Pawl.

Rajagopalan, R. 2000. '"Restoring Normalcy": The Evolution of the Indian Army's Counterinsurgency Doctrine'. *Small Wars and Insurgencies* 11(1): 44–68.

Rao, V. R., H. Thansanga, and N. Hazarika. 1987. *A Century of Government and Politics in North East India*, vol. 3: *Mizoram*. New Delhi: S. Chand.

Ray, S. 2000. *En-Gendering India: Woman and Nation in Colonial and Postcolonial Narratives*. Durham, NC: Duke University Press.

Reid, R. 1987 (1942). *History of Frontier Areas Bordering Assam 1883–1941*. Aizawl: Tribal Research Institute.

Renan, E. 1990. 'What Is a Nation?' In *Nation and Narration*, edited by H. K, 8–22. Bhabha. London: Routledge.

Riley, M., and A. D. Smith. 2016. *Nation and Classical Music: From Handel to Copland*. Woodbridge, UK: Boydell & Brewer.

Rokhuma, C. 2001. *The Anti-Famine Campaign Organisation, Mizoram Golden Jubilee*. Aizawl: Anti-Famine Campaign Organisation.

Roluahpuia. 2016. 'Ethnic Tension in Mizoram: Contested Claims, Conflicting Positions'. *Economic and Political Weekly* 51(29): 21–25.

———. 2018a. 'The Bru Conundrum in Northeast India'. *Economic and Political Weekly* 54(29): 16–18.

———. 2018b. 'Memories and Memorials of Mizo National Front (MNF) Movement: Problems and Politics of Memorialization'. *Economic and Political Weekly* 53(25): 38–45.

———. 2021. 'Unsettled Autonomy: Ethnicity, Tribes and Sub-National Politics in Mizoram, Northeast India'. *Nations and Nationalism* 27(2): 412–426.

———. 2022a. 'Nation'. In *Routledge Companion to Northeast India*, edited by J. P. Wouters and T. B. Subba, 359–363. Oxon: Routledge.

———. 2022b. 'Border Nation: Indigenous Peoples, State, and the Border in Indo-Myanmar Borderlands'. *Journal of Borderlands Studies*. DOI: 10.1080/08865655 .2022.2076250.

Ropianga, R. 2014. *Zoram Khua A La Var Ang*. Aizawl: Author.

Roy, S. 1999. 'Instituting Diversity: Official Nationalism in Post-Independence India'. *South Asia: Journal of South Asian Studies* 22(1): 79–99.

Saha, S. K. 1986. 'Historical Premises of India's Tribal Problem'. *Journal of Contemporary Asia* 16(3): 274–319.

Said, E. 1988. 'Introduction'. In *Blaming the Victims: Spurious Scholarship and the Palestinian Question*, edited by E. Said and C. Hitchens, 1–20. London: Verso Books.

Saikia, Y. 2011. *Women, War and the Making of Bangladesh: Remembering 1971.* New Delhi: Women Unlimited.

Sailo, S. 2010. 'Mizoram Buai Leh Kei'. In *Rambuai Leh Kei*, vol 1, 13–23. Aizawl: Mizoram Upa Pawl.

Sailo, T. 1981. *Speeches and Writings of Brig. T Sailo AVSM (RETD) Chief Minister, Mizoram.* Aizawl: Information, Public Relations, and Tourism, Government of Mizoram.

———. 2000. *A Soldier's Story.* Calcutta: Author.

Samaddar, R. 2006. 'Law and Terror in the Age of Colonial Constitution Making'. *Diogenes* 53(4): 18–33.

Sangkima. 1992. *Mizos: Society and Social Change (1890–1947).* Guwahati: Spectrum Publications.

Schultz, A. 2013. *Singing a Hindu Nation: Marathi Devotional Performance and Nationalism.* New York: Oxford University Press.

Scott, D. 1995. 'Colonial Governmentality'. *Social Text* 43: 191–220.

Scott, J. 1990. *Domination and the Arts of Resistance: Hidden Transcripts.* New Haven: Yale University Press.

———. 2009. *The Art of Not Being Governed: An Anarchist History of Upland Southeast Asia.* New Haven: Yale University Press.

Ségor, D. A. 2006. 'Tracing the Persistent Impulse of a Bedrock Nation to Survive within the State of India: Mizo Women's Response to War and Forced Migration'. PhD thesis, Fielding Graduate University, Santa Barbara, CA.

Sen, S. 1984. 'MNF Chief Laldenga's Recorded Message from London Does the Trick for Congress(I)'. *India Today*, 31 May. https://www.indiatoday.in/magazine/indiascope/story/19840531-mnf-chief-laldengas-recorded-message-from-london-does-the-trick-for-congressi-803649-1984-05-30. Accessed on 12 August 2017.

Shah, A. 2013. 'The Intimacy of Insurgency: Beyond Coercion, Greed or Grievance in Maoist India'. *Economy and Society* 42(3): 480–506.

Shakespear, J. 1912. *The Lushei Kuki Clans.* London: Macmillan and Co.

Sheth, D. L. 1989. 'Nation-Building in Multi-Ethnic Societies'. *Alternatives* 14(4): 379–388.

Shimray, U. A. 2007. *Naga Population and Integration Movement.* New Delhi: Mittal Publication.

Shneiderman, S., and A. Snellinger. 2014. 'Situating Political Transformation in South Asia'. Hot Spots, *Fieldsights*, 24 March. https://culanth.org/fieldsights/situating-political-transformation-in-south-asia. Accessed on 9 August 2018.

Siama, V. L. 1953. *Mizo History.* Aizawl: Lengchhawn Press.

Singh, G. 1996. 'Disorder, Order, and Legitimacy'. *Asian Survey* 36(4): 410–421.

Singh, G., and G. Shani. 2021. *Sikh Nationalism: From a Dominant Minority to an Ethno-Religious Diaspora.* Cambridge, UK: Cambridge University Press.

Singh, K. S. 1982. 'Transformation of Tribal Society: Integration vs Assimilation'. *Economic and Political Weekly* 17(33): 1318–1325.

Sirnate, V., and R. Verma. 2013. 'From Insurgency to Electoral Democracy'. *The Hindu*, 30 November 2013. http://www.thehindu.com/opinion/lead/from-insurgency-to-electoral-democracy/article5405661.ece. Accessed on 6 August 2018.

Smith, A. D. 1986. *The Ethnic Origin of Nations*. Malden: Wiley-Blackwell.

———. 2001. *Nationalism: Theory, Ideology, History*. Cambridge, UK: Polity Press.

———. 2008. *The Cultural Foundations of Nations: Hierarchy, Covenant and Republic*. Oxford: Wiley.

———. 2009. *Ethno-Symbolism and Nationalism: A Cultural Approach*. Oxon: Routledge.

Sofsky, W. 1997. *The Order of Terror: The Concentration Camp*. Princeton, NJ: Princeton University Press.

Stokes, M. (ed.) 1994. *Ethnicity, Identity and Music: The Musical Construction of Place*. Oxford: Berg Publishers.

Stuligross, D. 1999. 'Autonomous Councils in Northeast India: Theory and Practice'. *Alternatives: Global, Local, Political* 24(3): 497–525.

Suan, H. K. K. 2007. 'Salvaging Autonomy in India's Northeast: Beyond the Sixth Schedule Way'. *Eastern Quarterly* 4(1): 5–16.

Subba, T. B. 1991. *Ethnicity, State and Development: A Case Study of Gorkhaland Movement in Darjeeling*. New Delhi: Vikas Publishing House.

Subramanian, L. 2020. *Singing Gandhi's India: Music and Sonic Nationalism*. New Delhi: Roli Books.

Sundar, N. 2011. 'Interning Insurgent Populations: The Buried Histories of Indian Democracy'. *Economic and Political Weekly* 46(6): 47–57.

Sundar, N., and A. Sundar. (ed.) 2014. *Civil Wars in South Asia: State, Sovereignty, Development*. New Delhi: SAGE Publications.

Suny R. G., and M. D. Kennedy (ed.) 1999. *Intellectuals and the Articulation of the Nation*. Ann Arbor, MI: University of Michigan Press.

Surahmar. 2010. 'Grouping of Villages "Saddest Chapter" in Mizoram'. 8 September. https://surahmar.wordpress.com/2010/09/08/grouping-of-villages-saddest-chapter-in-mizoram/. Accessed on 12 December 2018.

Syiemlieh, D. R. 2014. *On the Edge of Empire: Four British Plans for North East India, 1941–1947*. New Delhi: SAGE Publications.

Talbot, I., and G. Singh. 2009. *The Partition of India*. New York: Cambridge University Press.

Thanga. L. 1978. *The Mizos*. Guwahati: United Publishers.

Thankima, R. 2014. 'Ram Buai Lai- Sialsuk-ah'. In *Rambuai Leh Kei*, vol. 2, edited by C. Chhuanvawra, 1–10. Aizawl: Mizoram Upa Pawl.

Thirangama, S., and T. Kelly. 2010. 'Introduction: Spectres of Treason'. In *Traitors: Suspicion, Intimacy and the Ethics of State-building*, edited by S. Thiranagama and T. Kelly, 1–23. Philadelphia: University of Philadelphia Press.

Thirumal, P., Laldinpuii, and C. Lalrozami. 2019. *Modern Mizoram: History, Culture, Poetics*. New Delhi: Routledge.

Times of India. 1955. 'Unfair Treatment of Hill Tribes'. 20 November.

———. 1967. 'Successful Re-Grouping of Mizo Villagers, a Tribute to the Army'. 11 August.

———. 1986. 'Laldenga Asks for Greater Mizoram'. 23 August.

Toffin, G., and J. Pfaff-Czarnecka. 2014. 'Introduction: Globalisation and Belonging in the Himalayas and in Trans-Himalayan Social Science'. In *Facing Globalization in the Himalayas: Belonging and the Politics of the Self*, edited by G. Toffin and J. Pfaff-Czarnecka, 1–44. New Delhi: SAGE Publications.

Uberoi, P. 2002. '"Unity in Diversity?" Dilemmas of Nationhood in Indian Calendar Art'. *Contributions to Indian Sociology* 36(1–2): 191–232.

Upadhya, C. .2011. 'Colonial Anthropology, Law, and Adivasi Struggles: The Case of Jharkhand'. *In Doing Sociology in India: Genealogies, Locations, and Practices*, edited by Sujata Patel, 266–289. New Delhi: Oxford University Press.

Vadlamannati, K. C. 2011. 'Why Indian Men Rebel? Explaining Armed Rebellion in the Northeastern States of India, 1970–2007'. *Journal of Peace Research* 48(5): 605–619.

Vajpeyi, A. 2009. 'Resenting the Indian State: For a New Political Practice in the Northeast'. In *Beyond Counter-Insurgency: Breaking the Impasse in Northeast India*, edited by S. Baruah, 25–48. New Delhi: Oxford University Press.

Vanhnuaithanga, R. 2009. *Rokunga Hlate: A Critical Study and Appreciation*. Aizawl: B. Bualchhumi.

Vanlalauva, K. 2015. *Independence Puan Leh Underground Sawrkar*. Aizawl: Author.

Vanlawma, R. 1989. *Ka Ram Leh Kei*. Aizawl: Zalen Publishing House.

Vanlallawma, C. 2014. 'Rambuaia innghat thawnthu'. In 'Rambuai Literature: Seminar Papers', 48–59. Aizawl: Government Hrangbana College.

Vanthuama, H. 2001. *Mizoram Politics Chanchin (1952 Hmalam)*. Aizawl: Vanlalmawii.

Varghese, C. G., and R. L. Thanzawna. 1997. *A History of the Mizos*. Delhi: Vikas Publishing House.

Varshney, A. 2002. *Civic Life and Ethnic Conflict: Hindus and Muslims in India*. New Haven: Yale University Press.

Visweswaran, K. (ed.) 2013. *Everyday Occupations: Experiencing Militarism in South Asia and the Middle East*. Philadelphia: University of Pennsylvania Press.

Vizenor, G. R. 1999. *Manifest Manners: Narratives on Postindian Survivance*. Lincoln: University of Nebraska Press, 1999

————. (ed.) 2008. *Survivance: Narratives of Native Presence*. Lincoln, NE: University of Nebraska Press.

Vumson. 1988. *Zo History*. Aizawl: Author.

Walker, L. 2019. 'Decolonization in the 1960s: On Legitimate and Illegitimate Nationalist Claims-Making'. *Past and Present* 242(1): 227–264.

Whittaker, H. 2012. 'Force Villagization during the Shifta Conflict in Kenya, ca. 1963–1968'. *International Journal of African Historical Studies* 45(3): 343–364.

Wilmsen, E. N., and P. McAllister. 1996. *The Politics of Difference: Ethnic Premises in a World of Power*. London and Chicago: University of Chicago Press.

Wimmer, A. 1997. 'Who Owns the State? Understanding Ethnic Conflict in Post-Colonial Societies'. *Nations and Nationalism* 3(4): 631–665.

Wouters, J. J. P. 2014. 'Performing Democracy in Nagaland: Past Polities and Present Politics'. *Economic and Political Weekly* 49(16): 59–66.

Wouters, J. J. P., and T. B. Subba. 2013. 'The "Indian Face", India's Northeast, and the "Idea of India"'. *Asian Anthropology* 12(2): 126–140.

Xaxa, V. 1999. 'Transformation of Tribes in India: Terms of Discourse'. *Economic and Political Weekly* 34(24): 1519–1524.

————. 2008. *State, Tribes and Society: Issues in Post-Colonial India*. New Delhi: Pearson.

————. 2016. 'Tribes and Indian National Identity: Location of Exclusion and Marginality'. *Brown Journal of World Affairs* 23(1): 223–237.

————. 2018. 'Tribes in the Democratic Politics of India'. *Explorations: E-Journal of the Indian Sociological Society* 2(2): 3–21.

Xaxa, V., and Roluahpuia (2021). 'Indigenous Peoples and the Nation Interface in India'. In *Indigeneity and Nation: Key Concept in Indigenous Studies*, edited by G. N. Devy and Geoffrey V. Davis, 85–101. Oxon: Routledge.

Yuval-Davis, N. 1993. 'Gender and Nation'. *Ethnic and Racial Studies* 16(4): 621–632.

Zairemthanga. 1992. *Tripura Mizo History*. Jampui: Kailuia Zote.

Zama, C. 2005. *Mizo Hnam Hla (1961–1986)*. Aizawl: Author.

————. 2008. *Chengrang A Au Ve!* Aizawl: Author.

————. 2011. *Lo Thlaphang Suh Kan Zoram*. Aizawl: Author.

————. 2014. *The Untold Atrocity*. Aizawl: Author.

Zama, M. Ch. 2005. 'Origin Myths of the Mizo: Mizoram'. *India International Centre Quarterly* 32(2–3): 7–11.

Zama, M. Ch., and C. L. Vanchiau. 2016. *After Decades of Silence, Voices from Mizoram: A Brief Review of Mizo Literature*. New Delhi: Amber Books.

Zamawia, R. 2012. *Zofate Zinkawngah Zalenna Mei a Mit Tur Ani Lo* (In the Journey of Zo People: The Torch of Freedom Must Not Die). Aizawl: Author.

Zawla, K. 1964. *Mizo Pi Pute Leh An Thlahte Chanchin* (History of Mizo Ancestors and their Descendants). Aizawl: HA Press.

Zoramthanga. 1980. *Zoram Zalenna Lungphum*. Chhimtlang: Government of Mizoram.

Zorema, J. 2007. *Indirect Rule in Mizoram, 1890–1954*. New Delhi: Mittal Publication.

Zou, D. V. 2010. 'A Historical Study of the "Zo" Struggle'. *Economic and Political Weekly* 45(14): 56–63.

Zutshi, C. 2003. *Languages of Belonging: Islam, Regional Identity, and the Making of Kashmir*. New Delhi: Permanent Black.

Index

Aizawl Theological College (ATC), 24–25
All India Radio (AIR), 37, 119
All Party Hill Leaders Conference
(APHLC), 84–85
Ambedkar, B. R., 32, 102
Anderson, B., 19, 93
    Imagined Communities, 98, 166
Anti-Famine Campaign Organization
(AFCO), 86
Armed Forces (Special Powers) Act
(AFSPA) (1958), 103, 113, 116, 130, 139n4
Assam, 8, 10–11, 15, 20–21, 35, 38, 40–42,
44, 46, 48, 54, 57, 62, 67–68, 72–73, 75,
79n13, 81, 84–87, 89, 117, 125, 148, 154
Assam accord 1985, 141, 154
Assam Lushai Hills District (Acquisition
of Chief's Rights) Act (1954), 71
Assam Maintenance of Public Order
(AMPO) (1968), 120
Assam Pradesh Congress Committee
(APCC), 84–85, 87
Assam Rifles (AR), 45, 70, 118, 151
    lammual, 141, 159, 164n2
autonomy, 12, 24, 27, 31, 34–35, 38, 40–
41, 43, 50–51, 60–61, 66–73, 162–163, 167

Bangladesh (erstwhile East Pakistan), 14,
77, 98, 100, 103, 105, 110n3, 119, 153, 156,
163
Bawichhuaka, H. K., 68–69, 87
Barua, Hem, 44
Bezbaruah Committee, 46
Bharatiya Janata Party (BJP), 1, 44–45, 165
Billig, M.
    Banal Nationalism, 10
Bordoloi Committee (Advisory
Subcommittee [ASC]), 41–42, 65, 67
Bru refugees, 1–2, 15, 162

Central Young Mizo Association (CYMA),
1, 92, 159, 163
Chaliha, B. P., 125
Chaliha, Kuladhar, 42
Chakma Autonomous District Council
(CADC), 106, 152–153
Chaudhuri, Rohini Kumar, 42
Chawnga, R. B., 11
Chenoy, Anuradha, 129
chiefs, 7, 11, 16–17, 19, 41, 48–50, 52–55,
57–67, 70–71, 74, 76, 104, 167–168 to
hate, 56

Chin Lushai Expedition (1890–1891), 44
Chin National Front (CNF), 106
Chittagong Hill Tracts (CHTs), 67, 103–
104, 119, 128, 143, 163
Christianity, 29n4, n5, 94, 107–108
        Mizos conversion into, 4–5, 20
Chuaungo, Pu Lalnunmawia, 1
church, 5, 15, 17, 20, 65, 91, 93, 98, 107,
111n20, 122–123, 129–131, 150–154,
159, 163
circle interpreter (CI), 52
Committee on Emotional Integration, 37
Constituent Assembly (CA), 31, 40, 42–
43, 69
Constitution of India
        Article 371(G), 141
counter-insurgency, 7, 14, 22, 28, 96, 107,
109, 112–115, 118, 127, 133–134, 137, 151
        aerial attack on, 118–119
        Home Guard establishment for,
        139n19
        India's northeast as laboratory of,
        116
        kawktu use for, 124
        Operation Sadbhavana, 117
        village groupings, 119–123
Counter-Insurgency Jungle Warfare
(CIJW), 115
cultural mainstream, 33

dahthat, 125, 139n13
Das, V., 132–133
Defence of India (DoI) Rules (1962), 112,
120, 139n1
democracy, 65, 142
        electoral, 116
        and politics, link between, 50
        securitized, 116
        vernacularization of, 49

elite, 6–7, 12–13, 18–21, 38–42, 49, 60,
62, 66, 82–83, 88–90, 168–169
Elwin, Verrier, 30–31

ethnicity, 2, 18–19, 21, 110n4, 163
ethnic separatism in South-East Asia, 36
Ex-Mizo National Army (Ex-MNA), 25
Extended Loop Areas (ELAs), 120

Gandhi, Indira, 143
Ghurye, G. S., 30–31
gaonburahs, 52
Goswami, B. B., 12, 18
government of India, 14, 28, 70, 88, 100,
102–104, 106–107, 109, 127, 138, 141,
143–146, 148–154, 156–157, 159–160,
162–163, 167
Guha, R., 30, 83, 134
Guru, G., 32, 34, 83

hills
        Jaintia, 47n1
        Lushai/Lusei, 10–11, 15–17, 20, 29,
        41, 44, 47n1, 48–52, 54–55, 57, 60,
        67–77, 79n12, 79n16, 88, 106–107,
        168
        Mizo, 3, 10–11, 40–41, 48, 71–72,
        75, 77–79, 81–82, 84–88, 103–107,
        109, 112, 118–120, 124–125,
        127–129, 138
        North Cachar, 47n1, 79n13
hla, 4, 8, 60, 64, 166
        hnam, 3–8, 13, 23, 28, 81, 90–91,
        95–96, 109, 110n13, 159, 167–169
        kaihlek, 29n4, 65
        party, 5, 7–8, 13, 27, 29n3, 49–50,
        59, 62, 65, 166–167
        rambuai, 7–8, 13, 114–115, 133–
        134, 166
        thu leh, 166
Hluna, J. V.
        Zawlkhawpui Senmei Chan Ni, 119
Hmar National Union (HNU), 78
Hmar People's Convention (Democratic)
(HPC-D), 26
hnamchawm, 54, 73–74
Human Rights Committee (HRC), 131

identity, 5–6, 8
    consciousness, 9
    national, 10
inclusion, 18, 27, 33–34, 41, 43–46, 70,
74, 142, 156
INC(I), 142–143, 150
Indian National Congress (INC), 21, 28,
48–49

Janata Party (JP) government, 143
jhum land, 121, 128, 139*n*5

kaihlek hla, 4, 29*n*4, 65
kawktu, 124–125, 127
Kawnpui Convention (1965), 78–79
Khasi Hills/states, 35–36, 41, 47*n*1
khawkhawm, 134
Khuangchera, 44–46, 97
Kuki National Assembly (KNA), 78

Lai Autonomous District Council, 79*n*16,
106–107, 128, 139*n*3
Laldenga, 7, 11, 14, 20, 28, 98–102,
106–109, 111*n*22, 127, 138, 141, 143–148,
150–156, 166
    Mizoram Marches towards
    Freedom, 23, 82–83, 97–99
    Zalenna Thuchah, 97
Lalhmingthanga, 14, 101, 109, 148
    Exodus Politics, 23, 83, 97–98, 100
Lalthanhawla, Pu, 143, 150, 155–156
lambus, 52, 79*n*1
Lushai Hills District (Change of Name)
Bill, 1954, 77
Lushai Hills District (Village Councils)
Act, 1953, 71
Lushai Student Association (LSA), 74–75

McCall, A. G.
    Lushai Chrysalis, 16
Maintenance of Internal Security Act
(MISA), 145–146
Manekshaw, Sam, 119

Manipur, 1, 3, 10, 14, 16–17, 22, 24–27,
35, 40, 44, 46, 51, 67–70, 73–74, 78, 79*n*1,
*n*13, 90, 104–105, 107, 118–119, 127, 129,
139*n*19, 160–161
Manipur State Constitution Act (1947), 69
Mara Autonomous District Council, 106
martyr, 45, 157, 160–161
mautam, 41, 81, 86, 110*n*2
Medhi, Bishnuram, 85–86
Meghalaya, 10, 15, 35, 40, 44, 77, 84, 119,
129
militarization, 46, 113, 116–118, 129–130
Mizo/Mizos, 1, 12, 34, 73–74, 78, 92, 108,
133–134, 136
    agrarian society, 8
    arte thih, 123, 139*n*11
    as *bawrhsap*, 52
    challenged colonial policy of
    exclusion, 49
    commoners, 53
    construed as Lusei-centric, 106
    counter-insurgency experience,
    133
    democratic politics, 49
    history of, 14–18, 48
    hnam hla songs popular among,
    3–4, 23
    hnam hnatlang, 2–3
    identity formation, 14–18
    left wing, 61–62
    lengkhawm zai, 136, 140*n*25
    Mizo Accord, 14, 21, 109, 142–143,
    155, 157, 159
    nation, 82, 88, 96, 141, 168
    pasaltha, 44–45, 97
    political future, 60–61
    politics, 11–14, 27
    nationalism, 2–3, 8–9, 18–22, 81
    saphun, notion of, 100–101
    sociopolitical transformation of
    commoners, 49
    territorial integration, 88
    violation of human rights, 129–132

women experiences, 133
Mizo Cultural Society (MCS), 11, 20
    Mizo National Army (MNA), 90,
97, 105, 110n11, 147, 151
Mizo National Famine Front (MNFF),
11–12, 20, 86–87
Mizo National Front (MNF), 4, 7–9,
11–14, 28, 78–79, 81, 83–84, 91, 94–100,
102–107, 109, 111n22, 118-119, 122–133,
139n7, n13, 141–163, 166–169
    agenda of *zalenna*, 92
    movement, 18–25, 28, 47, 51, 82,
    138
    and nationalist mobilization,
    87–90
    Peace Accord MNF Returnees
    Association (PAMRA), 25
    rise of, 84–87
    vernacularization of nationalism
    by, 83
Mizo National Volunteers (MNVs), 90
Mizo Peace Accord (1986), 21–22, 25, 28,
138, 152, 158–159
Mizoram, 1–3, 10–12, 14–17, 20–24, 26–
28, 29n3, 40, 44, 46, 54, 56–57, 67, 73–75,
77–78, 87, 89–90, 94, 98–100, 102–104,
107, 109, 110n1, 111n20, 114–115,
118–121, 127–128, 130–131, 135, 138,
141–143, 145–151, 153–154, 156–157,
159–163, 167, 169
Mizoram Evangelical Activity (MEC), 107
Mizoram Kohhran Hruaitute Committee
(MKHC), 153
Mizoram State Archives (MSA), 24–25
Mizo Zirlai Pawl (MZP), 1, 44, 75, 119
Mizo Union (MU), 5, 7, 11, 19, 24, 27, 41,
48–51, 53–67, 69–78, 79n13, n14, 81–82,
84–87, 92, 98, 127–128, 148, 167–168
    decline of, 84–87
muanna, 142, 150, 157

National Council (NC), 67
Naga National Council (NNC), 36

Naga National League (NNL), 70
Nag, S., 20–21, 61, 81–82, 86, 107, 130
National Archives of India (NAI), 24
national integration, 9, 27, 32–39, 101, 165
nationalism, 2, 5–7, 10, 12, 14, 18–22,
33–34, 44, 46, 48, 81, 84, 89–102, 104,
108, 167–169
    cultural, 9
    ethnic, 19, 36, 142
    ethno-nationalism, 19
    importance of, 165
    Indian, 3
    pan-Indian, 8–9
    peripheral, 8
    regional, 8
    right-wing, 165
    vernacular, 13, 82–83, 166
nationalist historiography in India, 83
nations, 2, 6–9, 13, 29n1, 31, 38, 45, 47, 79,
89–90, 93, 95, 97, 100, 116, 129, 131, 167
    -building, 19, 30, 32–33, 35, 101,
    113
    defined, 19, 83
    -state, 5, 19, 32, 34, 36–37, 46, 84,
    99–102, 115–118, 122, 166
New Grouping Centres (NGCs), 120
newspapers
    Mizo Chanchin Laisuih, 98
    Mizo Leh Vai Chanchinbu, 98
nghawngkawl battalion, 123, 139n10
northeast India, 6, 8, 10–12, 14–15, 27,
31, 35, 40, 42, 47, 49, 51, 57, 69, 77, 84, 98,
104, 113, 115–117, 142, 166–167

Operation Jericho (1966), 102
oral culture, 5–7, 22–23, 47, 82–83, 91,
134, 166
orality, 1, 5, 7, 23, 28, 114

Pachuau, J. L. K., 10, 24, 52, 66, 74, 83,
107–108, 119, 138, 162
    Being Mizo, 18
Pandian, M. S. S., 37, 151

Partially Excluded and Excluded Areas, 30, 35, 47n1

pasaltha, 44–45, 97

Pawi-Lakher Regional Council (PLRC), 71–72, 106

Pawi-Lakher Tribal Union (PLTU), 71–72

People's Conference (PC), 28, 128, 138, 139n15, 145–151, 153, 164n6

Phizo, Angami Zapu (AZ Phizo), 36

political integration, 33, 35–37, 46, 169

Protected and Progressive Villages (PPVs), 120, 136

puakphurh, 122, 139n9

puma zai, 4, 29n4

ram leh hnam, 6–7, 10, 13, 21, 28, 46, 82–84, 90, 92, 97, 107–109, 166–169

Rashtriya Swayamsevak Sangh (RSS), 2

rebels, 7, 13–14, 21–24, 82–83, 87–88, 103, 108, 112, 119, 124, 128, 132–134, 142–143, 147–149, 151, 155, 158, 160, 167

regionalism, 7, 9, 21, 37

remna, 152–153, 163

remna leh muanna, 141–142, 150–151, 153

Remna Ni (Day of Peace) celebration, 157–159

resistance, 33, 48–49, 66, 114, 133, 138

anti-colonial, 5, 50

to integration into nation-state, 35, 166

Rokunga, 13, 21, 23, 81–82, 84, 91–92, 94–96, 109, 110n13, n17, 159, 168

Roy, Nichols, 42

Sailo, Thenphunga, 28, 128, 131, 138, 145–149, 153, 164n6

Schedules

Fifth, 42–43

Sixth, 40–43, 50, 70, 73, 75, 79n17

Shakespear, John

The Lushei Kuki Clans, 16

Shashank, S. B., 1–2, 169

Shastri, Lal Bahadur, 89, 104

Singh, Jaipal, 42

Singh, G., 146

Smith, A. D., 6, 9, 21, 82, 84, 95, 97, 104, 117

songs, 3–7, 13–14, 21–23, 27–28, 29n3, 50–51, 60, 62–66, 70, 81–84, 88, 90–98, 108–109, 111n19, 114, 133–137, 167–169

Special Force (SF), 127, 139n15

statehood, 40–41, 72–73, 84–87, 141, 154

Swell, G. G. and Roy, J. J. Nichols

Suppression of Mizos in India: An Eye Witness Report, 129–130

Syiem, U. Tirot Sing, 44

Tawna, L., 68

thingfak, 102–109

Tikendrajit, Bir, 44

tlawmngaihna, 44, 47n2, 91, 110n14

tribes, 2, 11, 30–31, 34

Chakma, 1, 15–16, 24, 106, 128, 139n3, 153, 156, 162–163

colonial exclusion policy of, 12

Garo, 35, 77

Hmar, 24, 70

as internal other, 33

Jaintia, 35

Lai, 15, 24, 71–72, 74, 79n16, 106

Mara, 15–17, 27, 71–72, 74, 79n16, 107, 128, 139n3, 163

Paite, 24

savagery, 8

Scheduled Tribes (STs), 10, 30

Tripura, 1, 3, 10, 14, 16–17, 24–27, 35, 40, 51, 67–68, 70, 73–74, 79n17, 104–105, 127, 129, 160

Tripura Tribal Autonomous District Council (TTADC), 79n17, 90

United Mizo Freedom Organization (UMFO), 7, 11, 27, 50, 61–64, 67 *vai sipai*, 121, 124, 131–132, 134, 139*n*6, 150

Vanlawma, R., 11, 42, 56, 61, 98

Vanvasi Kalyan, 2

village council president (VCP), 122, 125, 127, 130

Voluntary Grouping Centres (VGCs), 120

violence, 13–14, 22, 26, 28, 40, 46, 66, 105, 107, 109, 116, 118, 134–135, 141–143, 145–146, 148–151, 162–163

    collective, 81

    colonial, 114

    counter-insurgency, 113, 115, 117–132

    and governmentality of Indian states, 113–114

    history, 113

    military, 138

    routinized, 114

    sexual, 133

Young Mizo Association (YMA), 9, 15, 27, 44, 74, 81, 110*n*1, 159

Xaxa, Virginius, 33, 43, 49, 66, 83

zalenna, 7, 12–14, 21, 23, 25, 28, 82, 84, 90, 92, 95, 97–109, 111*n*24, 143, 166–167

Zama, C., 92, 95–96, 105, 108, 130, 134

    The Untold Atrocity, 119

Zoram, 3, 64, 90–92, 94, 100, 108, 110*n*3

Zoramthanga, 7, 14, 22, 97–100, 109, 111*n*22, 148, 152

    Zoram Zalenna Lungphum, 23, 83, 97–99

Zuala, R., 11